THE INDIGENOUS PEOPLES OF
Trinidad and Tobago

THE INDIGENOUS PEOPLES OF Trinidad and Tobago

FROM THE FIRST SETTLERS UNTIL TODAY

Arie Boomert

Sidestone Press

Published by Sidestone Press, Leiden
www.sidestone.com

ISBN 978-90-8890-353-3
Lay-out & cover design: Sidestone Press

Front cover illustrations: © Altinosmanaj | Dreamstime.com: View of coast of northern Trinidad just west of Maracas Bay.
La Venezuela; statue of a Warao Amerindian, artist unknown. Santa Cruz Valley, Trinidad, ca. 1900.

Also available as:
e-book (PDF): ISBN 978-90-8890-354-0

Universiteit Leiden

NEXUS 1492

[TRINIDAD]

'*This Iland is called by the people therof Cairi, and in it are diuers nations* [...]'

Sir Walter Ralegh (1595)

[TOBAGO]

'*This island is called Urupaina in the Indian language, meaning big snail; it is inhabited by Carib Indians* [...]'

Antonio Vásquez de Espinosa (1628)

Contents

List of illustrations

19. Large pottery jar, probably representing a male effigy, found underwater at Bombshell Bay, offshore Caspar Grande (Gasparee) Island (SGE-37), Trinidad. Saladoid series, Early Ceramic Age, ca. AD 350–650/800.
20. White-on-red painted, asymmetrical ceramic bottle, showing a human/animal-like face design, found at Erin (SPA-20), Trinidad. Saladoid series, Early Ceramic Age, ca. AD 350–650/800.
21. Partially red-painted pottery bowl, showing a bat-shaped head lug, found at Atagual (VIC-30), Trinidad. Saladoid series, Early Ceramic Age, ca. AD 350–650/800.
22. Slate-like, thin stone slab, decorated with incised motifs, found at Erin (SPA-20), Trinidad. Barrancoid series, Early Ceramic Age, ca. AD 350–650/800.
23. King vulture-shaped stone (serpentine?) pendant, found at an unknown location in Trinidad. Saladoid series, Early Ceramic Age, ca. AD 0–350.
24. Ceramic bowl showing two tube-shaped extensions, most likely used to pour tobacco juice into the nose in order to induce an ecstatic-visionary trance, found at St. Bernard (MAY-4), Trinidad. Saladoid series, Early Ceramic Age, ca. AD 350–650/800.
25. Threepointed stones, probably used in shamanic rituals to promote the growth of food plants, found at (left) Mount Irvine 3 (TOB-19), Tobago, and (right) Blue River (CAR-1), Trinidad. Saladoid series, Early Ceramic Age, ca. AD 350–650/800.
26. Layout of the second occupation at Manzanilla 1 (SAN-1), Trinidad, showing three round to oval house structures, burials, pits, and hearth. Arauquinoid series, Late Ceramic Age, ca. AD 650/800–1400.
27. Inhumation burial of a ca. ten year old individual of unknown sex, who was deposited half seated, half lying on the back with flexed legs. The skull was resting on a large pebble, with two more stones on each side of the head. Manzanilla 1 (SAN-1), Trinidad, Arauquinoid series, Late-Ceramic Age, ca. AD 650/800–1400.
28. Pottery ocarina (whistle), showing four holes, found at Grant's Trace 1 (SPA-25), Trinidad. Arauquinoid series, Late Ceramic Age, ca. AD 650/800–1400.
29. Ceramic roller stamp, used for body painting, found at Los Iros (SPA-22), Trinidad. Arauquinoid series, Late Ceramic Age, ca. AD 650/800–1400.
30. Reddish-brown, fine-ware pottery bowls, probably used for ceremonial purposes, found at Great Courland Bay (TOB-23), Tobago. Troumassoid series, Late Ceramic Age, ca. AD 1150–1400.
31. Fragment of a greyish, coarse-ware pottery cauldron (a) and handled jar (b), both showing scratched surfaces, most likely used for domestic purposes, found at Great Courland Bay (TOB-23), Tobago. Troumassoid series, Late Ceramic Age, ca. AD 1150–1400.
32. Two quartz crystal beads, a turquoise pendant, and a pottery bead, found at Great Courland Bay (TOB-23), Tobago. Troumassoid series, Late Ceramic Age, ca. AD 1150–1400.
33. Part of an ink and watercolour manuscript map, probably drawn by Willem Mollens in 1654, showing an Amerindian village situated northwest of the Courlander fort Jekabs (here not shown) at present Plymouth, Tobago.

Preface

This book was written on the request of many. It forms the outcome of a long-standing active involvement and study of the archaeology and indigenous ethnohistory of Trinidad and Tobago. After having been employed as a Senior Research Fellow in Archaeology at The University of the West Indies (UWI), St. Augustine, Trinidad, between 1980 and 1988, the author has continued his archaeological research in the two islands at regular intervals, mainly under the auspices of the Faculty of Archaeology of Leiden University, The Netherlands, the former National Archaeological Committee of Trinidad and Tobago, and the Tobago Museum, Scarborough. It was during a seminar on archaeological heritage management in Trinidad and Tobago, organized by the National Trust of the twin islands and The University of Trinidad and Tobago (UTT) in March 2014, that the author realized that his numerous academic writings on the archaeology and ethnohistory of Trinidad and Tobago needed a modest overarching sequel exclusively intended for the general public. Not least important, this was expressed by members of today's indigenous groups in Trinidad following the author's presentation at this meeting. This seminar and the present book form the results of a series of cooperative ventures between the Caribbean Research Group of the Faculty of Archaeology, Leiden University, led by Professor Corinne L. Hofman, and the Academy for Arts, Letters, Culture and Public Affairs of UTT, led by its Provost, Dr. Fazal Ali. The publication of this book was made possible by the Caribbean Research Group of the Faculty of Archaeology, Leiden University. The research leading to the writing of this book received funding from the European Research Council under the European Union's Seventh Framework Programme (FP7/2007-2013) / ERC grant agreement No. 319209 under the direction of Professor C.L. Hofman.

As an introduction to the cultural history of the indigenous peoples of Trinidad and Tobago, this book is directed in particular to students, history teachers and generally speaking interested adult citizens of the twin-island republic who wish to learn about the results of the archaeological excavations in both islands of the past century, and the picture that arises of Amerindian society and culture if the documentary sources of the European–Amerindian contact period are consulted. Accordingly, in writing this account, for as far as possible, I have tried to avoid academic jargon. As it is not feasible to neglect all technical phrases, a glossary has been appended in order to explain the (limited) specific terminology used. Besides, textual and footnoted references to the relevant professional literature have been omitted. For the latter, the reader is referred to the (select) bibliography. Finally, an appendix listing the institutions and museums with significant archaeological holdings from Trinidad and Tobago has been added.

The author wishes to gratefully acknowledge his debt to Professor Emerita Bridget Brereton, Department of History, UWI, St. Augustine, Trinidad, who meticulously scrutinized the manuscript of this book, signalling inconsistencies in the English text and suggesting numerous improvements. Furthermore, I am indebted to all those involved in the organization of the 2014 seminar on archaeological heritage management, which became the incentive for writing this book, especially (in alphabetical order): Dr. Fazal Ali, UTT, O'Meara, Trinidad; Mr. Jalaludin Khan, formerly of the National Trust of Trinidad and Tobago, Laventille, Trinidad; Dr. Hollis U.L. ('Chalkdust') Liverpool, UTT, Port-of-Spain, Trinidad; and Dr. Neil H. Lopinot, Missouri State University, Springfield, MO, USA. Also, I wish to thank those scholars and non-academics who assisted me at various stages during my 2014 stay in Trinidad, and during the writing of this book, notably (in alphabetical order): Mr. Gérard A. Besson, Paria Publishing Company Ltd., Port-of-Spain, Trinidad; Mr. John C. Correia, Port-of-Spain, Trinidad; Mr. Marc C. Dorst, Historic Buildings Conservation and Archaeology, Dordrecht Municipality, The Netherlands; Professor Maximilian Forte, Concordia University, Montréal, Canada; Mr. Christopher Harris, London, UK; Chief Ricardo B. Hernandez, The Santa Rosa First Peoples Community, Arima, Trinidad; Dr. Lodewijk A.H.C. Hulsman, The University of Amsterdam, The Netherlands; Dr. Lorraine Johnson, The National Museum and Art Gallery of Trinidad and Tobago, Port-of-Spain, Trinidad; the late Professor Emeritus Keith O. Laurence, Department of History, UWI, St. Augustine, Trinidad; Mr. Dennis C. Nieweg, Miramar Sea Museum, Vledder, The Netherlands; Dr. Amy Strecker, Leiden University, The Netherlands; and Mr. Louis Vilain, Museum of Tobago History, Scarborough, Tobago. Thanks are due also to Mr. Julijan A.M. Vermeer, Faculty of Archaeology, Leiden University, The Netherlands, for embellishing and finalizing the illustrations. Finally, I would like to thank my wife, Marion Boomert-Heukelom, for her unremitting support and interest during the writing of this work.

I wish to dedicate this book to Peter O'Brien Harris (1935–2013), a dear friend and colleague with whom the author co-operated in numerous archaeological surveys and excavations as well as documentary projects. Attached successively to the Trinidad and Tobago Historical Society (South Section), the Department of History of UWI, and as a Research Fellow to UTT, Peter Harris fulfilled a pivotal role as the organizer of epoch-making archaeological research in the two islands. Moreover, he was most successful in establishing and training a group of young avocational archaeologists who assisted him during some of his excavations, especially those of his UTT years. Outreach to the general public was one of Peter's major interests, and as such this publication answers to one of the tasks he had set for himself, but which due to his untimely death he was unable to fulfill.

Abbreviations

NMAG	National Museum and Art Gallery, Port-of-Spain, Trinidad
SRFPC	Santa Rosa First Peoples Community, Arima, Trinidad
THM	Tobago Historical Museum, Scarborough, Tobago
UTT	University of Trinidad and Tobago, O'Meara, Trinidad
UWI	University of the West Indies, St. Augustine, Trinidad
WIC	Dutch West India Company
WFT	Wild Fowl Trust, Pointe-a-Pierre, Trinidad
YPM	Peabody Museum, Yale University, New Haven, Connecticut, USA

1. Introduction

Consisting predominantly of people of African, Indian, and to a lesser extent European, Chinese and Lebanese descent, the citizens of Trinidad and Tobago represent one of the most cosmopolitan populations in the world. The ancestors of the majority of the present inhabitants of both islands came to the West Indies as slaves or indentured labourers during the era of colonial rule when Trinidad and Tobago were successfully exploited by the metropolitan countries of Europe as plantation colonies producing cash crops such as sugar, cocoa, coffee, and copra for the world market. At present the descendants of the original inhabitants of the twin-island republic, i.e. the indigenous peoples who lived in Trinidad and Tobago at the time of the European encounter (1498), constitute only a small minority among the residents of both islands. This was quite different in the past since as late as the mid-eighteenth century, these indigenous peoples, also known as Amerindians, still formed the most numerous population component both in Trinidad, then part of the Spanish empire, and Tobago, at that time unoccupied by any of the European powers.[1]

In spite of their insignificant presence as a population group, still today the linguistic and cultural heritage of the Amerindians of Trinidad and Tobago considerably influences the complicated fabric of the two islands' society, albeit it is rarely recognized as such. First of all, by far the majority of place names (toponyms) of Trinidad are derived from the indigenous languages formerly spoken in the island. This number is much smaller in Tobago, reflecting the limited population of Amerindians still living in the smaller island at the beginning of its unbroken colonial settlement in 1763. Besides, considerable linguistic loans and transference of ways of living took place between the indigenous inhabitants of the twin islands and the peoples of African and European descent who came to replace them. Transmission of lifeways occurred predominantly between the Amerindians and the African slave population of colonial times as well as the island peasantry which evolved out of the latter after the abolition of slavery. They involved a wide range of ecological knowledge, subsistence practices with respect to horticulture, hunting, fishing and food collecting, and techniques of food preparation, material culture, traditional medicines, and religion. Especially the African slaves and their descendants were profoundly influenced by the Amerindian cosmological concepts and religious practices. Thus far the significance and impact of these transfers are insufficiently appreciated in Trinidad and Tobago, or for that matter in the other islands of the West Indies.

---

1 'Amerindian' is a somewhat unfortunate term which was coined when it was realized that Columbus was fully mistaken in assuming that in 1492 he had discovered a western route to Asia ('India'), as a consequence of which he referred to the inhabitants of the continent he had come across as *indios*.

Both the pre-Columbian ('prehistoric') past of the indigenous peoples of Trinidad and Tobago, as well as their vicissitudes in colonial times, will be reviewed here. At the outset it is important to realize that Trinidad is the oldest settled island of the Caribbean and, besides, was probably traversed by Amerindians even when it was still part of the South American mainland. Thousands of years of cultural development followed in which the indigenous communities of the twin islands experienced a significant development of their society, involving considerable population growth, progress in subsistence practices, food preparation and material culture, as well as substantial deepening of spiritual beliefs. As the Amerindians had not mastered the art of writing, our knowledge of the pre-Columbian past is entirely based on archaeological excavations, during which sites where the indigenous peoples left material traces are dug up. The first documents on the Amerindian lifeways in Trinidad and Tobago appeared with the third voyage of Columbus to the West Indies. The written accounts from the European–Amerindian contact period also inform us about the names of the indigenous peoples living in the two islands at the time.

Geographical situation and natural environment

Situated on the South American continental shelf, both Trinidad and Tobago can be considered to form a geographical extension of the mainland, moreso as both islands once were attached by land bridges to South America (Fig. 1). This continental character sets them apart from the oceanic islands of the West Indies. Due to their geographical situation as the southernmost links between the Caribbean archipelago and the mainland of South America, the two islands formed the natural gateway for human movement, exchange and diffusion of culture from the continent, especially the Orinoco Valley, to the islands of the West Indies, as well as from the Venezuelan coast to the Guianas and vice versa. As a result, at one stage in pre-Columbian times the twin islands formed part of an extensive indigenous 'interaction sphere', i.e. a dense contact network closely knit by ties of kinship, language, exchange, war, and culture, encompassing parts of the Orinoco Valley, the Guianas and the Paria peninsula. This region is interconnected by an extensive web of sea channels, rivers, lagoons, and estuaries, which formed the favorite channels of Amerindian communication and transport and, consequently, facilitated dense interaction among the indigenous peoples living here. This contact network, in which Amerindian peoples of varying ethnic identities and cultural backgrounds participated, continuously warring and trading, exchanging people, news, tales, songs, and customs, still functioned in the early contact period after 1498.

Formerly communication to and from Trinidad and Tobago was largely determined by the prevailing winds and the system of sea currents around both islands. The major sea current affecting the twin islands is the Guiana Current which approaches Trinidad from the southeast. Part of this stream flows through the Columbus Channel into the Gulf of Paria while another portion moves to the north, subsequently encircling Tobago in order to continue flowing in a

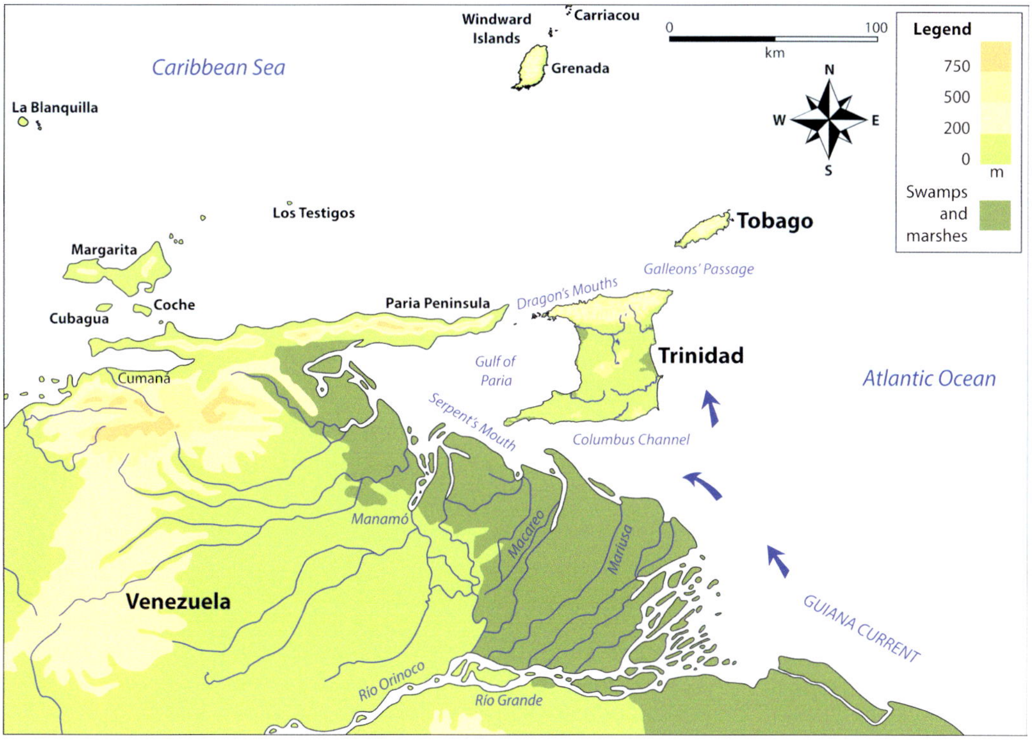

Figure 1. Geographical situation of Trinidad and Tobago, with nearby islands and parts of the South American mainland, showing edge of the continental shelf (200 m below mean sea level).

generally western direction. In the wet season the enormous amount of muddy, yellowish-brown freshwater discharged by the Orinoco River reinforces the velocity of the current, and reduces the salinity of the Gulf of Paria to such a degree that its condition approaches that of freshwater, while it is near-oceanic during the dry portion of the year. The Orinoco outflow carries floating mats of vegetation from the delta of this river to Trinidad as well as caimans, lizards, snakes and freshwater turtles, while similarly alligators from the mainland are known to have washed ashore on Tobago. Interaction between the two islands is facilitated by the circumstance that the northeastern part of Trinidad is almost always within view from south-central Tobago and vice versa. In pre-Columbian times the route most frequently taken by the Amerindians led from Matura Bay, Balandra Bay and Cumana Bay on the northeast coast of Trinidad to Canoe Bay (the name is no coincidence) and La Guira in southwest Tobago. Intra-island communication primarily took place along the two islands' littoral; overland routes were apparently used to a much lesser extent. Clearly, the island mass especially of Trinidad formed a barrier reducing interior interaction.

Both Trinidad and Tobago show a remarkably varied physical make-up (Fig. 2). As a result, both islands offered an extensive series of alternative subsistence potentials to their pre-Columbian inhabitants. Trinidad is geomorphologically most complex and has

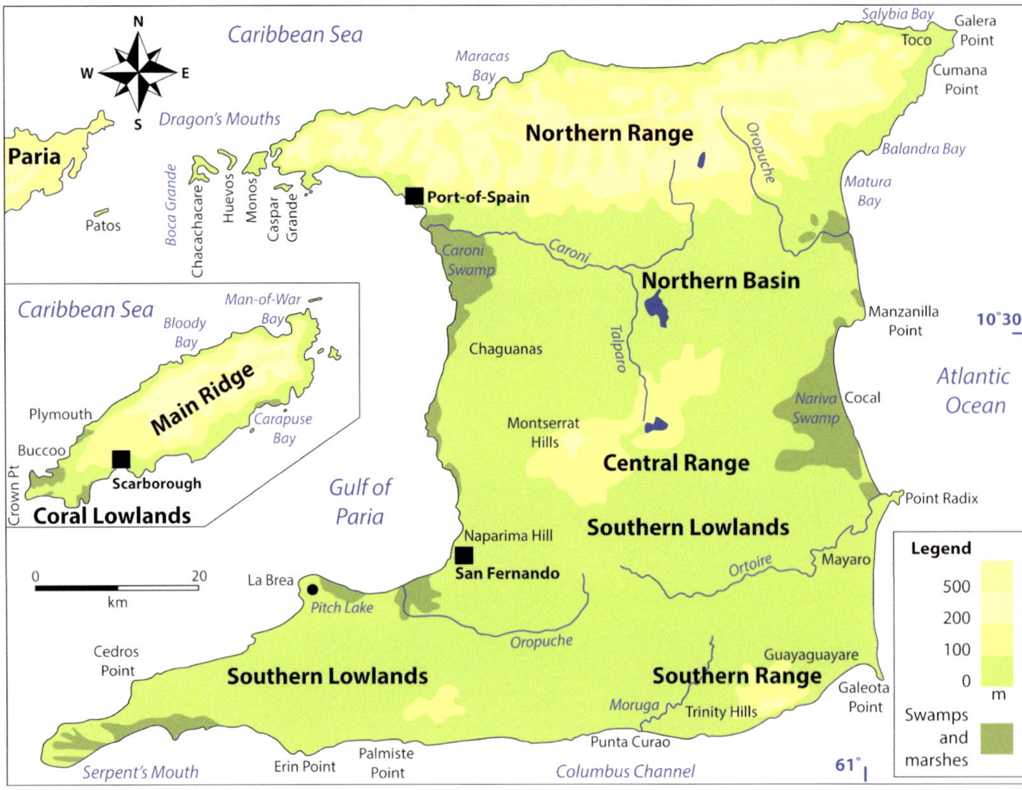

Figure 2. Map of Trinidad and Tobago (inset), showing major physiographic features.

a quite diversified landscape with its three mountain chains and two intervening lowlands. The Northern Range, which contains the highest mountains of the island, rises steeply from the coast and effectively separates the valley of Trinidad's major stream, the Caroni River, also known as the Northern Basin, from the northern littoral. It is dissected by a series of valleys, containing perennial streams, which formed excellent areas for Amerindian habitation. Hematite ('red iron stone') belongs to the useful minerals found in the Northern Range while sources of lignite (coal) and chert, a hard and dense rock type used in pre-Columbian times for the manufacture of small tools, have been encountered in the Central Range. The underground of southern Trinidad is renowned for its deposits of oil and natural gas with related geological phenomena such as the world-famous Pitch Lake (Fig. 3) and other asphalt seepages, for instance in Mayaro, as well as the low mounds bringing up mud and traces of petroleum known as 'mud volcanoes', which are scattered throughout the entire Southern Basin and the Southern Range. Useful minerals of this part of Trinidad include asphaltite (manjak or 'glance pitch') and lignite. Tobago consists of two landscape units, the Coral Lowlands, an elongated coral limestone plateau, and the Main Ridge, a heavily dissected central dorsal ridge of highland which forms the backbone of the island. Tobago's geological make-up is different from that of

Figure 3. Dome-shaped islands in the Pitch Lake, Trinidad.

Trinidad and, as a result, it yields sources of rock materials useful for the pre-Columbian Amerindians, not found in the larger island.

Trinidad and Tobago possess a rich natural fauna and a highly varied vegetation cover, both of which reflect the entirely continental character of the twin islands. Most uncultivated and not built-over parts of the two islands are covered by Tropical Rain Forest ('high woods'), although at present much forest has been severely affected by man due to clearing operations for monocropping, logging and slash-and-burn cultivation, and, as a result, takes the form of secondary growth. Due to the fact that the northern and eastern parts of Trinidad receive much more rainfall than the island's western portion, forests are densest in the Northern Range and the Central Range. As, consequently, vegetation was more open in the west and thus easier to clear for agriculture, this part of Trinidad became the major area of sugar cane cultivation in colonial times. Forests as well as the other ecosystems of the twin islands, such as rivers, swamps and marshes, show a great variety of animals and birds. Some of the latter ecosystems take the form of palm 'islands' fringing small savannas, i.e. grassy plains with scattered trees. The land fauna is enriched by the aquatic life forms to be found at the interface of land and sea in such coastal habitats as mangroves and coral reefs. Of course, the food resources offered by the sea surrounding the two islands were as important to the indigenous peoples of Trinidad and Tobago as those of the land.

The 'high woods' form the habitat of numerous birds and mammals, the latter including for instance howler monkeys (*macaques rouge*), anteaters, ocelots, porcupines, tayras, squirrels, and opossums (*manicous*) which live in the upper storey of the forest, while the forest floor is the domain of brocket deer (*biches*), agoutis (*goutis*), pacas (*lappes*), and peccaries (*quenks*). Here smaller animals such as armadillos (*tatoos*), spiny rats, tortoises, frogs, toads, and snakes are to be found as well. Thick undergrowth is the favourite habitat of Tobago's national bird which, after its raucous call, is known as the *cocrico*. A very special fauna inhabits the limestone caves of Trinidad's Northern Range. These are occupied by thousands of bats and colonies of oil birds which only emerge at night in order to feed on fruits, using sonar for navigating. Typical swamp dwellers are raccoons, otters, water rats, turtles, anacondas, and caimans. At present, manatees (*lamantins*) can only be seen occasionally in some of the extended swamps of the island. Of course, Trinidad's national bird, the scarlet ibis, is a typical swamp dweller which especially inhabits the mangroves of the Caroni Swamp in the northwest. Only a small selection of the animals and birds of the twin islands can be mentioned here, but it is obvious that no island of the West Indies shows such a varied landscape and natural flora and fauna as Trinidad and Tobago. Besides, as both islands are situated at the southern fringe of the Caribbean hurricane zone, fortunately destructive tropical storms of hurricane force pass over them only very infrequently, up to two times per century.

The indigenous peoples of Trinidad and Tobago

Popular belief has it that at the time of Columbus the West Indies, including Trinidad and Tobago, were occupied by two major indigenous groupings, Caribs and Arawaks. The Arawaks are depicted as gentle and peaceful Amerindians who were well-disposed towards the European explorers while the Caribs would have been their antithesis, being fierce, warlike and man-eaters. Of course, these stereotypes are mirrored by our brand names *Arawak* for chicken meat ('lacking courage') and *Carib* for beer ('manly, dauntless'). This ethnic classification is based on gross misunderstanding and presents a caricature of the actual indigenous peoples living in the Antilles at contact. It is largely based on the uncritical acceptance of the first Spanish impressions of the original inhabitants of the Antilles, which were thoroughly mixed with preconceived images partially suggested by medieval thought. Besides, the issue was confused by the inability of archaeologists and anthropologists to distinguish between linguistic and ethnic groupings among the Amerindians of the Caribbean. It is important to realize that ethnic identity, the expression of a feeling of belonging to a particular 'people' (nation), is a matter of self-ascription. In stateless societies such as those of the pre-Columbian Caribbean, ethnic unity was expressed and reinforced by the use of a common name, by particular forms of body ornamentation and dress, and by adherence to an ideology involving recognition of a common origin, and sharing hostile feelings to and stereotyped images of other peoples.

Columbus described the Amerindians of the Greater Antilles as gentle, pacific and obliging people, naming them *indios*, a term which subsequently remained in use among the Spanish as indicating harmless and docile natives who could be easily subjugated. While soon afterwards the Spanish attempts at colonizing Hispaniola would provoke massive armed resistance by the natives, remarkably the original stereotype remained. In other words, the Amerindians turned out to be as peaceful, or warlike if you wish, as the Spanish. When in the nineteenth century scholarly interest in Antillean indigenous society and culture awakened, linguists applied the name 'Island Arawaks' to the peoples of the Greater Antilles. They had discovered that the language spoken by most Amerindians of the Greater Antilles in the contact period is related to that of the 'Lokóno' or 'Arawak' ('Aruac'), a tribal ethnic grouping at present still inhabiting the coastal zone of the Guianas, but formerly living in south Trinidad and the Lower Orinoco Valley as well. Both languages, albeit mutually unintelligible, can be assigned to the Northern Arawakan linguistic family which is widespread on the mainland of South America.[2] It is noteworthy that 'Arawak' was never a name the Amerindians of the Greater Antilles used for themselves. 'Taíno' is another collective term which was coined for the indigenous peoples of the Greater Antilles by nineteenth-century linguists. Actually, *taíno* is a native adjective meaning 'good, noble', forming the root of the noun *nítainos* which was used to indicate the aristocracy in the hierarchical (chiefdom-type) indigenous societies of at least Hispaniola and Puerto Rico.

The use of the term Island or Insular Arawak, with the adjective frequently omitted, for the contact-period inhabitants of the Greater Antilles was adopted, especially in the anglophone Caribbean, by the authors of history textbooks for primary and secondary schools and for this reason gained major popularity here. Moreover, amongst the general public the application of the term Arawak to both the indigenous peoples of the Greater Antilles and the Lokóno, also known as the 'True Arawaks', has given rise to the mistaken belief that a close ethnic relationship existed between these groups of people. However, it should be kept in mind that the speakers of even closely related languages may consider themselves as belonging to quite different ethnic unities ('peoples, nations'). Think for instance of the English, Scots, Irish, Americans, Canadians, and the nations of the anglophone Caribbean, all speaking English but nevertheless thinking of themselves as quite different peoples and thus referring to themselves by entirely different names.[3] This applied to the indigenous peoples of pre-Columbian times as well. Clearly, the term Arawak should be abandoned when reference is made to the Indians of the Greater Antilles. It should be applied only to the Lokóno or Arawaks of the mainland and Trinidad, who used both names to refer to themselves. This is not to say that Taíno is an appropriate name for the contact-period inhabitants of the

---

2 This language family was called as such since the language of the Lokóno or Arawaks of the Guianas was the first of its numerous individual member languages which was thoroughly described. If the speech of the related Goajiro nation of west Venezuela would have been the earliest well documented Arawakan language, it would have been called instead the Goajiroan family.

3 Similarly, although English, together with for instance Dutch, German, Danish, and Swedish, belongs to the Germanic group of languages, the English would not think of it calling themselves Germans.

Greater Antilles. Contrary to what is often thought, these Indians never employed an overall name for themselves, as a sense of communality amongst them simply did not exist. Instead, most likely they used the names of the local (chiefdom) polities to which they belonged as self-ascriptions, in this way expressing feelings of ethnic unity.

Columbus portrayed the Amerindians of the Lesser Antilles as the mental and behavioural opposites of the *indios* of the Greater Antilles. Tales from the latter during his first voyage to the West Indies induced the Admiral to believe that a race of belligerent, agressive and anthropophagous (man-eating) Indians, variously called *canima*, *caniba*, *caníbales*, *caríbales* or *caribes*, who instilled the inhabitants of Cuba and Hispaniola with deadly fear, occupied islands rumoured to exist towards the east and southeast of the Greater Antilles. Obviously, the original form of the name may have been *caniba* which was modified to *caníbales* and *caribes*. Unfortunately, the veracity of Columbus' writings on this matter is difficult to gauge. The problem of communicating between the Spanish and Indians during the first voyage, and the Admiral's original belief that he had met followers of China's Great Khan, may well have influenced the reliability and accuracy of the notes in his *diario*. It is quite obvious that for the Spanish the name *caribes* never had a specific, well-circumscribed ethnic meaning: it just signified fierce, supposedly anthropophagous Amerindians who were difficult to subjugate. It was their supposed cannibalism which in 1503 induced the Spanish Crown to authorize their enslavement, as a result of which, from then onwards, the Spanish colonists in the West Indies applied the name *caribes* to as many Amerindian peoples as possible, both in the Caribbean and beyond. Nevertheless, 'Caribes' (English 'Caribs') represents the name under which a particular tribal ethnic group of Amerindians has become known, which at contact times inhabited parts of Trinidad, the Orinoco Valley and the coastal zone of the Guianas, and the Windward Islands and the southernmost Leeward Islands.

The present Caribs of the Guiana coastal zone and Venezuela call themselves 'Kali'na' or 'Kari'na' (meaning 'person, people'). These 'Mainland Caribs' (also known as Galibis) speak a language belonging to the Cariban linguistic family, which like Arawakan forms one of the most widespread language stocks of the South American tropical lowlands. Linguistically the Caribs, who formerly occupied the Windward Islands and Guadeloupe, Montserrat and St. Kitts, were quite different from their kinsmen on the South American mainland. These 'Island Caribs' spoke two variants of what was basically Northern Arawakan, i.e., a female and a male register, of which the latter shows numerous Cariban vocabular borrowings. Their common name, which was recorded in the mid-seventeenth century, expresses strong feelings of ethnic unity with the Caribs of the mainland, since the male Island Caribs used the same name as the latter to indicate their people (nation): they called themselves 'Kali'nago' which is obviously derived from the name Kali'na. Consequently, while considering themselves ethnically to belong to the Cariban-speaking Caribs of the mainland, the Island Caribs spoke principally Arawakan. In the seventeenth century the Island Carib males explained this situation by claiming that the origin of their people stemmed from a migration

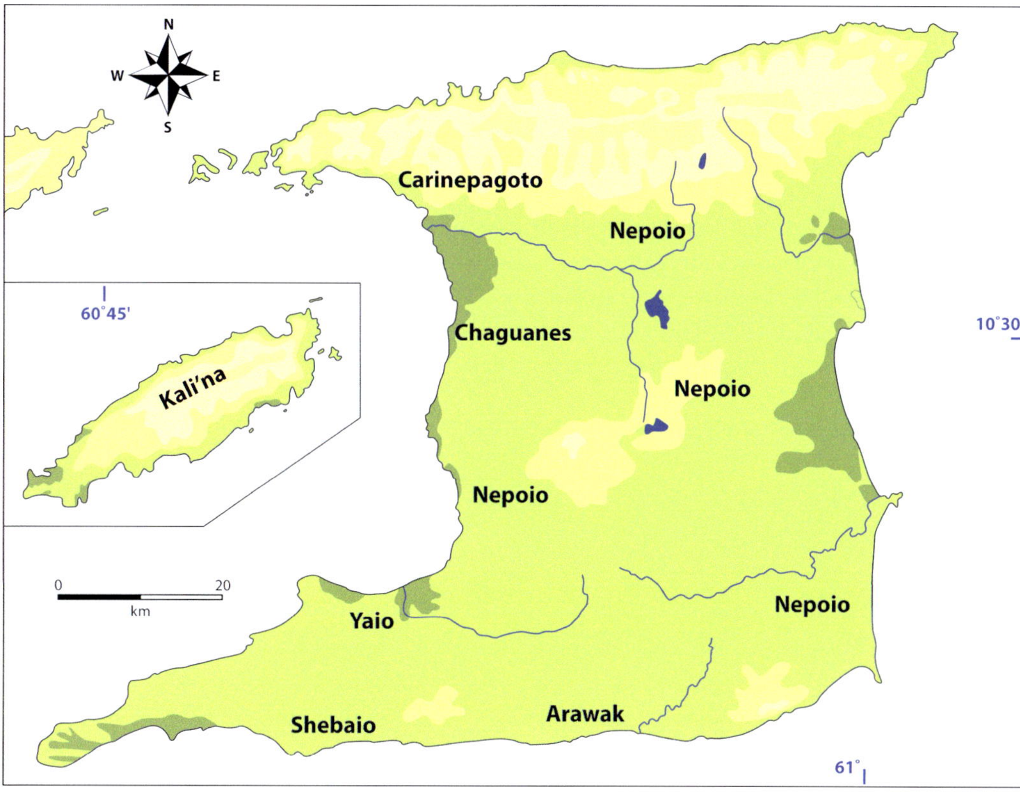

Figure 4. Map of Trinidad and Tobago (inset), showing Amerindian ethnic groups in the contact period (ca. 1500).

from the coast of the Guianas, in the process of which the males of the original inhabitants of the Lesser Antilles were killed, while the females were taken as slaves and concubines. The latter would have preserved their original, Arawakan, language while the males lost most of their own speech in the new environment.

At the time of the European encounter Trinidad was a complex multiethnic and multilingual conglomerate of Amerindian 'nations' (Fig. 4). It was not until the 1590s that the names of these various indigenous peoples were recorded. According to Sir Walter Ralegh, Trinidad was inhabited by five different Amerindian groupings: Carinepagoto, Arawak, Shebaio, Yaio, and Nepoio. In the sixteenth century the Carinepagoto lived in northwest Trinidad. Their name is clearly derived from that of the Kali'na, to which *-pa* ('place') and *-goto* have been affixed, the latter being a terminal commonly added to tribal names of Cariban-speaking Amerindians. All of this suggests that the Carinepagoto formed a Mainland Carib tribal segment. Apart from the Carinepagoto, two other, now extinct, Cariban-speaking tribal peoples inhabited Trinidad in the contact period, the Yaio and the Nepoio. The Yaio lived in southwest Trinidad. They may have been related especially with the Cariban-speaking peoples living on the Venezuelan coast who were ethnically different from the Kali'na (and Kali'nago). The documentary sources suggest that the Yaio were multilingual. They were to be found also in the western coastal zone of the Guianas. The central and eastern parts of Trinidad were occupied by Nepoio, but they inhabited stretches of the Lower Orinoco valley and delta as well.

A mainland connection is similarly seen among the Arawakan-speaking Amerindian tribal groupings of Trinidad: the Arawaks (Lokóno) and Shebaio. These two (now amalgamated) ethnic groups inhabited the central and western parts of the island's south coast. Finally, a sixth Amerindian people, the Chaguanes, is reported to have lived close to the central-western coastal zone of Trinidad about 1600. (The place name Chaguanas is derived from their name.) The Chaguanes (Siawani) formed a subtribe of the Warao, a major Amerindian grouping still

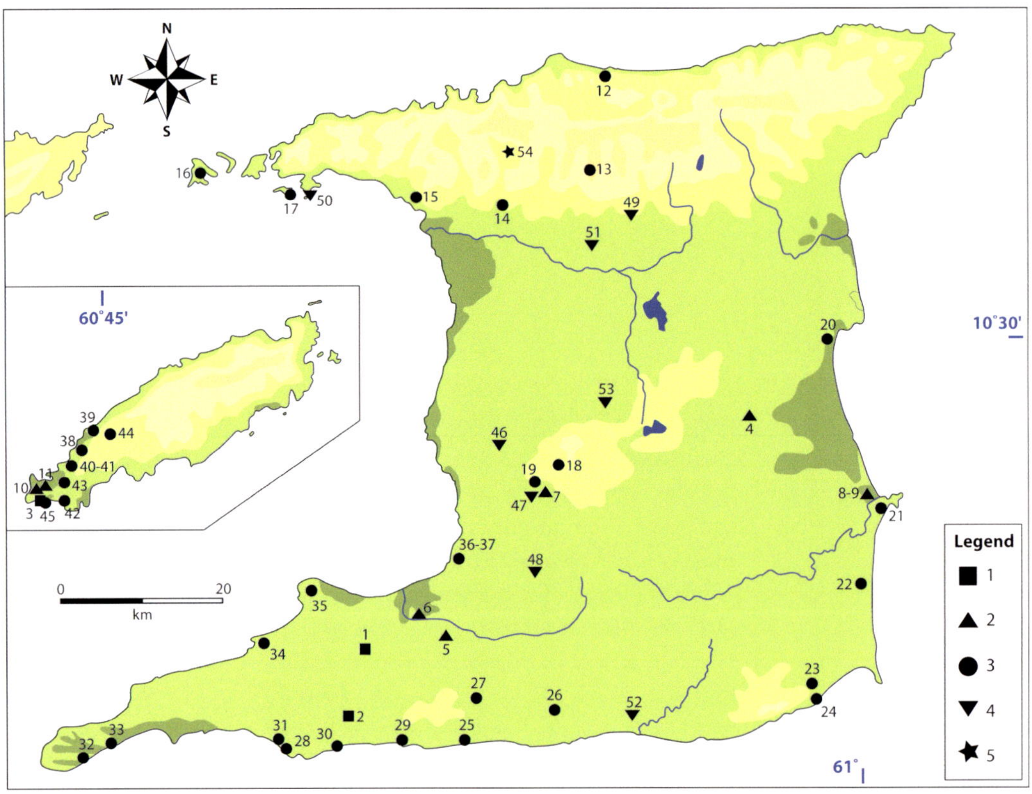

Figure 5. Map of Trinidad and Tobago (inset), showing major palaeontological and archaeological sites. Legend: (1) Fossil mammal sites; (2) Lithic/Archaic Age sites; (3) Ceramic Age sites; (4) Historic-Amerindian sites; (5) petroglyphs. Key to sites: (1) Forest Reserve; (2) Los Bajos; (3) Robinson Crusoe Cave; (4) Biche; (5) Banwari Trace; (6) St. John; (7) Poonah Road; (8) Ortoire; (9) Cocal 1; (10) Milford 1; (11) Bon Accord 1–5; (12) Blanchisseuse; (13) La Reconnaissance; (14) St. Joseph 2; (15) Red House; (16) Sanders Bay, Chacachacare Island; (17) Bombshell Bay, Caspar Grande Island; (18) Atagual; (19) Whitelands; (20) Manzanilla 1; (21) St. Bernard; (22) Lagon Doux 1; (23) St. Catherine's; (24) Guayaguayare; (25) Batîment Crasé; (26) Marac 2; (27) Grant's Trace; (28) Los Iros; (29) Quinam; (30) Palo Seco; (31) Erin; (32) Icacos; (33) Cedros; (34) Otaheite; (35) Pitch Lake 1–2; (36) Bontour; (37) San Fernando–Harris Promenade/High Street; (38) Great Courland Bay; (39) Lovers' Retreat; (40) Mount Irvine 1; (41) Mount Irvine 3; (42) Friendship; (43) Golden Grove; (44) Courland River; (45) Crown Point; (46) Savaneta 2; (47) Mayo; (48) Princes Town 1; (49) Arima; (50) Carrera Island; (51) Golden Grove; (52) Moruga Road/Esmeralda; (53) Mamoral; (54) Caurita.

living in the delta of the Orinoco and the western portion of the Guianas. They speak an independent language (Waraoan), not related to Arawakan or Cariban. Warao from the Orinoco delta visited south Trinidad regularly until recently. In the contact period Tobago was, unlike Trinidad, inhabited by only one Amerindian ethnic group. From the early sixteenth century onwards it is recorded that Caribs occupied the smaller island. Whether these were Mainland Caribs (Kali'na) or Island Caribs (Kali'nago), thus speaking Cariban or basically Arawakan, is not entirely clear. The first possibility appears to be the most likely one.

It should be kept in mind, that linguistic affiliation and ethnicity are concepts which are almost completely beyond archaeological retrieval, the reason why archaeologists have to classify their units in terms of cultural traditions ('series') rather than, for instance, in terms of 'ethnic groups' or 'peoples'. Besides, as we have seen, due to the lack of written documents in pre-Columbian times, indigenous tribal names, such as those listed above for the contact period, cannot be assigned to the prehistoric cultural traditions archaeologists are able to identify. And indeed, their linguistic affiliations can only be guessed at. We are simply unable to give a name, such as Yaio, Carib, Arawak or Nepoio, to archaeological finds which can be dated to prehistoric times. Consequently, archaeologists use names of archaeological sites to refer to the cultural traditions they can distinguish in the pre-Columbian era. Thus, they speak for instance of the Cedros and Palo Seco cultural complexes in Trinidad, both belonging to the Saladoid series, when referring to two subsequent local cultural traditions typified by the Cedros and Palo Seco sites on the island's south coast, which belonged to one overarching and long-lasting tradition, called Saladoid after the site of Saladero on the Lower Orinoco River in Venezuela.

Discovery of archaeological sites

Interest in the pre-Columbian antiquities of Trinidad and Tobago was first roused in the second half of the nineteenth century. During exploration surveys of especially the coastal areas of both islands at various locations, large deposits of shells were discovered which could not be interpreted as natural phenomena. Besides, many of these shell heaps, clearly the refuse middens of villages or hamlets inhabited by the pre-Columbian inhabitants of the twin islands, yielded pottery fragments and tools made of stone, bone, shell and/or coral, and occasionally Amerindian inhumation burials. The scientific study of these former settlements through archaeological excavations was initiated in the early twentieth century and has accelerated during the past decades. To date some 300 registered archaeological sites are known in Trinidad and Tobago, although some have been destroyed in the recent past (Fig. 5). Site density is lowest in central and north Trinidad as well as interior Tobago. This, obviously, is due to the history of archaeological investigation in both islands which has seen a concentration of research in south Trinidad and southwest Tobago. Unfortunately, the legal protection of these places of cultural heritage in the two islands leaves much to be desired. Fortunately, the urgent necessity of

Figure 6. Archaeological settlement site at Plum (SAN-6) in the Nariva area, Trinidad, showing ploughed field with shell midden deposit, dating to the Late Ceramic Age, ca. AD 650/800–1400.

enacting adequate protective legislation of archaeological sites by the government is a matter which at present forms a prime area of interest by the National Trust of Trinidad and Tobago.

Most archaeological sites in Trinidad and Tobago represent chance discoveries, caused by natural or human action. Often site relocation results from the caving in of river banks and beach erosion. Otherwise, archaeological sites have been discovered due to human activities such as the construction of houses, dams, roads, jetties, and (formerly) fortifications, as well as from excavation works in order to place water lines or sewer pipes, the erection of oil derricks, ploughing sugar cane fields or gardens, quarrying building materials, and (in the old days) digging for loam (*tapia*) for plastering the wattle-work walls of cottages built in the Spanish fashion. In south Trinidad numerous sites have been discovered during field surveys by archaeologically interested oil geologists. Also, the formerly quite frequent removal of shells for gravelling local roads and yards has led to both the location of sites and the destruction of large parts of them. Besides, as many midden sites show uniformly dark-coloured habitation layers rich in organic matter, phosphorus and calcium, they are sought after as garden earth, which in various instances has again led to the discovery and the complete or partial disappearance of sites.

Figure 7. Pre-Columbian petroglyphs (rock drawings) at Caurita (SGE-9), north of St. Joseph in the Northern Range, Trinidad.

Several different categories of archaeological sites can be distinguished in Trinidad and Tobago. The first group includes settlement sites, yielding deep midden (refuse) deposits, speckled with numerous finds of Amerindian material culture, and soil features. Food debris such as animal and fish bone remains, as well as shells, are characteristic. In south Trinidad such sites are often locally known as *chipchip* hills, after the vernacular name of the most popular edible bivalve of the island, the donax clam, which in various instances indeed forms the major component of these refuse heaps (Fig. 6). Settlement sites are often characterized by numerous individual or collective inhumation burials. Pottery deposits represent another category of sites. They include surface scatters of ceramics and other artifacts, lacking appreciable amounts of food remains. In most cases such pottery deposits indicate temporary camp or bivouac sites, utilized briefly by the Amerindians during hunting, fishing or collecting expeditions. Flint deposits, i.e. refuse or workshop areas at which no pieces of pottery and negligible amounts of food remains are found, constitute another type of archaeological sites. Individual finds of especially Amerindian stone implements represent a special category of sites: they may indicate the locations where special activities took place such as manufacturing canoes, collecting vegetable foods or invertebrates such as crabs and shells, and horticultural work.

The age of most archaeological sites and the material remains they yield can be determined by a series of methods, including dating using the so-called radiocarbon method of organic remains, especially charcoal. There is one category of sites, however, for which this is possible only under exceptional circumstances: petroglyphs. These are Amerindian rock drawings, which no doubt originally formed the centre of particular religious ceremonies. At present only one example is still to be seen and visited, pecked and chiselled by the pre-Columbian inhabitants of Trinidad into the surface of a big quartzite boulder situated north of Caurita ravine in the Northern Range. It is certainly one of the most interesting and mysterious monuments the prehistoric inhabitants of the twin islands have left us. No rock drawings are known from Tobago, while a petroglyph, which reportedly formerly was to be seen close to the Lagon Doux (Marie Rose) River in Mayaro, has since been covered with a few metres of sand due to a change in the river bed. The rock drawings of Caurita are to be found in the high forest southeast of El Tucuche (Fig. 7). They consist of a number of human-like heads and figures, pecked into the rock surface. One central figure, which has been likened to a pregnant woman, can be discerned: it has a diamond-shaped body, raised arms and an oval head in which eyes, mouth and nose are indicated by pits. At least three other faces, showing similarly executed features, are represented. Who made the Caurita rock drawings and when remains a mystery; the only thing we know is that they are pre-Columbian in age. Besides, the meaning of these rock drawings can only be guessed at. Perhaps they are representations of the culture heroes, spirits or other supernatural beings in Amerindian mythology. They may have been chiselled into the rock by the indigenous shaman (medicine man) under the influence of hallucinogenic drugs, which were taken to induce an ecstatic trance in order to contact the spirit world.

2. The first settlers (ca. 8000–300 BC)

It was not until about 7000/6000 BC that, due to the global sea level rise after the close of the Last Ice Age, Trinidad became an island. Only a millennium or so afterwards it got its present contours, making Trinidad the fifth largest island of the Caribbean. Tobago, too, is a continental island, but its land bridge with the mainland was broken at a much earlier stage, perhaps by 11,000 BC. Throughout the final part of the Last Ice Age the landscape of Trinidad and Tobago was quite different from that of today. Mean annual temperature was some 4–5°C lower than at present and, most importantly, there was much less rainfall. As a result forests were much more open and mainly restricted to the mountain ridges of both islands. Besides, savannas, i.e. wide grasslands with scattered trees, were much more extended. Small relics of such savannas are to be found nowadays at only a few places, for instance at Aripo in the Caroni Valley of north Trinidad. To a certain extent these Ice Age savannas resembled the *llanos*, i.e. the extended grassy plains of present Venezuela and Colombia.

This original landscape of both Trinidad and Tobago was roamed by a fauna which is entirely different from that of nowadays as it consisted predominantly of oversized ('megafaunal') animals which are now extinct. Remains of these Ice Age animals have been encountered at sites in southwest Trinidad, mainly now filled-in stream channels or ponds where they came to drink and bathe (Fig. 5). All of these large animals were slow movers, feeding on grasses, twigs or leaves. They include for instance giant ground sloths, the *Megatherium* and *Mylodon*, and glyptodonts, i.e. large mammals related to the present armadillo (*tattoo*), and huge tusked animals, ancestors of today's elephant, known as mastodons or mammuts. In 1957 an entire *Glyptodon* skeleton, found during digging for an oil well, was excavated by the geologist Dr. Kenneth W. Barr at Forest Reserve in southwest Trinidad. Glyptodont remains have been recovered also from the famous Robinson Crusoe Cave in southwest Tobago. Glyptodonts had the size of a small car and when a *Megatherium* stood on its hind legs and stretched itself, it could reach the branches of trees as high as 3 m. Bones of a *Megatherium* found at Los Bajos in 1935 are exhibited in the National Museum and Art Gallery in Port-of-Spain. All of these 'megafaunal' animals became extinct at the close of the Ice Age. Now the landscape of Trinidad and Tobago changed tremendously. The climatic conditions improved: it became warmer and much wetter. As a result the existing forests became denser and expanded into areas formerly clad with savannas. The latter almost disappeared.

The earliest Trinidadians

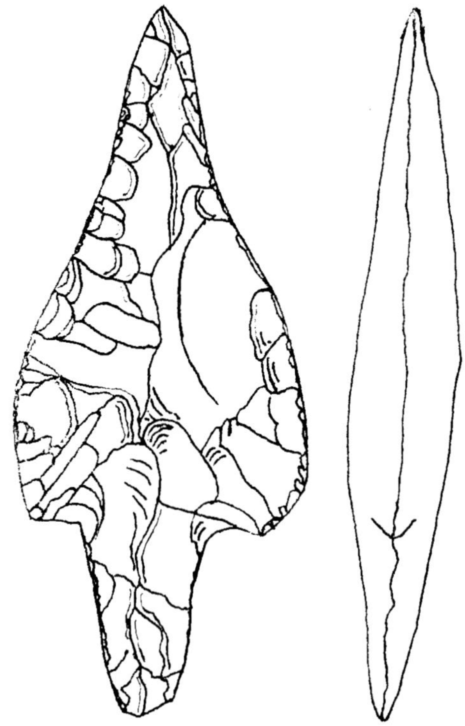

Small wandering bands of Amerindians mainly subsisting on hunting and foraging visited Trinidad infrequently long before the island became detached from the South American mainland. A single, nicely chipped stemmed spearhead, found by a schoolboy in his father's yard at Biche in the eastern part of the Central Range (Fig. 8), suggests that the lifeway of these Amerindians, who are known to have roamed the then relatively open landscapes of present Venezuela and the Guianas by about 9000–8000 BC, was primarily based on hunting for small-game animals and perhaps some fishing. Their diet must have been supplemented by gathering wild fruits and plant foods, honey, eggs, mollusks, berries, palm nuts, etc.

Figure 8. Bifacially chipped, stone spearhead found at Biche (NAR-9) in the Central Range, Trinidad, dating to the Lithic Age, ca. 8000 BC. Length 9.2 cm. Coll. UWI.

Perhaps these Amerindians combined forces for collective hunting in the most productive seasons of the year, dispersing into small family groups during other times. This first era of human development in the Americas is known as the Lithic Age as it was the period that stone chipping was first practised. When Trinidad definitely became an island, about 7000/6000 BC, obviously further movement to and from the mainland by humans was prevented without adequate watercraft. And it would take another millennium or so that the present contours of the island were reached due to the gradual submergence of the Gulf of Paria. By then other immigrants from the mainland had long been settled in Trinidad (Fig. 9).[4]

Two major habitation sites of these early Trinidadians, Banwari Trace and St. John, have been discovered at the southern edge of the Oropuche Lagoon in southwest Trinidad (Fig. 10). This shallow river is brackish at its mouth, supporting a large mangrove stand. Both sites are situated on hillocks at the edge of swampy terrain, at a distance of some 5 km from each other. They represent extended deposits of discarded shells which were collected by the Amerindians from the lagoon, and yielded also other food remains and stone and bone tools. Banwari Trace and St. John may have been central base camps, i.e. dwelling sites which formed the focus of the major subsistence activities shown by these Amerindians. They are considered to belong to an archaeological tradition ('series')

4 The oral traditions of the present Warao Amerindians of the Orinoco delta still speak of the times when the Serpent's Mouth was dry land and a land bridge connected Trinidad with the mainland. They attribute the origin of the Columbus Channel to a violent hurricane as a result of which 'the trees of the forest came crashing down with a noise like thunder', the soil 'split open, and the waves of the ocean filled the cracks'.

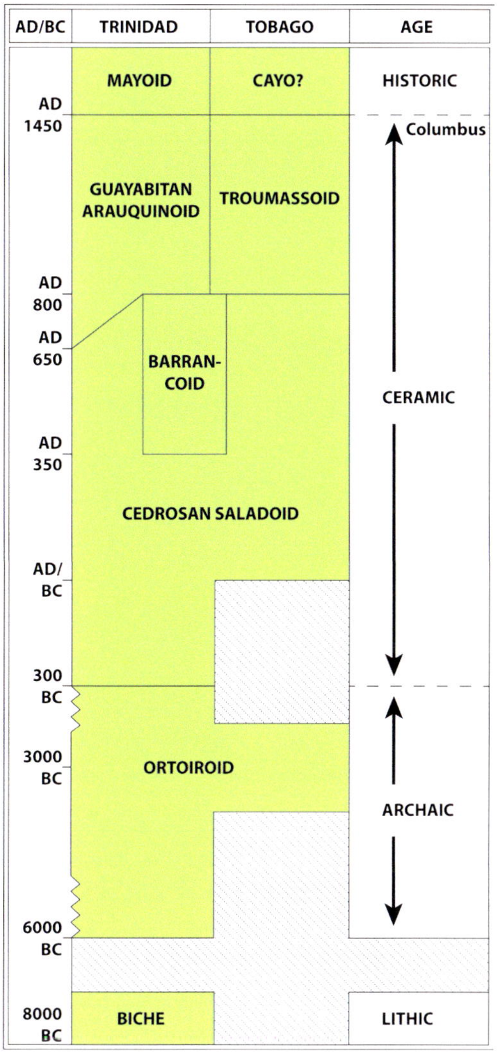

Figure 9. Chronological chart of Trinidad and Tobago, showing the sequence of pre-Columbian cultural traditions, reconstructed from archaeological excavations, and their dating. Hached episodes in the columns, uninhabited or occupation yet unknown.

called Ortoiroid (called after the similar but much more recent Ortoire site in Mayaro). As the people of Banwari Trace and St. John had not yet mastered the art of pottery making, the era of the Ortoiroid tradition is known as the Archaic Age. This pre-Columbian period, which followed the Lithic Age, would last for thousands of years during which the Ortoiroid peoples spread through the West Indies.

It was due to the unceasing efforts of local avocational archaeologists, members of the Trinidad and Tobago Historical Society (South Section) led by Peter O'Brien Harris, that in October 1969 archaeological excavations started at the Banwari Trace site located near San Francique. They would last well into 1971 and were resumed by Harris, assisted by a group of young volunteer archaeologists, in 2005. St. John was excavated as early as 1953 by a team led by the 'father' of Caribbean archaeology, Professor Irving Rouse of Yale University, New Haven, USA. While at present the St. John site is completely destroyed, the now remaining portion of the Banwari Trace site was acquired by the government of Trinidad and Tobago in 2000, in this way guaranteeing its protection as a truly national site of cultural heritage. Dating of charcoal and shell samples from both sites using the radiocarbon method established their age, between 6000 and 4000 BC.

The Amerindians of Banwari Trace and St. John were hunters, fishers, foragers, and incipient horticulturalists (gardeners). By diversifying their subsistence strategies in this way, they were able to consume a large variety of foodstuffs: they had a 'broad-spectrum diet'. Formerly it was thought that horticulture was introduced to the West Indies at a much later date, but many of the stone implements used by the Banwari people were intended for the processing of plant foods. Besides, analysis of starch grains trapped in fissures and pores of stone pestles found at St. John yielded evidence that the Archaic Amerindians who lived at this site consumed maize (corn), chili peppers, and ground provisions such as sweet potatoes, Indian shot (*achira*), perhaps Indian yam and coontie (zamia). The latter is a highly toxic, wild tuberous plant, which was perhaps tended by the inhabitants of St. John. Processing coontie would have involved grinding the tubers into mash that had to be left to ferment

Figure 10. View of the Oropuche Swamp, directly west of the archaeological site of St. John (SPA-11), Trinidad, dating to the Archaic Age, ca. 6000–4000 BC.

until maggots appeared, signalling detoxification. Further research is necessary to deepen our understanding of the horticultural practices of the Banwari people. In addition, they may have collected wild food plants, palm starch, grass seeds, and edible fruits. Cultivation would have taken place primarily in small-sized house or kitchen gardens, typically showing a seemingly chaotic packing of cultivated plants, each of which is represented by only a limited number of individuals. These house gardens would eventually develop into true 'swiddens', i.e. horticultural plots, generally less than a hectare in size, which were tilled systematically and planted with a small number of ground provisions, seed crops and fruit trees. The clearing of these fields took place by simple slash-and-burn techniques. Most of them were only productive for a few years.

Hunting and fishing were important subsistence activities of the Archaic Amerindians living at the edge of the Oropuche Lagoon. Hunting took place primarily in the forests away from the lagoon, where mammals such as howler monkeys, common opossums, nine-banded armadillos, spiny rats, agoutis, pacas, collared peccaries, and red brocket deer were caught. Fishing took place both in the Oropuche Lagoon and the Gulf of Paria; almost half of the fish caught belonged to the sea catfish family. Gradually fishing became

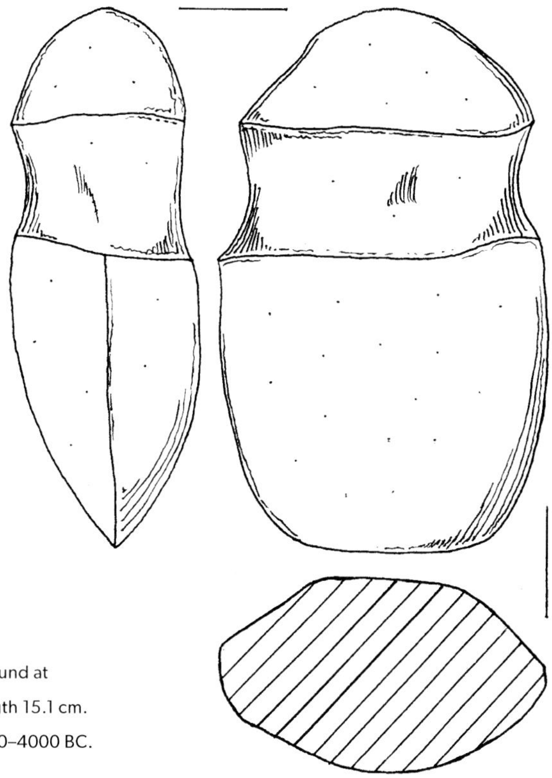

Figure 11. Grooved stone axe head, found at Banwari Trace (SPA-28), Trinidad. Length 15.1 cm. Ortoiroid series, Archaic Age, ca. 6000–4000 BC. Private coll.

more and more important at the expense of hunting. While hunting and fishing were most likely male occupations, the collecting of shells may have been typically the activity of women and children. They gathered gastropods such as river conchs and nerites, and bivalves including tiger lucinas and, from the lagoon's mangroves, West Indian crown conchs, and two species of oysters, i.e. 'Coon oysters and Caribbean oysters. (Indeed, as early as 1595 Sir Walter Ralegh noted approvingly about the oysters from the Oropuche Lagoon that they 'were very salt and well tasted'.) In addition, blue crabs and hairy (*callaloo*) crabs were caught for food.

The Banwari people used a variety of ground stone tools for processing especially the vegetable foods they cultivated and gathered, such as conical pestles, pitted stones or anvils (for cracking palm nuts) and various types of grinding stones, including 'faceted' or 'side' grinders showing traces of grinding exclusively round the (narrow) edges (for grinding and/or mashing both root and seed crops). They had sizeable ground stone axes (Fig. 11) for cutting trees and the manufacture of dugout canoes,[5] while they used small, irregular flake and core tools made of quartz, flint, chert or other local rock materials for a variety of purposes, *e.g.* cutting meat, scaling fish, prying shells open, scraping skins, finishing wooden arrowshafts, and processing vegetable fibres for making baskets. Besides, small

5 Trees were cut by alternately charring the trunk with fire and cutting away the burned wood. Consequently, the stone axes were used as bruising rather than as cutting instruments. In a similar way dugout canoes were made.

Figure 12. Bone projectile points and bipointed fishhooks, found at Banwari Trace (SPA-28) and St. John (SPA-11), respectively, Trinidad. Length smallest artifact 4.2 cm. Ortoiroid series, Archaic Age, ca. 6000–4000 BC. Harris Coll., UTT.

stone mortars were used for grinding red ochre in order to obtain pigment for *e.g.* body painting. Bone fishhooks and projectile points were made for hunting and fishing (Fig. 12). Conspicuously smooth and pointed antler tips and bone needles may have been used as perforators. Crude stone choppers, finally, were perhaps utilized as woodworking tools or wedges. All in all the men and women of Banwari Trace and St. John had a sophisticated technology in order to exploit their environment, make themselves a living, and secure a varied, balanced and tasty diet.

Habitation sites such as Banwari Trace and St. John functioned as the dwelling places (hamlets) where especially the women and children of the band lived on a semi-permanent basis. Some group members, especially the men, probably departed temporarily in order to occupy small, sometimes seasonal, camps, quarry sites or workshops to pursue specialized tasks such as building canoes, producing stone tools, collecting vital raw materials, or engaging in subsistence activities. Such special activity sites dating from this period have indeed been found in southwest Trinidad. They include individual finds of stone implements or flint deposits, i.e. workshops for producing small stone flake and core tools. That watercraft formed an integral part of the Banwarian cultural heritage is shown by the presence of stone implements at Banwari Trace and St. John, the raw materials for which were apparently procured during overseas voyages to the Venezuelan coast, Tobago or the Windward Islands. A unique fragment of a serpentinite bowl was found at Banwari Trace; most likely it originated on the Paria Peninsula of Venezuela. Large amounts of broken and crumbling stones, mostly soft sandstones, have been found at both Banwari Trace and St. John. Most likely they functioned as heating (cooking) stones, used in hearths for cooking large fish, game meat and edible tubers. At St. John a possible hearth was found consisting of a thick sand bed with a clay centre. It resembles the dome-shaped hearths the present Warao are accustomed to construct in their pile dwellings.

The excavations of Peter Harris at Banwari Trace would lead to the uncovering of the skeleton of Trinidad's oldest resident, the famous 'Banwari Person', dating back to about 5000–4350/4000 BC. Close analysis of the skeleton was recently carried out by a specialist on Caribbean human remains, Professor Alfredo Coppa of Rome, Italy. Although originally identified as a male skeleton, Professor Coppa concluded that its gracial nature and pelvic structure suggest that it could be the remains of a woman as well, who, according to her dental characteristics, may have died at an age of approximately 25–30 years. Lifted entirely from the soil, the skeleton of Trinidad's oldest resident was transported to the Zoological Museum of the Department of Life Sciences at the University of the West Indies, St. Augustine, where it has been curated since. The 'Banwari Person' was carefully buried, deposited in flexed position (with bent knees) and positioned on the left side, along a northwest axis. Two mortuary gifts were found by the excavators accompanying the skeleton. A smooth oval pebble was encountered close to the skull and a bone needle point by the hip. Of course, the latter find strengthens the likelihood that this (inhumation) burial represents a woman. Groups of human bones, apparently assembled and bundled for secondary interment after exhumation of the original burials, were found as well. They illustrate a belief in the afterlife and care for the remains of the ancestors.

The first Tobagonians and late Archaic times in Trinidad

It is likely that the first Amerindians of Tobago came from Trinidad. Habitation sites of the Ortoiroid series are only known from the southwestern part of Tobago, close to the mangrove swamps of Bon Accord Lagoon (Fig. 5). The local Archaic culture is known as the Milford complex, after Tobago's only shell midden site, Milford 1, dating from this period. Besides, individual stone artifacts of distinctly Archaic affiliations have been encountered at a number of locations in the Bon Accord area just northeast of the Milford site. Unfortunately, the few available radiocarbon measurements of shells and animal bone from this site have yielded widely diverging dates between 3500 and 1000 BC. The stone artifacts found at Bon Accord and Milford 1 resemble those encountered at the Poonah Road site in Trinidad, and although no reliable dates are available for this latter complex, it can be seen as having developed out of the Ortoiroid tradition of Banwari Trace and St. John. As such a date close to approximately 3500/3000 BC would be most likely. Poonah Road is a site in the interior of Trinidad's Central Range which was excavated by Harris in 1971 and 1972. It yielded Archaic stone implements such as

Figure 13. Bottle-shaped stone pestle, found at Poonah Road (VIC-29), Trinidad. Length 7.6 cm. Ortoiroid series, Archaic Age, ca. 3000 BC. Harris Coll., WFT.

axes, mortars, faceted (side) grinders, and highly distinctive bottle-shaped pestles (Fig. 13). Most of these tools are made of local quartzitic sandstone. The site may have been a temporary (seasonal) camp site used to collect and process plant foods and/or vegetable fibers.

A relationship between Poonah Road and the Tobagonian Archaic sites is suggested especially by the presence of typically bottle-shaped pestles among the stone finds made at Bon Accord. Other stone tools encompass conical pestles, pitted anvils, axes, grinding stones and hammerstones. They suggest that wild and perhaps cultivated vegetable foods, probably including edible roots, palm starch and seeds, formed part of the Archaic diet in Tobago. A series of small, irregular stone flakes and chunks, produced by unsophisticated direct percussion, was encountered at the Milford 1 shell midden. They may have served for a multitude of purposes as needed. Apart from wild plant collecting and possibly incipient horticulture, the Archaic Tobagonians subsisted by fishing, hunting, turtling, and shellfish collecting. They fished for reef fish such as parrotfishes, snappers and groupers, probably using fish pots, and pelagic fishes such as tunas and flying fishes. Hunting concentrated on mammals such as collared peccaries and agoutis, but pacas, red howler monkeys, nine-banded armadillos, and iguanas were caught as well. Abundant bone fragments of sea turtles attest to the capturing of these oversized reptiles by the Archaic Tobagonians while they were nestling on the island's beaches. Shell collecting took place in various habitats, although mainly marine to brackish species, notably queen conchs (*lambis*), hawk-wing conchs, West Indian topshells (*whelks*), and thick lucinas, were gathered. Crabs made up the most noteworthy non-shell invertebrate food source.

Several archaeological sites in Trinidad can be dated to late Archaic times, which can be taken to cover approximately the last few millennia BC. The best known of these sites are Ortoire and Cocal 1, situated close to each other just north of the mangrove-fringed estuary of the Ortoire (Guataro) River in Mayaro. Both occupy a sand bar which separates the Nariva Swamp from the Atlantic Ocean. Charcoal samples from Ortoire have been dated by radiocarbon to about 950 BC. Cocal 1 was excavated as early as 1915 by the American archaeologist Theodoor de Booy on behalf of the Museum of the American Indian, New York, while Ortoire was investigated by Irving Rouse of Yale University in 1953. Both sites are shell middens predominantly consisting of marine bivalves at home in a muddy, sandy-bottom habitat, i.e. mainly trigonal tivelas (*wacoo*) and less donax clams (*chipchip*).[6] At present especially the latter shells are collected by digging them out in the intertidal zone at low tide; they are boiled and made into the locally renowned *chipchip* soup. Clearly, this Mayaro tradition may go back as far as Archaic times. The Ortoire site yielded several clay hearths showing abundant ash, charcoal, fire-cracked stones as well as burned shells and bones. Large quantities of red ochre pebbles and flat, tabular heating (cooking) stones of local sandstone were found at both sites.

Apart from shellfish collecting, hunting, fishing and probably incipient horticulture formed major subsistence activities. Red brocket deer, peccaries, armadillos, land turtles, crabs, and birds were hunted. It is likely that fishing concentrated on catching especially inshore/estuarine fish. A series of perforated clam shells may have served as fishing lures or as net or line sinkers. Relatively few man-made artifacts were encountered. All are made of stone and bone. Tools related to hunting and fishing include flat, angle projectile points of bone and small stone netsinkers. Most implements were apparently meant for woodworking and the processing of various raw materials and plant foods. Such tools include hammerstones, small stone mortars, occasionally showing red colouring due to the grinding of hematite, pitted anvils for the cracking of palm nuts, and grinding stones. Most ground stone artifacts are made of local quartzite; the presence of pieces of blackish dolerite at Ortoire suggests contacts with Tobago. Pieces of quartz crystal are numerous at both sites. At present such quartz chips are prized shamanic charms thought to possess curative properties among the Warao and other Amerindian peoples of the mainland. Moreover, quartz or quartzite pebbles often serve as healing stones, symbolizing guardian spirits, in the gourd rattles used by the local religious specialist, the shaman, to contact the spirit world.

The present Warao of the Orinoco delta and northwest Guyana, of whom a subtribe, the Chaguanes, is known to have lived in Trinidad around 1600, have often been seen as the direct descendants of the Archaic peoples of the mainland and Trinidad. Clearly, their lifeways must have resembled those of the Ortoiroid peoples to a large extent. Until recently fishing, hunting and collecting wild and tended vegetable foodstuffs, especially the starchy pith and nuts of the moriche palm, formed the mainstay of Warao subsistence. The moriche palm occurs in managed groves occupying swampy terrain. Its starch is baked into bread by spreading it out on stones or iron plates on a fire. The moriche palm further yields numerous useful raw materials. The trunk is often used in house construction

6 Both these names are derived from Cariban terms, still current in Venezuela, i.e. *guacuco* and *chipichipe*.

while its leaves serve as material for thatching. A strong fibre is extracted from the young, unopened leaves, which, after soaking in water, boiling, washing and drying, is made into a twine, employed for making hammocks, fishing thread, female loincloths, and the ceremonial head gear of men. The moriche palm leaves also yield the material for various forms of basketry. Being accomplished manufacturers and traders of dugout canoes, pottery making was traditionally unknown to them. Warao settlements are small, typically consisting of a few rows of up to ten rectangular, open pile dwellings, set parallel to the river bank. As a whole, the Warao are often felt to have been pushed back into their present swampy abode by the horticulturalist Amerindians of Ceramic times, the ancestors of the present Arawak and Kali'na.

3. New immigrants: the first ceramists (ca. 300 BC–AD 650/800)

The last few centuries before the beginning of our era saw the gradual movement of new groups of indigenous people from the South American mainland to Trinidad and Tobago (Fig. 9). Called after the archaeological site of Saladero on the Lower Orinoco River, they are known as the Amerindians of the Saladoid tradition. After having moved from the Orinoco to the Venezuelan coast by ca. 800–500 BC, the Saladoid peoples came into contact with the local peoples of the Ortoiroid tradition who lived here and on islands such as Margarita and Cubagua. These Amerindians were accomplished seafarers and had become acquainted with Trinidad, Grenada and Los Testigos. Learning from the Venezuelan Amerindians about the existence of these islands and the necessary maritime technology and navigational requirements to reach them, the Saladoid peoples subsequently settled in Trinidad and afterwards in Tobago, also venturing out into the West Indies and finally travelling as far as Puerto Rico. Eventually all of the islands of the Lesser Antilles and Puerto Rico would be densely inhabited by the Amerindians of the Saladoid tradition. Unfortunately, the reasons behind the Saladoid migrations are badly understood. Perhaps a combination of causes propelled these movements, which may have been carried out principally by small groups of adventurous young men who were attracted by the favourable settling conditions of the Antillean archipelago. The Saladoid peoples introduced the art of pottery making to Trinidad and Tobago, and that is why they are considered to have initiated the Ceramic Age of pre-Columbian times. Besides, it has been suggested that they spoke a language belonging to the Arawakan linguistic family.

Saladoid settlement sites in Trinidad and Tobago

Some sixty archaeological sites in Trinidad and Tobago can be attributed to the Amerindians of the Saladoid tradition. Most of them are habitation sites, but camp ('bivouac') sites and other special activity sites are known as well. They are distributed all over Trinidad and Tobago, both in the coastal zone and the interior of the twin islands. One of the best known Saladoid habitation sites is to be found at Palo Seco on the coast of southwest Trinidad. This is one of the first excavated sites of the Saladoid tradition in the island. It consists of a series of shell midden deposits in the middle of Petrotrin's Palo Seco beach camp, occupying the top and flanks of a gently sloping sand ridge. Discovered as early as 1906, the site was recognized as a pre-Columbian Amerindian settlement in 1917. By this time it was being dug for shells used for road gravelling by Trinidad's Public Works Department. It was John A. Bullbrook, a British-born oil geologist, who succeeded in convincing the colonial government to have this stopped. Subsequently, Bullbrook received a grant to excavate the site, which he did in 1919, thereby becoming the first local archaeologist of Trinidad and Tobago. He discovered that the Palo Seco site was built up of two different shell layers, each accompanied by many pottery sherds, stone, bone and shell tools, as well as food remains. In addition, Bullbrook encountered hearths (more or less oval, pink areas containing ash, charcoal and burned shells), and in all eleven human burials, all except one interred in strongly flexed ('foetal') position. In 1920 part of the Palo Seco site was demarcated as a Crown Reserve in order to protect it from further deterioration. This made it the first archaeological site in the twin islands which was acquired by the government because of its cultural heritage value. In 1946 and 1969 the site would be investigated further by Professor Irving Rouse of Yale University. Finds from Palo Seco are exhibited in the National Museum and Art Gallery, Port-of-Spain.

Cedros, Atagual, Blanchisseuse, Manzanilla 1, St. Bernard, Erin, Quinam, and Whitelands, all in Trinidad, and Golden Grove (I), Courland River, Friendship, and Mount Irvine 1, all in Tobago, are other important Saladoid habitation sites (Fig. 5). By far most of the Saladoid settlement locations of both islands are to be found at a distance of less than 500 m from a source of potable water, either a freshwater stream or a spring, and generally at contour elevations of less than 100 m above mean sea level. All are situated on dry and level or almost level terrain, sufficiently high to escape flooding in the wet season. The majority of these sites occupy areas consisting of generally fertile soils, covered with seasonal forest, suggesting a certain preference for village locations offering possibilities for hunting activities and horticulture in their surroundings. Many habitation sites are in the coastal zone of the two islands, providing excellent marine fishing opportunities nearby. Such coastal settlements typically occupy low, forested hills or terraces close to the lower reaches of a stream, with easy access to a sandy beach. This is the case with for instance the Saladoid settlement that is currently being excavated in the Red House, Port-of-Spain. It was situated on the bank of the former bed of the St. Ann's River, not far from its mouth in the Gulf of Paria. (The lower reaches of the St. Ann's river were diverted to the east as the Dry River in 1787.) At least one habitation site is known from one of Trinidad's offshore islets, Chacachacare. A minority of Saladoid habitation sites are to be found on ridges or hilltops in the interior of Trinidad and Tobago, sometimes allowing a commanding view of the surrounding areas. Small groups of human burials have been found at the periphery of various sites, but extended cemeteries are unknown. Most burials consist of primary inhumations without apparent mortuary gifts, although exceptional interments, provided with one to four pottery vessels and occasionally one or two stone artifacts, have been found as well.

The general character of the Saladoid habitation sites in the twin islands is relatively uniform. Most coastal sites yield deep refuse deposits consisting of literally tens of thousands of mollusks (shellfish), and crab remains, animal and fish bones, all food debris, as well as cultural relics. The largest midden accumulations are typically to be found on the slopes and at the foot of the hill or ridge on top of which the

Amerindian settlement was located originally. Obviously, the refuse was discarded by throwing it down the hill slopes. Sometimes the midden deposits show complicated vertical stratifications, being built up of layers of closely-packed food debris, alternating with layers primarily containing humus, ash, charcoal, and cultural remains. The horizontal structure of several sites on Trinidad's south coast shows that the communal dump was deliberately located to the leeward side of the village. Dimensions of these refuse accumulations vary. The most extended midden at the Quinam site has been estimated to measure some 50×15 m, those of Manzanilla 1 roughly 40×20 m. At Trinidadian habitation sites such as Atagual, Palo Seco and St. Bernard charcoal is especially found in the bottommost layers of the Saladoid refuse deposits examined. This can be interpreted as the result of the forest clearance operations which were necessary prior to the construction of the settlement.

Layout of the villages and the form and structure (morphology) of the individual dwellings and other structures are badly known. Partially this is due to the lack of area excavations in Trinidad and Tobago. Besides, many Saladoid settlement sites continued to be occupied by Amerindians in late-prehistoric times, thus long after the disappearance of the Saladoid tradition, which complicates interpretation of the archaeological sample excavations executed at such 'multicomponent' sites. A 'single-component', purely Saladoid habitation site such as St. Bernard shows a layout consisting of a series of discrete, round to oval, as much as 170 cm thick, mound-like accumulations of refuse, measuring up to 15×6 m, distributed over an area of at least one hectare, suggesting the former existence of a number of small houses close to each other. The St. Bernard site was first examined by the Dutch-American archaeologist Theodoor de Booy on behalf of the Museum of the American Indian, then based in New York, in 1919. An archaeological survey consisting in all of 68 shovel tests at the Blanchisseuse site on Trinidad's north coast, undertaken in 1999 by Anne A. Stokes and David W. Steadman of Southeastern Archaeological Research, Florida, yielded evidence of the former presence of a Saladoid village community centred around a central open square (plaza). The latter is indicated by an oval space lacking finds of potsherds, while the surrounding habitation area produced heavy quantities of such finds. The site, which measures some 2 hectares, is located on a flat to gently sloping bluff overlooking the Caribbean Sea to the north and the Marianne River to the west. During excavation works for the construction of a road in 1967, John T. Llanos and Thomas C. Cambridge encountered a series of post moulds at the Mount Irvine 1 site, which occupied the western slope of a hill overlooking Little Courland Bay on Tobago's leeward coast. From these post moulds the floor-plans of two circular Saladoid houses could be reconstructed. The only one of these former dwellings that was fully excavated had a diameter of 12.8 m and showed in all 12 posts. Comparable structures of Saladoid habitation sites, composed of round to oval dwellings surrounding an open plaza, have been encountered in the smaller islands of the West Indies.

Saladoid ceramics and Barrancoid intrusion

The pottery vessels made by (most likely the women of) the Saladoid peoples belong to the artistically most attractive items of material culture of the pre-Columbian Caribbean. Generally speaking, pottery fragments are the most common archaeological finds at sites dating from the Ceramic Age such as those of the Saladoid tradition. While objects manufactured of organic materials other than shell practically always decay in the soil, pottery and stone tools represent the items of material culture which are preserved under all circumstances. Bone artifacts and food remains such as animal and fish bones often decompose below the surface. Even shells and shell implements occasionally perish. The same applies to human burials. A comparison between the archaeological record and, for instance, the rich variety of items made traditionally by the Amerindians of the Guianas, suggests that 80–90% of the objects of prehistoric material culture have decayed in the soil, including implements, weapons, ornaments, domestic requisites, clothes, musical instruments, etc. made of organic materials such as cotton, plant fibres, bamboo, feathers, leather, bark, skin, wood, and calabash. In Trinidad pre-Columbian wooden artifacts have been preserved only in the Pitch Lake due to the protection the asphalt offers against decay of objects made of organic materials. Clearly, our impression of the past Amerindian material culture in Trinidad and Tobago, or for that matter the entire West Indies, is highly skewed.

As to manufacture, form and decoration, the Saladoid earthenware is highly characteristic and detailed research on the chronological development of its style differences shown in Trinidad and Tobago has led to the identification of two parallel series of largely subsequent stages ('styles' or 'complexes') called after the pottery of typical sites: Cedros, followed by Palo Seco in Trinidad, and Courland and Mount Irvine, succeeded by Friendship in Tobago. The term Cedrosan (after the Cedros complex) is often used as an overarching phrase denoting all of the local Saladoid 'complexes' of the West Indies and the coastal zone of South America. Generally speaking, Cedros, Early Palo Seco, and Courland belong to the Early Cedrosan episode (also known as the Early Ceramic A phase), which can be dated between ca. 300 BC to AD 350. They are followed by Late Palo Seco and Friendship between ca. AD 350 and 650/800, characterizing the Late Cedrosan episode or Early Ceramic B phase (Fig. 9). The reconstruction of this framework of Saladoid chronology was initiated by Professor Irving Rouse of Yale University for Trinidad and by Geoffrey H.S. Bushnell of Cambridge University for Tobago in the 1940s and 1950s. It was subsequently expanded by Peter Harris and the author for both islands. The individual Saladoid 'complexes' of the twin islands can be affiliated with comparable pottery assemblages elsewhere in the West Indies.

Saladoid pottery was manufactured by carefully attaching clay coils to each other on top of a wooden board, afterwards smoothing the wet vessel surface with small polishing stones, drying, and finally firing the vessels in an open fire. In order to prevent breakage during firing, prior to modelling, the pottery clay was thoroughly mixed ('tempered') with either crushed shell, quartz sand, siltstone, or finely ground potsherds (grog). The Saladoid vessel repertoire and its ornamentation are exceptionally varied. The domestic containers range from small bottles (furnished with removable stoppers) and bowls or dishes, occasionally provided with horizontally protruding ('flanged') rims, to vessels with 'keeled' profiles, double-spouted jars and asymmetrically 'necked' specimens. Most of these vessels were used for storage or the cooking of food. Others may have been used as serving vessels or for displaying food. Forms such as the bottles and double-spouted jars were apparently intended for the keeping or transportation of liquids, either water or, in case of the larger forms, beer made by fermenting cassava cakes. Many vessels show red, white and, rarely, black painted decorative motifs which were applied before firing. The inner surfaces sometimes have a thick, black coating that may have been achieved by burning an organic resin under the inverted container, as was done traditionally by the Amerindians of the Guianas in order to make the pottery watertight. Otherwise, black pigment on Saladoid pottery from La Reconnaissance in Lopinot Valley of the Northern Range probably derives from bitumen collected either at the Pitch Lake or at La Brea in Mayaro. White-on-red (WOR) painted designs are typical; they were often achieved by partially scraping off the white slip in order to reveal the underlying red pigment. Thin-line incised motifs were applied with a pointed stylus. Zoned-incised-crosshatched (ZIC) patterns are characteristic as well as wavy lines, zigzags, spirals, and multiple, parallel semi-circles or stepped lines. Modelled ornamentation, finally, includes a bewildering variety of highly typical, geometric, breast-shaped ('mammillary') and human- and/or animal-like ('anthropozoomorphic') sculptured projections ('lugs'), so-called *adornos*, which often surmount D-shaped strap handles. Such lugs often show hollow backs and highly conventionalized features. Identification of the individual animal or bird species is difficult. Besides, many of these *adornos* show combined human-animal features. Beautifully modelled examples of these anthropozoomorphic head lugs are exhibited in the National Museum and Art Gallery.

Study of the stylistic development of the Saladoid pottery repertoire in Trinidad and Tobago shows a growing influence by another ceramic tradition, the Barrancoid 'series', called after the site of Los Barrancos on the Lower Orinoco River, from ca. AD 350 onwards. The gradual adoption of Barrancoid stylistic features ('modes') by the Saladoid potters of Trinidad and Tobago reflects the growing interaction between the Saladoid communities of the twin islands and the mainland Amerindians in this period. It is suggestive of frequent contacts which were formalized by ceremonial exchanges. In this way, apart from influencing the local Saladoid earthenware, typically Barrancoid pottery vessels reached due to exchange as far as Tobago where they were used as mortuary gifts, illustrating the high prestige these exotic items had among the local Saladoid population. This Saladoid/Barrancoid exchange network formed part of a wide-ranging 'interaction sphere' encompassing parts of the mainland and the twin islands. Saladoid–Barrancoid interaction would culminate in Late Cedrosan times, eventually resulting in the settling of Barrancoid immigrants from the mainland in south Trinidad about AD 500–650/800. Although specimens of the local Trinidadian Barrancoid pottery tradition, known as the Erin 'complex', have been found as exchange items at various Saladoid sites in the central and southern parts of the island, and, as we have seen, in Tobago, truly substantial amounts of Erin materials are known only from four 'multicomponent' sites on the

Figure 14. Ceramic bowl, showing hollow rim modeled in the form of an originally red-painted snake-like creature with protruding tongue, found at Erin (SPA-20), Trinidad. Width of fragment 24.6 cm. Barrancoid series, Early Ceramic Age, ca. AD 350–650/800. Coll. NMAG.

Figure 15. Ceramic bird-shaped head lug (*adorno*), perhaps representing a king vulture, found at Erin (SPA-20), Trinidad. Width 6.9 cm. Barrancoid series, Early Ceramic Age, ca. AD 350–650/800. Coll. NMAG.

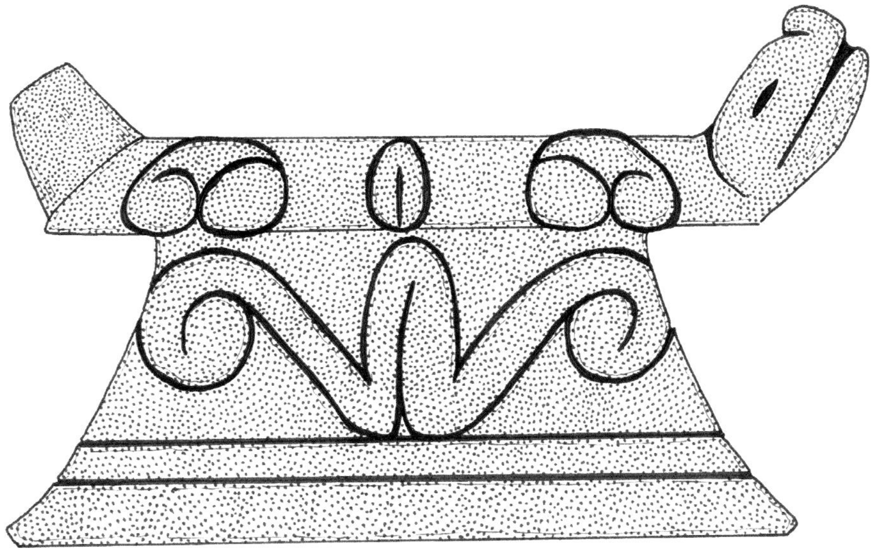

Figure 16. Red-painted, ritual ceramic pot rest, modeled as a sea turtle, found at Guayaguayare (MAY-16), Trinidad. Maximum height 10.7 cm. Barrancoid series, Early Ceramic Age, ca. AD 350–650/800. Harris Coll., WFT.

south coast. Here they occur in consistent association with Late Cedrosan pottery, suggesting that people of the Barrancoid tradition settled on Trinidad by AD 500–650/800 in order to live side-by-side, and no doubt intermarry, with the Saladoid inhabitants of the island.

Erin ceramics represent the artistic as well as technological climax of pre-Columbian material culture in the twin islands (Fig. 14). They are well known from the research by the American archaeologist Jesse W. Fewkes of the Museum of the American Indian at the Erin site on Trinidad's south coast in 1913. More extensive work at Erin was carried out by Irving Rouse in 1946. Made by coiling and fired in an open fire, just like Saladoid pottery, the Barrancoid earthenware is thicker and stronger while showing darker vessel surfaces than the latter. Besides, 'temper' is quite different, consisting predominantly of abundant quantities of deliberately crushed quartz particles, resulting in a dense, gritty clay paste. In Late Erin times the clay is mixed also with fine quartz sand and, rarely, freshwater sponge spicules (*cauixí*) or a mixture of the latter and pieces of crushed quartz. The Erin vessel repertoire is less varied than that of the Saladoid peoples. Typical forms include round or oval, open bowls showing externally thickened rims, triangular in cross section, outward-bulging hollow rims or heavy rim flanges. They are provided with flat or footed bases. Double-spout-and-bridge-bottles represent the most specific shape of the Erin ceramic assemblage. Just like the Saladoid earthenware, most vessels were intended for cooking, storing, serving, drying or displaying food, and for keeping liquids or using as travelling canteens. Pottery decoration comprises painting, incising, punctation, and modelling. All-over red painting and partially (black) smudging and subsequently polishing of vessel surfaces are characteristic, as is broad incision of straight ('rectilinear') and curved ('curvilinear') lines, including designs such as spirals, scrolls, lines ending in crossbars or dots, Y-shaped lines, and zigzags. Modelling includes a wide variety of modelled-incised, strongly sculptural, geometric and anthropozoomorphic head lugs (Fig. 15) and human as well as animal limbs, hands, claws and feet. The latter design elements suggest that animal-shaped ('effigy') vessels took a prominent position in the Erin vessel assemblage (Fig. 16). Some fine examples of Barrancoid pottery are exhibited in the National Museum and Art Gallery.

Saladoid/Barrancoid subsistence and food processing

Essentially the striving towards a 'broad spectrum' diet by tapping as many natural resources as possible formed the central objective of the subsistence strategies of the Saladoid and Barrancoid peoples. Accordingly, they preferred settlement in and exploitation of the boundary zones ('ecotones') between ecological areas ('habitats') such that between water and land where a large variety of high-quality edibles could be obtained. By combining horticulture, hunting, fishing, and collecting wild vegetable and invertebrate food stuffs, the Amerindians of Early Ceramic times were able to achieve a dietary balance between the input of carbohydrates provided by the cultivation of starchy root crops and the resources of proteins and fats which had to be secured by hunting, fishing and foraging. Archaeologically these subsistence activities are reflected by the occurrence of special activity sites identified by individual archaeological finds and temporary camp ('bivouac') sites characterized by individual finds or by small pottery deposits lacking appreciable food remains. Such temporary camps were apparently utilized during fishing, crab-catching, shell-collecting and/or hunting expeditions, while others on river banks or beaches may have served as landing stages for canoes. Besides, individual finds of polished stone axe heads probably indicate garden sites as they may have been lost or abandoned during clearance of swidden plots in the forest. Calculations of the catchment areas utilized for different subsistence strategies by the Saladoid/ Barrancoid peoples in Trinidad and Tobago suggest that their basic subsistence needs could be satisfied within a zone of some 1–3 km around the habitation. Only in the case of specific procurement activities this territory had to be extended as far as 3–5 km from the settlement.

It can be assumed that the Saladoid and Barrancoid cultivation practices resembled those of the present Tropical Forest peoples of the South American mainland. Accordingly, horticulture apparently concentrated on raising a wide variety of food crops and fruit trees in the indigenous kitchen gardens and swidden fields. Circumstantial evidence attests to the cultivation of bitter or sweet cassava, sweet potatoes and other ground provisions such as Indian yam and tannia, along with maize. Still at present these crops and pigeon peas, which were originally cultivated in Africa, are allotted most space in West Indian 'provision grounds' such as those of Tobago. Apart from tubers and cereals, most likely fruit trees such as avocado, guava, mammee apple, and papaw were grown. Clearance of swiddens by slash-and-burn techniques ('making garden' as it is called in Tobago) takes place at the end of the dry season, planting follows when the first rains fall. As a rule, swiddens are used for 3–5 years, after which soil depletion, weed incursion or insect pests force vacation. Various tools were used for the processing of vegetable foods in Early Ceramic times. Large, thick ceramic platters (griddles) served for baking cassava or maize cakes, while wooden mortars and conical stone pestles were used for processing root crops other than cassava as well as moist or leafy vegetable foods. Such a mortar forms one of the unique wooden objects which were retrieved from the Pitch Lake.[7] Small stone chips, originally inserted as 'teeth' in wooden cassava grater boards, stone grinding stones and pieces of fossil coral, used for similar purposes, have been found at numerous Early Ceramic sites in the twin islands.

Hunting and fishing were major subsistence occupations. Indeed, chunks of meat and fish or crabs, peppers and *casareep*, the thickened juice extracted from bitter cassava pulp, formed the major ingredients of the 'pepperpot' stew, which together with cassava cakes formed the major dish of the Tropical Forest Amerindians. Although little is known about the specific hunting strategies employed, it is certain that from Saladoid times onwards the dog invariably accompanied the indigenous hunters. Spears, bows-and-arrows and possibly harpoons were used for hunting. Arrowheads made of stone, bone or fish spines have been found at various sites in Trinidad and Tobago as well as stone arrowshaft polishers. Hunting took place in the forest environment, along small streams and near old garden plots, as during the period of fallow abandoned swiddens attract a variety of terrestrial game. Red brocket deer, collared peccaries, agoutis, pacas, nine-banded armadillos, black-eared opossums, tortoises, and iguanas were the terrestrial mammals and reptiles preferred by the Amerindians of Trinidad and Tobago in Early Ceramic times. In Tobago especially peccaries were highly ranked prey, as a result of which they were probably overexploited. Aquatic mammals and reptiles including manatees and sea turtles were similarly targeted. Red howler monkeys and tapirs were captured less frequently; birds were rarely caught. Fishing took place by using hooks and lines, fishpots, fishing-nets, bows-and-arrows, harpoons, and probably by fish poisoning. Fishhooks, including bipointed ones, made of bone and stingray spines, and net weights, suggesting the use of seines (dragnets), have been found at several sites. In Trinidad most fishing occurred in the inshore-estuarine environment where species such as sea catfishes, mullets, snooks, tarpons, jacks, sharks, and rayfish were caught. Fishing was much more diversified in Tobago where the inshore-estuarine, the offshore-pelagic as well as the marine banks/reefs habitats were exploited, predominantly the latter environment, catching mainly parrotfishes, tunas and mackerels, toadfishes, surgeonfishes, snappers, flyingfishes, and needlefishes. It is likely that reef species such as parrotfishes and snappers were overexploited. Obviously, fishing, or for that matter aquatic travelling in general, was impossible without proper dugout canoes. None has been found in archaeological context in the twin islands, but in all four, nearly identical, wooden paddles have been retrieved from the Pitch Lake. One of them is exhibited in the National Museum and Art Gallery.

7 Two large potsherds found at the Golden Grove (I) site in Tobago show deposits of a thick, carbonized vegetable cake, possibly cassava, adhering to their inner sides. These vegetable residues show a branched cracking and fibrous appearance. Golden Grove (I) yielded also a piece of fungus, suggesting that mushrooms formed an important dietary supplement.

Apart from cultivated food plants, the Saladoid/Barrancoid Amerindians consumed a variety of (sometimes tended) wild fruits and vegetables such as palm seeds. Stone anvils ('pitted stones') were used together with small hammerstones in order to crack such nuts. Collecting terrestrial and aquatic invertebrate food sources such as crabs, mollusks and sea urchins ('sea eggs') further added to the Early Ceramic diet. Remains of land crabs, both blue crabs and hairy (*callaloo*) crabs, are frequent in the Saladoid sites of both Trinidad and Tobago. Mollusks are the most common food remains encountered. Numerous species of gastropods, bivalves and chitons (*pacro*) were consumed by the Early Ceramic peoples in the two islands. Deer bone awls, occasionally made of sharpened antler beams still showing the burr, may have been used as picks for prying out the gastropod animal from its shell. The shell contents of the investigated middens suggest that a few particular mollusk species were targeted while a variety of others were collected only as people came across them when searching for the preferred species. On Trinidad's south and east coasts sandy-beach bivalves as donax clams (*chipchip*) and trigonal tivelas (*wacoo*) were preferred next to mangrove species such as Caribbean ('tree') oysters, tulip mussels and West Indian crown conchs. Terrestrial snails formed a minority. The shellfish species collected in Tobago differed markedly from those in Trinidad due to the dissimilar biotic character of the marine environment around the smaller island. Here reef species such as queen conchs (*lambis*) were gathered extensively, and rocky-shore gastropods such as West Indian top shells (*whelks*) and chitons. Sandy-bottom bivalves as venus clams, mangrove oysters and mussels and gastropods such as crown conchs were targeted as well.

Saladoid/Barrancoid population, society and religion

Although apparently the pre-Columbian peoples were quite successful in tapping the natural resources of Trinidad and Tobago, it is difficult to make more than educated guesses about human population size and density in the two islands in Early Ceramic times. Assuming that the Saladoid/Barrancoid villages were inhabited by some 150 people each, the total population of the twin islands in this period could have been some 6000 persons, provided that all sites are contemporary and known (which is unlikely). At any rate, the gradual increase of the number of habitation sites throughout Saladoid/Barrancoid times is suggestive of steady population growth, splitting of villages and increasing population density. The patterns of settlement, subsistence and population of the Early Ceramic peoples in the two islands closely resemble those of a range of present and former 'tribal' societies or 'local groups' typical of the South American tropical lowlands. Such systems represent essentially egalitarian societies consisting of a series of semi-independent local communities, each often made up of only a few kinship groups or extended families, integrated by non-residential clans (descent groups), elaborate networks of trade and exchange, political and military alliances, and 'regional fields' of ceremonial and shamanic cooperation. Individual tribal systems often share a common culture, language, territory, and name, thus forming separate ethnic groups and polities. Division of labour is primarily based on sex and age

Figure 17. Wooden bench in the form of a jaguar (?), recovered from the Pitch Lake (SPA-6), Trinidad. Length 57.2 cm, maximum height 20.1 cm. Saladoid (?) series, Early Ceramic Age, ca. AD 500. Coll. YPM.

while semi-specialists operate only on the community level. Status variation is small: leadership is temporary, personalized and context-dependent. Due to personal qualities some headmen are able to dominate in war and trade as 'great men', attracting large followings through gift giving, but their leadership is not hereditary.

Two wooden artifacts retrieved from the Pitch Lake are associated with this kind of status differences within the Trinidadian Saladoid communities: a bench carved in the form of an animal, perhaps a jaguar, and an asymmetrical, high-backed seat. The zoomorphic bench (Fig. 17) is carved of a single block of wood and has been dated by radiocarbon to about AD 500. It has a concave seat which is very smooth through use; its underside still shows the original hewing marks. Such benches are typically male-associated pieces of furniture in the present Amerindian dwellings of the South American tropical lowlands, only used by the headman or shaman (religious specialist) of the village. The high-backed, somewhat 'hammock-shaped', seat from the Pitch Lake (Fig. 18) resembles the chiefly stools the Amerindians of the Greater Antilles used in contact times and may represent a 'prototype' of the latter. Such seats played important roles during the communal festivities which are or were held by the Tropical Forest peoples on various occasions, including the initiation rituals of young warriors, the burials of chiefs, the settlement of peace treaties, and the contracting of marriages. Cassava beer

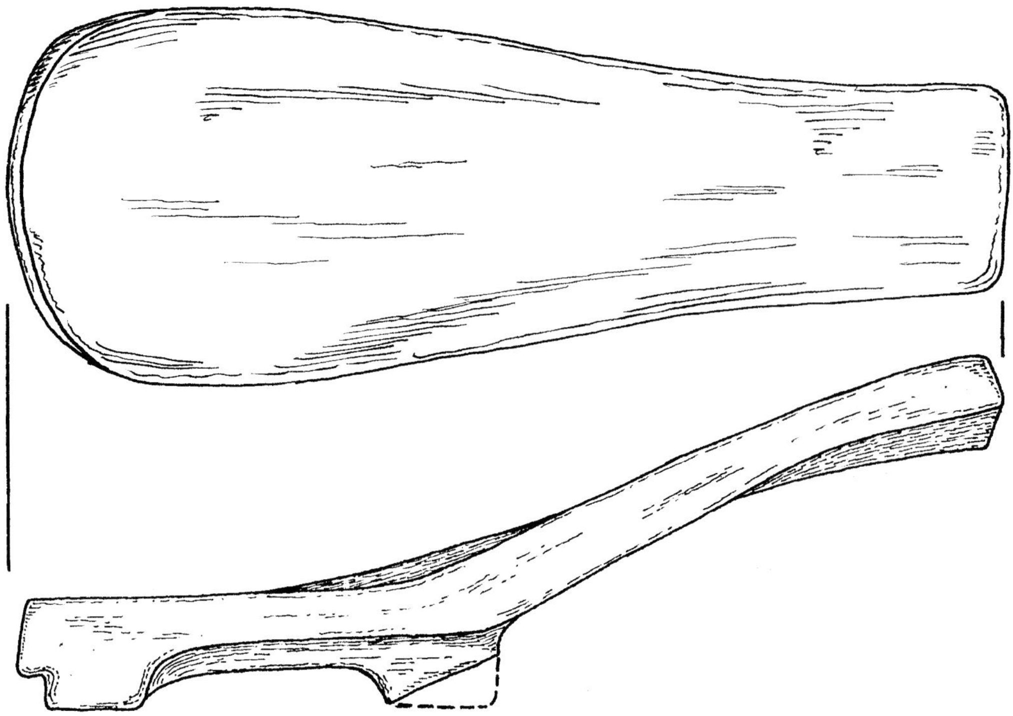

drinking, singing and dancing formed invariable ingredients of these fêtes which may have lasted three or four days. Actually, the only archaeological evidence pointing to such village parties are massive vessels used for brewing the cassava beer that was consumed in large quantities during the festivities.[8] An especially rare example of such a huge container is represented by a large pear-shaped ('aryballoid') jar showing a convex neck with an human-like face design and three vertical handles (Fig. 19). The placement of these handles suggests that the vessel in fact represents a male effigy. It was found by a scuba diver at a depth of 5 m below the surface of Bombshell Bay, offshore Caspar Grande (Gasparee) Island in 1990. Exact parallels of this jar are only known from Saladoid sites in Puerto Rico.

Figure 18. 'Hammock'-shaped wooden seat, recovered from the Pitch Lake (SPA-6), Trinidad. Length 77.5 cm, maximum height 27.0 cm. Saladoid (?) series, Early Ceramic Age, perhaps ca. AD 500. Coll. NMAG.

Elaborate ceremonies accompanied traditionally 'passage rites' such as birth, initiation, marriage, and death, but only the latter is known archaeologically. Among the Amerindians of the South American tropical forest the methods of disposal of the dead and the associated ceremonies vary primarily according to the social status of the deceased. The primary burial of high ranking (male) individuals is often unearthed again after a number of years, followed by separation of the skull and/or some long bones for keeping in the dwelling in

8 Nicely decorated bowls of pottery and halved calabashes were used traditionally to serve cassava beer during these feasts. For obvious reasons the gourd dishes have not been retrieved archaeologically.

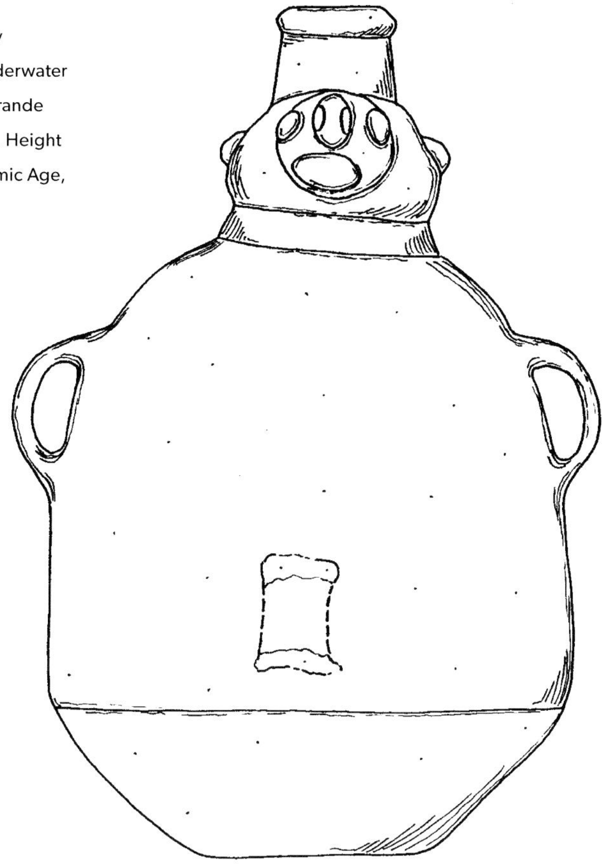

Figure 19. Large pottery jar, probably representing a male effigy, found underwater at Bombshell Bay, offshore Caspar Grande (Gasparee) Island (SGE-37), Trinidad. Height 43.0 cm. Saladoid series, Early Ceramic Age, ca. AD 350–650/800. Private coll.

order to consult the dead ancestor's spirit whenever necessary. It is succeeded by reburial of the remainder of the skeleton. Many Early Ceramic sites in Trinidad and Tobago have yielded primary and/or secondary inhumations, several of which appeared to be accompanied by mortuary gifts such as pottery vessels, no doubt originally filled with food for placating the spirit world, and personal possessions. Most skeletons show burial in more or less flexed ('foetal') position; orientation varies. These inhumations have yielded occasionally exceptional ceramic finds: while the pre-Columbian pottery retrieved from midden sites was generally deposited in heavily fragmented condition, vessels were placed undamaged as mortuary gifts in burials. Such a find is the famous Erin 'waterbottle', a finely WOR-painted asymmetrical bowl, which was recovered by John A. Bullbrook in 1944 and is now exhibited in the National Museum and Art Gallery (Fig. 20). Together with its bottle stopper and three other, similarly painted vessels, it formed the mortuary gift of a probably male burial.

Another special burial at the Erin site, similarly exhibited in the National Museum and Art Gallery and excavated by Bullbrook (in 1941/1942), is represented by the flexed primary inhumation of a young, probably male, adult

Figure 20. White-on-red painted, asymmetrical ceramic bottle, showing a human/animal-like face design, found at Erin (SPA-20), Trinidad. Height 23.1 cm. Saladoid series, Early Ceramic Age, ca. AD 350–650/800. Coll. NMAG.

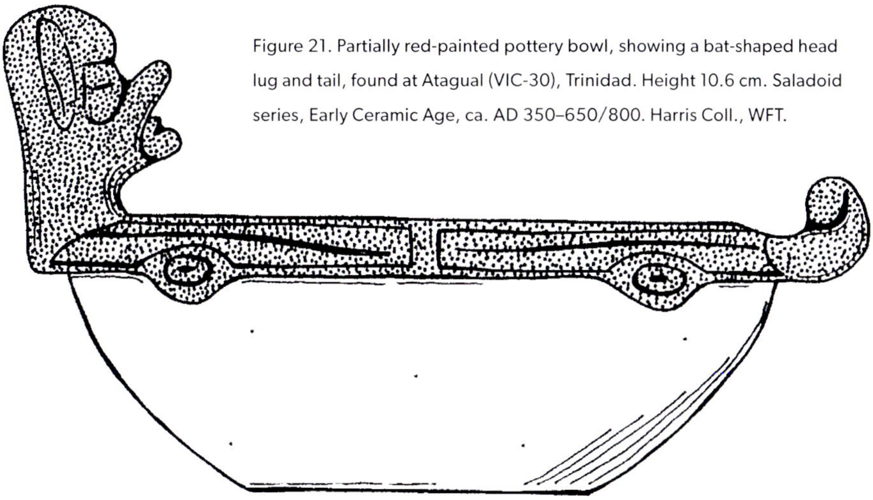

Figure 21. Partially red-painted pottery bowl, showing a bat-shaped head lug and tail, found at Atagual (VIC-30), Trinidad. Height 10.6 cm. Saladoid series, Early Ceramic Age, ca. AD 350–650/800. Harris Coll., WFT.

Figure 22. Slate-like, thin stone slab, decorated with incised motifs, found at Erin (SPA-20), Trinidad. Length 5.5 cm, width 4.5 cm. Barrancoid series, Early Ceramic Age, ca. AD 350–650/800. Coll. NMAG.

who was deposited on his right side, accompanied by a large Saladoid bowl with hollow rim, which originally functioned as a rattle, a hammerstone and a small bowl showing a bird-like head lug. An exceptionally rich burial was encountered at Atagual and dug up by Peter Harris and the author in 1981/1982. It contained a probably north–south oriented, flexed skeleton of an adult who was accompanied by four Saladoid vessels and a greenstone oval ('petaloid') axe head. A white-painted bottle was found resting on top of an inverted bowl which, in turn, covered the leg bones of the deceased. Two other vessels were found close by, including a second bowl showing a bat-head *adorno* (Fig. 21) and a hammock-shaped vessel decorated with WOR-painted and incised motifs. Another Atagual burial yielded a north–south oriented adult skeleton of which the skull was covered with an inverted oval-shaped bowl decorated with bat-head *adornos* at both ends. In Tobago, the most exceptional Saladoid burials are known from Lovers' Retreat where a group of five adult interments was found by Thomas C. Cambridge in 1948, accompanied by 18 vessels and 27 petaloid stone axes, including three miniature specimens.

Study of a series of skeletons from the Palo Seco and St. Bernard sites suggests that the Saladoid peoples of Trinidad practiced artificial skull modification which, together with tattooing, body painting, bodily accoutrements, and dress, forms a method of expressing status and ethnic distinctions in Amerindian society. Indeed, stone or coral rubbing tools showing a red dye may have been used for processing hematite for body painting as well as pottery decoration. Ceramic spindle whorls, recovered from numerous sites, point to the spinning and weaving of (cultivated) cotton twine and the manufacture of girdles, waistbands and hammocks. Besides, two wooden weaving sticks ('separators') were retrieved from the Pitch Lake. A wealth of carved bone, stone and shell pendants, beads and other ornaments is known from the Early Ceramic sites in Trinidad and Tobago. The simplest, obviously locally made, ornaments include flat and barrel-shaped bone, shell and pottery beads, and pottery ear plugs and beads made of fish vertebrae. A clearly male-associated category of adornments, showing prowess, is formed by perforated or (yet) undrilled peccary tusks and pendants made of caiman's and shark's teeth. At Palo Seco a circular pendant was found, manufactured of a probably human skull, perhaps that of a slain enemy, which was perforated four times. Various pendants are known made from the valves of local freshwater mussels (naiads) from which the external layer was removed in order to expose the brilliant mother-of-pearl underneath. Other pendants include perforated miniature axe heads ('pygmy celts'), small stone trinkets which may have been suspended as danglers during dancing ceremonies. An unmodified, greyish stone pendant, found at Atagual, was clearly shaped to be suspended from the lowest part of the nose.

Quite sophisticated bodily adornments found in Trinidad comprise exotic artifacts such as pendants made of lignite, occasionally showing strongly Barrancoid incised designs, which most likely originated in the Lower Orinoco Valley. A similarly decorated, thin slab of a slate-like rock material encountered at Erin probably derived from this same region (Fig. 22). Other exotics include beads made of semi-precious stones such as tourmaline, serpentinite or chlorite, and turquoise, probably deriving from the Paria Peninsula or elsewhere on the South American mainland. Frog-shaped pendants, made of green-coloured stone or shell, have been found in Saladoid context as well. At least one of these ornaments is made of chlorite. The two undoubtedly most spectacular, zoomorphically sculptured, stone pendants from Trinidad were purchased in the island by Jesse W. Fewkes in 1904. The first one represents an unidentifiable animal, possibly a turtle, of which the legs and other features are indicated by Barrancoid-like broad-line curvilinear incision. The second pendant, which is most likely made of serpentinite, represents a king vulture carrying an animal in its claws (Fig. 23). It may have been an exchange item which originated as far north as Vieques, a small island

Figure 23. King vulture-shaped stone (serpentine?) pendant, found at an unknown location in Trinidad. Length 4.3 cm. Saladoid series, Early Ceramic Age, ca. AD 0–350. Coll. Smithsonian Institution, Washington, DC.

directly east of Puerto Rico, on which a workshop manufacturing this kind of king vulture pendants was located. Local beads and pendants made of shell, bone and stone, are well known from Tobago as well. Most interestingly, the smaller island appears to have been a major bead-manufacturing site throughout Late Cedrosan times (and afterwards). As research by Peter O'B. Harris and the author has shown, diorite formed the natural rock predominantly used for this purpose. This black-and-white mottled material, which is found in a wide zone across central and east Tobago, was utilized to manufacture numerous button- and barrel-shaped beads at the Golden Grove (I) site in the southern part of the island. Apart from blanks and finished diorite beads, this workshop site yielded also polishing stones which show deep, wide grooves resulting from carefully smoothing the beads.

Diorite beads made in Tobago may have spread beyond the island as the result of exchange relationships with the Saladoid peoples elsewhere in the West Indies. Unfortunately, diorite is a rock material which occurs naturally throughout the Caribbean and a possible Tobagonian origin of the diorite beads found on the other islands of the region is difficult to ascertain. However, it is almost certain that Tobago played an important role in the distribution of rock materials used for the manufacture of cutting tools in Trinidad. The smaller island possesses extensive sources of the metamorphic and igneous (volcanic) rock materials which were used for Saladoid/Barrancoid axe and adze head manufacture in Trinidad, while these rock materials are almost entirely lacking in the latter island. Besides, the presence of shell axe heads ('celts') made of queen conchs, perhaps used for canoe manufacture, and of grinding and polishing slabs of fossil coral at various Saladoid sites in south Trinidad, may similarly point to interaction with Tobago. This, of course, is suggested also by the Barrancoid pottery vessels of ceremonial character, originating in Trinidad or the Lower Orinoco Valley, which have been encountered in mortuary contexts at Saladoid sites on southwest Tobago. In contrast, a mother-of-pearl pendant made of the valve of a freshwater mussel, found at Golden Grove (I), may represent a social valuable deriving from south Trinidad. Ethnohistoric documents suggest that such valuables were exchanged among the pre-Columbian communities of the West Indies and beyond during feasts held on the occasion of, for instance, the formation of political alliances associated with marriage pacts, burials of high-status persons, and initiation rituals. In this way complex systems of interethnic relations could knit together extended territories as 'interaction spheres' in both the South American tropical lowlands and the West Indian archipelago. Wide-ranging communication and interaction are indicated by, for instance, the presence of exactly similar incised decorative patterns on some of the Saladoid earthenware encountered at sites on south Tobago (Mount Irvine), the northern coastal area of Trinidad (Blanchisseuse), the central coast of Venezuela, and the Lesser Antilles.

Numerous highly desired exchange items derived their prestige in Amerindian society from specific religious connotations. The profusion of anthropozoomorphic head lugs ornamenting the Saladoid/Barrancoid pottery of the twin islands adequately reflects the 'animistic' nature of Early Ceramic religion, which centred around a profound belief in the total spirituality of the universe, and placed humans, animals and spirits on an equal level, involving unlimited transformations from one manifestation to another. The profusion of these anthropozoomorphic head lugs on Saladoid/Barrancoid pottery illustrates the high value placed by the pre-Columbian Amerindians on communication with the spirit world in order to ensure health, fertility, social order, and group survival. Utilization of these vessels in rituals even as profane as village festivals or communal meals seems indicated. Many Early Ceramic vessel forms are really effigies, representing 'mythic transforms' of creatures which also act as the major natural symbols of present South American mythology. They reflect a cosmology which identifies a series of twofold oppositions, associated with a fundamentally sexual symbolism. The Saladoid zoomorphic *adornos* include highly conventionalized representations of birds and animals such as monkeys, bats, dogs, armadillos, rodents, felines, turtles, frogs, lizards, and caimans. Besides, many of these head lugs show a form of pictorial dualism involving the occurrence of divergent images when seen from contrasting points of view. It has been suggested that the most common head lugs shown on these vessels, portraying fruit-eating bats and frogs, can be taken to represent the predominant iconographic symbols of the male and female principles, respectively, in Early Ceramic religion. The other animals and birds can be identified similarly. The human mammillary *adornos*, known from Saladoid and Barrancoid contexts, clearly refer to fruitfulness and propagation.

Two 'ceremonial' sites can be identified in the twin islands: the Pitch Lake, which represented a place of offering wooden artifacts and/or specific human burials, and Crown Point, a small cave in southwest Tobago. As with caves and lakes on the South American mainland, most likely the Amerindians considered both sites as portals to the spirit world. As in present Amerindian religion, the village shaman ('lookman') functioned as a curer, advisor and seer, contacting the realm of the spirits through trances invoked by the intake of hallucinogenic drugs. Several find categories can be identified as shamanic paraphernalia. Small pottery bowls showing pairs of tube-shaped extensions, so-called 'nostril' or 'sniffing' bowls, were apparently used for pouring tobacco or pepper juice into the nose, so as to induce an ecstatic-visionary trance (Fig. 24).[9]

9 A fine example, recovered by Basil E. Josa from a disturbed burial at St. Bernard, is on exhibit in the National Museum and Art Gallery.

Figure 24. Ceramic bowl showing two tube-shaped extensions, most likely used to pour tobacco juice into the nose in order to induce an ecstatic-visionary trance, found at St. Bernard (MAY-4), Trinidad. Maximum width 14.7 cm. Saladoid series, Early Ceramic Age, ca. AD 350–650/800. Coll. NMAG.

Hollow pottery *adornos* containing small clay pellets or tiny pebbles, which functioned as rattling devices when moved quickly, obviously represent curing devices analogous to the rattles made of organic materials which present-day shamans use to invoke their tutelary spirits. Other shamanic aids found on Trinidad and Tobago include ceremonial vessel stands and cylindrical, bottomless vessels with nearly closed tops ('incense burners') which may have been used to kindle and inhale hallucinogenic drugs. The effigy vessels may have functioned during shamanic ceremonies as the temporary repositories for the shaman's guardian spirits when summoned for advice and assistance. An exceptional Barrancoid *adorno*, found at Whitelands, shows an intricately modelled-incised, so-called 'alter ego' (second-self) portrayal of a king vulture surmounting an anthropomorphic head, clearly representing a shaman keeping his hands to the chin and lower cheeks while in trance. It recalls South American mythological tales of king vultures as the prime guardian spirit of the shaman, taking him to heaven during a tobacco-induced ecstatic-visionary trance.

Finally, various examples of threepointed stones (Fig. 25), the most ubiquitous category of Saladoid shamanic paraphernalia, have been found on both Trinidad and Tobago; the smaller island probably was the origin of the only specimen known from Trinidad. These 'threepointers' may have been used for shamanic rituals intended to promote the growth of food plants. A most interesting find, illustrating the direct access of the Tobagonian Saladoid Amerindians to the Antillean exchange networks, is represented by a threepointer found at the Mount

Figure 25. Threepointed stones, probably used in shamanic rituals to promote the growth of food plants, found at (left) Mount Irvine 3 (TOB-19), Tobago, and (right) Blue River (CAR-1), Trinidad. Height 3.5 and 4.4 cm; width 3.5 and 6.7 cm, respectively. Saladoid series, Early Ceramic Age, ca. AD 350–650/800. Coll. THM.

Irvine 3 site. It is made of calci-rudite, a conglomerate which was specially collected on St. Martin in the Leeward Islands for the manufacture of threepointed stones on this island and Anguilla. Such calci-rudite threepointers ultimately spread due to ceremonial exchange throughout the Lesser Antilles and Puerto Rico.

4. Late-prehistoric cultural change (ca. AD 650/800–1498)

The period from AD 650 to 800 was one of exceptional dynamism, both on the mainland and in the islands of the West Indies. Major cultural, socio-political and ritual reformulations took place in both areas during these few centuries, the character and consequences of which are still poorly understood. Coincidentally or not, this cultural watershed was also an episode of climatic change, during which centuries of relatively abundant rainfall were replaced by a period characterized by dry conditions culminating in prolonged droughts and increased hurricane frequency. Throughout the region the Saladoid interaction sphere disintegrated rapidly. In Trinidad and Tobago the existing cultural relationships, political alliances and social networks connecting the twin islands' Amerindian communities were redefined essentially. As a result, the strong cultural unity between the two islands, which existed during Saladoid times, was definitely broken. Tobago was now drawn into the sphere of influence of the Troumassoid tradition which locally crystallized in the Windward Islands and Barbados, replacing the Saladoid series here.[10] Simultaneously, the inhabitants of Trinidad became increasingly affiliated with the peoples of the Arauquinoid tradition which first materialized on the middle reaches of the Orinoco River (Fig. 9). After having established themselves on the Lower Orinoco and the central Venezuelan coast, intermingling with the Barrancoid tradition, the Arauquinoid peoples spread to the coastal zone of the Guianas and both sides of the Gulf of Paria, here giving rise to the so-called Guayabitan subseries, called after the Guayabita complex of the Paria peninsula. In Trinidad a local Guayabitan ceramic assemblage, the Bontour complex, would gradually replace the Saladoid and Barrancoid pottery throughout the island, reflecting the merging due to intermarriage of the Saladoid/Barrancoid communities with groups of Arauquinoid immigrants. It would dominate the Late Ceramic phase of Trinidad until shortly before the contact period.

Arauquinoid settlement in Trinidad

The Arauquinoid (Guayabitan) immigration into Trinidad was foreshadowed by the Barrancoid ceramics of Late Erin times which display a number of features of Arauquinoid derivation such as the application of *cauíxi* (freshwater sponge spicules) temper, and distinctly haphazard and sloppily executed incised and modelled decorative motifs, clearly reflecting a slackening of the strict standards of ornamentation originally regulating Barrancoid ceramics. The development from Saladoid/Barrancoid to Arauquinoid is shown most clearly at the 'multicomponent'

10 It was called after the Troumassée site on St. Lucia in the Windward Islands.

sites of Trinidad's south coast. Here, the dense interaction taking place across the Columbus Channel with the Orinoco Valley and the coastal zone of the Guianas was reflected by the development of an independent Barrancoid/Arauquinoid pottery assemblage in the southeasternmost portion of the island. This St. Catherine's (II) complex closely resembles the so-called Late Mabaruma/Apostadero ceramics of coastal Guyana. It is characterized by a profusion of punctated and punctated-incised decorative motifs, including series of parallel lines ending in dots, trapezoidal and triangular rim lugs, punctated appliqué fillets, modelled-incised human faces, and animal-like *adornos*. St. Catherine's may represent a temporary outpost of people from the coastal zone of Guyana, established in order to facilitate exchange and communication with the Amerindians of south Trinidad. It would last for a few hundred years.

By AD 800 Arauquinoid (Bontour) pottery had replaced Saladoid/Barrancoid ceramics everywhere in the island. Bontour earthenware is characterized by coarse open bowls and simple jars with inflected contours, the ornamentation of which is reduced to a minimum (some 2–3% of the potsherds). The pottery clay is typically tempered with crushed shell fragments and, much less frequently, fine quartz sand or *cauíxi*. Decoration is restricted to sparse punctated and incised or gouged motifs. Remarkably, anthropozoomorphic head lugs, so obtrusive during Saladoid/Barrancoid times, have almost completely disappeared. This drastic decline in the quality of manufacture and decoration of the local Trinidadian pottery assemblage, which closely reflects the Arauquinoid ceramic development in the Lower Orinoco Valley and the east Venezuelan coastal zone, can be explained only by assuming that pottery had lost much of its ritual significance to other items of material culture. Perhaps ceramics were much less imbued by ceremonialism than during Saladoid/Barrancoid times and shamanic religious expression now manifested itself in artifacts made of perishable materials. All of this suggests that the transition from the Saladoid and Barrancoid to the Arauquinoid series in Trinidad and beyond meant a genuine cultural break. Of course, this does not mean that the original population of the island was completely replaced by newcomers. On the contrary, the gradual ceramic succession which culminated in the establishment of the Bontour complex suggests a steady development and cultural transition involving primarily a locally settled population. It would explain, for instance, the apparent continuity of some of the local modes of late Saladoid ceramic technology well into Arauquinoid times at the Manzanilla 1 site of east Trinidad.

Bontour pottery has been encountered at 56 archaeological sites, most of which are settlement sites (midden deposits), occasionally yielding inhumation burials. Coastal as well as inland sites occur. Increasing population density across the island is shown by the enhanced number of sites compared to Saladoid/Barrancoid times. The type site, Bontour, was excavated by Irving Rouse in 1946. Area excavations at the Manzanilla 1 site, carried out by teams of Leiden University, The Netherlands, between 1997 and 2007, have yielded most information about Bontour settlement structure. These digs, led by Marc C. Dorst, showed that this site represents a late Saladoid habitation which was occupied again, and much more extensively, in Arauquinoid times. The site covers in all some 200×250 m and occupies the

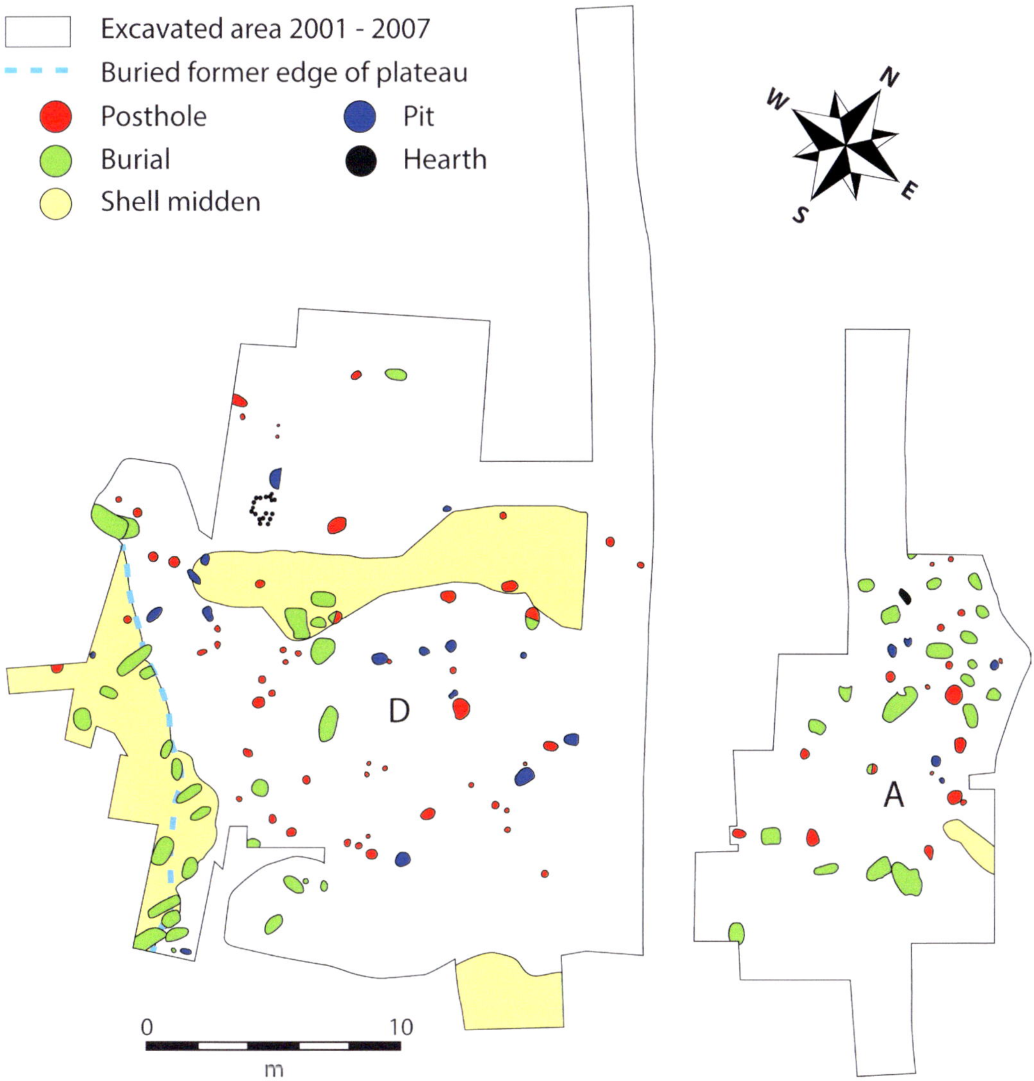

Figure 26. Layout of the second occupation at Manzanilla 1 (SAN-1), Trinidad, showing three round to oval house structures, burials, pits, and hearth. Arauquinoid series, Late Ceramic Age, ca. AD 650/800–1400. Courtesy Marc C. Dorst.

top of a 15-m tall hill close to the eastern shore. The layout of the Arauquinoid (Bontour) habitation consisted of four zones of almost equal extensions (60×30 m) lacking food debris, surrounded by thick shell deposits.[11] One of these zones, situated in the central portion of the site, was investigated in detail and appeared to be characterized by two complete and one partial, round to oval, house structures, located next to each other, associated with some pit structures, a short windbreak, a small midden deposit, and numerous inhumation burials (Fig. 26). The first of these dwellings (Structure A) measured

11 The total amount of donax clams at the Manzanilla 1 site, thus including both the late Saladoid and Arauquinoid occupations and not counting any other shell species, has been estimated by Dennis C. Nieweg at some 5.5 billion individuals with a total meat weight of around 280,000 kg.

6×8 m in diameter and showed one central post (of which the hole contained a secondary burial), seven side posts and one repair post. It was associated with at least 20 burials deposited immediately outside its walls. The second complete house (Structure D) was 9×12 m in diameter and showed two central posts and at least 15 side posts. It had a shallow hearth surrounded by stones and showed the soil marks of two small, three-legged structures. Seven side posts of a third round structure, situated at the edge of the plateau, could be identified. All houses may represent the dwellings of extended families, each counting at most some 15 to 20 members. They obviously showed a cone-shaped roof thatched with palm leaves.

The Manzanilla 1 site also yielded substantial informationon the burial ceremonies of Trinidad's Arauquinoid Amerindians. Primary as well as secondary inhumations were encountered, many showing signs of rituals such as the removal of long bones or skulls. Apparently, several graves were left open for a considerable period of time. The skull and some long bones of an over 50-year old person, initially buried in semi-flexed position inside Structure A, were removed when the burial pit was half filled. In this same dwelling a child was buried in extremely flexed, perhaps wrapped, position. Both house structures had at least one deposition of bone materials in a posthole, placed there after removal of the post. The central posthole of Structure A had the secondarily interred skeletal remains of two old individuals, probably a male and a female. They were perhaps deposited after the dismantling of the house and may represent the material evidence of rituals associated with the abandonment of the house. Similarly, a side post of Structure D had at its bottom a primary deposition of a very young child in seated position, accompanied by a shell pendant and a quartz crystal pebble as mortuary gifts. The immediate surroundings of this dwelling showed burials in (family?) clusters. The burial pit of one very old, primary interred individual, placed in extended position, was reopened after some time in order to place a compact bundle of human bones, containing two skulls and jaws, and some long bones and ribs, on top of the pelvic area. Finally, some burials had flat stones under the skull, arms, shoulders and/or spinal column (Fig. 27).

The Arauquinoid subsistence strategies, combining horticulture with hunting, fishing and the collecting of wild plant foods and invertebrates, did not alter from those of Saladoid/Barrancoid times. Isotope investigation of skeletal material from the Manzanilla 1 site has shown that the diet of its inhabitants was quite varied, including marine and terrestrial proteins as well as root and seed crops. The analysis of starch grains trapped in dental calculus ('tartar') shown by skeletons buried at this same site yielded evidence of the consumption of maize and coontie (zamia). The maize was perhaps eaten ground and baked as bread. Besides, ground provisions such as cassava and sweet potato would have been grown. Interestingly, dramatic changes in vegetation due to human-induced burning have been shown to have taken place by AD 1200 in the Oropuche Lagoon area, suggesting extensive landscape modifications in at least this part of Trinidad, but perhaps

Figure 27. Inhumation burial of a ca. ten year old individual of unknown sex, who was deposited half seated, half lying on the back with flexed legs. The skull was resting on a large pebble, with two more stones on each side of the head. Manzanilla 1 (SAN-1), Trinidad, Arauquinoid series, Late-Ceramic Age, ca. AD 650/800–1400. Courtesy Marc C. Dorst.

elsewhere as well, by the Bontour peoples.[12] According to the animal bone materials found at the Manzanilla 1 site, hunting of terrestrial mammals targeted especially agoutis, pacas, peccaries, and red brocket deer, less tapirs, armadillos, porcupines, crab-eating raccoons, and howler or capuchin monkeys. Besides, aquatic mammals and reptiles such as manatees, caimans and sea turtles were caught. Fishing took place mainly in the inshore-estuarine area, catching primarily catfishes, jacks, grunts, bonefishes, and sharks. The species of shells collected vary according to the site locations. On Trinidad's east and south coasts especially donax clams and trigonal tivelas were targeted (as at present), next to mangrove species including crown conchs and Caribbean oysters, while Arauquinoid sites such as Otaheite, Bontour, San Fernando–Harris Promenade/High Street, and St. Joseph 2 yielded predominantly tiger lucinas, ark shells, turret shells, crown conchs, fighting conchs, rock shells, tulip shells, murex shells, and Caribbean oysters, all collected on the shore of the Gulf of Paria or in the mangrove swamps fringing it.

12 This represents one of the results of a detailed augering project in various swamp areas on Trinidad and several other islands of the West Indies, led by Peter E. Siegel of Montclair State University, New Jersey.

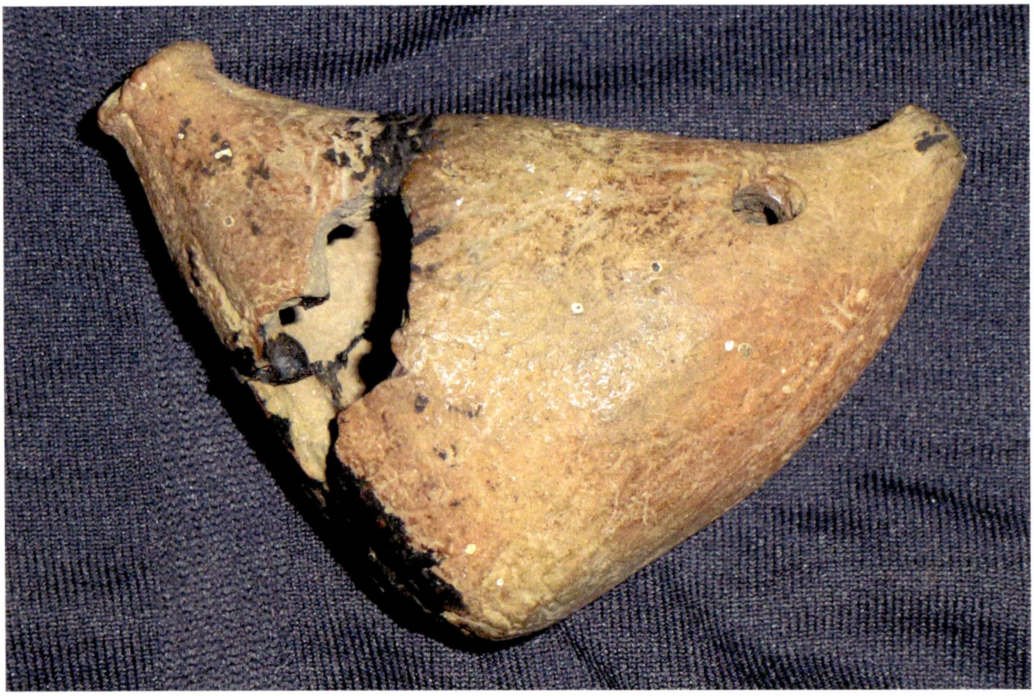

Most types of stone, bone, pottery, and shell artifacts recovered from the Arauquinoid sites of Trinidad closely resemble those of Saladoid/Barrancoid times. Pottery griddles (for baking cassava or maize bread) are common, but ceramic (cotton) spindle whorls and fragments of anthropomorphic figurines, especially

< Figure 28. Pottery ocarina (whistle), showing four holes, found at Grant's Trace 1 (SPA-25), Trinidad. Length 6.5 cm. Arauquinoid series, Late Ceramic Age, ca. AD 650/800–1400. Harris Coll., WFT.

< Figure 29. Ceramic roller stamp, used for body painting, found at Los Iros (SPA-22), Trinidad. Length 5.7 cm. Arauquinoid series, Late Ceramic Age, ca. AD 650/800–1400. Harris Coll., WFT.

feet, occur sparingly. Tools made of stone include polished axe heads, hammerstones, pestles, anvils, grinding stones, arrowshaft polishers, polishing stones, hematite rubbing stones, and irregular chert flakes and small cores which undoubtedly were used for a variety of purposes. Shell celts, pieces of fossil coral and bone spearheads are rare. A very exceptional find was made at Grant's Trace, a ridge top site close to Morne Diablo, some 4 km inland from Trinidad's south shore. Here a triangular pottery ocarina (whistle), showing four holes, was encountered associated with Bontour ceramics (Fig. 28). Personal accoutrements are known from several sites. Bone pendants, including a (yet) undrilled peccary tusk, were found at Bontour, close to the Gulf of Paria, and Marac 2, east of Grant's Trace, a shell bead as a burial gift at Manzanilla 1, while a bone labret/earspool was collected at Batîment Crasé on the south coast. Besides, the St. Joseph 2 site yielded a thin circular pendant with central perforation and an elliptical one with unfinished transfixion, both made of typically Northern Range micaceous schist.

Various objects indicate long-distance exchange contacts. This applies to, for instance, a turquoise pendant and a frog-shaped specimen, made of chlorite, both found at Manzanilla 1. The latter ornament may have been attached to a cotton band or belt. Both exotic accoutrements may have been imported from the mainland, perhaps the Paria Peninsula. Besides, a greenschist axe and diorite rock fragments found at the Otaheite site, located on the Gulf of Paria, most likely derive from Tobago. In addition, similarly Tobagonian diorite beads were found at the Manzanilla 1, Bontour and Marac 2 sites. Interaction with the Orinoco Valley is suggested by exceptional finds such as cylindrical (roller) stamps, no doubt used for body painting, which were discovered at Los Iros on the south coast, Grant's Trace and Marac 2. The Los Iros specimen is tempered with *cauíxi* (Fig. 29). Such roller stamps formed prestigious objects of ceremonial exchange between headmen of the Arauquinoid communities in the Orinoco Valley and the coast of Guyana. Pottery griddles, typically tempered with *cauíxi*, may equally represent trade objects originating on the mainland, as well as, indeed, all Bontour pottery (less than 5% of the potsherds) showing this specific additive. Besides, exchange pottery deriving from the contemporary Late Mabaruma/Apostadero communities of coastal Guyana now appeared at Icacos and Erin in the southwesternmost part of Trinidad. Conversely, shell-tempered Bontour pottery has been found in the Lower Orinoco Valley as well as on Tobago, Los Testigos and Carriacou (Grenadines). Intra-island interaction is suggested by the recovery of pottery tempered with river sand containing micaschist particles, typical of the Northern Range, at the Bontour sites of Trinidad's southern portion.

Interestingly, strontium isotope analyses of Manzanilla 1 skeletons by Jason E. Laffoon of Leiden University showed that at least three persons buried at this site were of nonlocal origin, illustrating the wide-ranging (marriage?) contacts of the Arauquinoid Amerindians of Trinidad. One adult male most likely derived from elsewhere on the island, while two other male individuals, according to their isotope signatures, clearly originated from the mainland. An adolescent, interred on his back with the legs in flexed position towards the torso, displaying the chlorite frog pendant referred to above, probably came from northeast coastal Venezuela, while a second adult male was probably born in the interior of the Guianas. Besides, the latter two individuals, together with another adult male skeleton, showed excessive dental calculus, which, according to Hayley L. Mickleburgh of Leiden University, is the result of the habitual chewing and/or sucking of plant materials in combination with lime, similar to the practice of coca (or perhaps tobacco) chewing among the South American Indians. By adding lime powder or other alkali to the quid of plants such as coca, the release of their active narcotic ingredients is facilitated. It is noteworthy that in the contact period the easternmost cultivation and chewing of coca took place on the Venezuelan coast. Finally, the study of the Manzanilla 1 skeletons indicated that several individuals showed signs of osteoarthritis of the joints due to old age. Besides, dental health was poor: caries was rampant while tooth loss and dental wear were severe.

Troumassoid occupation of Tobago

The incorporation of Tobago's Amerindian communities into the Troumassoid interaction sphere of the Windward Islands and Barbados meant a major cultural realignment for the smaller island, comparable to the transition of Saladoid/Barrancoid to Arauquinoid in Trinidad. Whether the onset of the Arauquinoid series in Trinidad was directly associated with the contemporary development from Saladoid to Troumassoid in the Lesser Antilles is utterly unclear. The latter is definitely not connected with major population movements, but particular Troumassoid ceramic expressions are duplicated in Trinidad's Bontour complex. At any rate, although contacts between the indigenous communities of the two islands across the Galleons' Passage never ceased, from now onwards Trinidad and Tobago became incorporated into separate interaction networks which expressed different cultural and perhaps also ethnic loyalties. Two successive pottery complexes characterized the Troumassoid episode in Tobago: Golden Grove (AD 800–1150) and Plymouth (AD 1150–1400/1450), respectively called after the Golden Grove (II) site in the middle of the island's Coral Lowlands and the Lovers' Retreat site on Tobago's leeward coast. In all 37 sites can be assigned to the Troumassoid tradition, most of which are camp/bivouac sites. While the Golden Grove complex includes in all eight sites, all restricted to the southern third of Tobago, the Plymouth complex encompasses totally fourteen sites, to be found all around the island, suggesting a certain measure of population growth and geographical expansion throughout Troumassoid times.[13]

All Troumassoid sites of Tobago are situated relatively close to the present coastline. Even an 'inland' site like Golden Grove (II) is to be found at a distance of only 1–1.1 km from the sea. Several of the settlement sites yielded human inhumation burials. All sites are located close to a source of potable water, generally a permanent freshwater stream, and offshore reef complexes and/or mangrove swamps. One of the best known Troumassoid sites, Great Courland Bay, stretches along Tobago's leeward coast for some 375 m, in between the mouths of two freshwater streams. It was examined by the author, followed by Léonid Kameneff and the Karrek Ven Training Group in 1998. The site can be divided into a midden area which extends to the sea shore and a residential portion 50 m toward the interior, situated at a slightly higher elevation. The dwelling area is characterized by a pattern of postholes representing a probably circular house structure and two primary inhumation burials. One of these represents a young adult of unknown sex who was buried in strongly flexed position, provided with a necklace consisting of two polished shark teeth. A ring of stones, possibly forming the remnants of a hearth, was found on top of this skeleton. (A reconstruction of this burial is on display in the Tobago Historical Museum, Scarborough.) Close by, a small child wearing a necklace of three diorite beads was buried in similarly flexed position. Interestingly, many plant species known to have been used for medicinal or otherwise curative purposes by the Amerindians of the Lesser Antilles during the contact period have been identified as growing at present in the area of the Great Courland Bay site. Lovers' Retreat occupies part of a rocky headland on Tobago's leeward coast. Troumassoid cultural remains are to be found in an area of ca. 120×80 m in the central and northern part of the promontory. Another important settlement site, Golden Grove (II), consists of a series of shell midden deposits close to the edge of a coral limestone plateau. A small permanent freshwater stream passes in a small valley below the site. This stream empties into an extended mangrove swamp fringing one of Tobago's leeward coastal bays. The refuse deposits are still visible as slight elevations.

The Troumassoid pottery of Tobago shows a division into basically two distinct, sand-tempered wares with specialized functions and, consequently, different occupational and gender associations. The most outstanding of these two wares is represented by high-quality, completely oxidized, reddish-brown to yellowish-orange, relatively thin, burnished pottery with even surfaces (Fig. 30), apparently principally serving ceremonial or at least non-domestic purposes, such as storing and presenting cassava beer or food during meals or festive communal and inter-village gatherings. This implies that these high-quality (fine ware) vessels were primarily associated with the male sphere of activities in the Troumassoid communities. The second major ware includes low-quality, incompletely oxidized, yellowish-grey to grey, relatively thick and badly smoothed pottery with uneven to

13 The available data regarding the remainder of the Troumassoid sites in Tobago are insufficient to allocate them to either the Golden Grove or the Plymouth complex.

Figure 30. Reddish-brown, fine-ware pottery bowls, probably used for ceremonial purposes, found at Great Courland Bay (TOB-23), Tobago. Height 15.4 and 7.8 cm, respectively. Troumassoid series, Late Ceramic Age, ca. AD 1150–1400. Coll. THM.

bumpy surfaces and a gritty, poorly kneaded paste, which was clearly used exclusively in household contexts (Fig. 31a-b). This low-quality ware typically shows either untreated, partially scraped or all-over scratched surfaces. The latter were apparently applied with a bundle of grass or twigs on the vessel surfaces when these were still 'leather dry'. No doubt this coarse ware was affiliated with the female sphere of activities and functioned as cooking pots, for storing liquids and fermenting cassava beer. Flat stone discs were used as vessel covers. It is noteworthy that surface scratching of pottery, although clearly representing a cultural trait dictated by a long-lived tradition of ceramic manufacture, may have had a distinctly functional aspect. Deep, overall scratching enlarges the surface of a vessel and, consequently, the vessel's contents will heat up more rapidly.

Typically high-quality vessel shapesinclude shallow round and oval bowls or dishes, restricted bowls, keeled jars and, in Plymouth times, biconical bowls, all with 'annular' (ring-shaped) bases. The low-quality pottery comprises handled jars (cauldrons) with inflected contours and sizeable open or closed bowls or cooking vessels. The largest of these containers may have been able to hold some 30 litres of liquid. Some potsherds from Great Courland Bay show tar, used for mending, along their edges. Indeed, one special vessel was apparently used for the melting of asphalt.[14] The high-quality ware is often decorated with incised or gouged, punctated or nicked, fingertipped, and modelled designs. In contrast, the coarse ware is rarely ornamented. The incised or gouged designs comprise horizontal parallel lines interrupted

14 Asphalt deriving from underwater seepages offshore Mayaro occasionally washes ashore on Tobago's southeast coast. Formerly it was used for medicinal purposes and burning in lamps as well as by fishermen for caulking their canoes.

a.

b.

Figure 31. Fragment of a greyish, coarse-ware pottery cauldron (a) and handled jar (b), both showing scratched surfaces, most likely used for domestic purposes, found at Great Courland Bay (TOB-23), Tobago. Height (a) 18.1 cm, (b) 15.5 cm. Troumassoid series, Late Ceramic Age, ca. AD 1150–1400. Coll. THM.

by loops, wavy lines and spirals while the upper exteriors of the Plymouth-type biconical bowls characteristically show rows of incised semi-circles. Oval bowls are often provided at both ends with modelled triangular or trapezoidal rim lugs decorated with incised and punctated designs, probably representing bat heads, wings and tails. Other zoomorphic *adornos*, mostly representing frogs and birds, are rare. Modelled human face designs typically adorn necked jars. Some coarse ware containers dating from Plymouth times show finger-indented rims. Ring-shaped 'potrests' were used for placing vessels with rounded bases securely on the ground.

Fine examples of the Troumassoid pottery of Tobago are exhibited in the Tobago Historical Museum, Scarborough.

The food remains recovered from Tobago's Troumassoid sites indicate that the subsistence practices of the late-prehistoric inhabitants of the island did not deviate from those of their Saladoid predecessors. Clearly, their subsistence economy was based on horticulture, notably the cultivation of cassava, maize and sweet potatoes, and hunting, fishing and food collecting, thus establishing a 'broad-spectrum' diet. Artifacts associated with the cultivation and processing of ground provisions include stone axe heads, stone pestles, grinding stones, and pottery griddles, which in Plymouth times were typically provided with 3–4 massive, slab-like feet. Besides, they show direct or upturned rims, triangular in cross section, suggesting that if used for cassava processing, they were used for baking cassava cakes as well as pellets (farinha). Stone anvils were probably used for cracking palm nuts. Pottery spindle whorls point to the cultivation of cotton. According to the archaeozoological remains encountered at Golden Grove (II), Lovers' Retreat and Great Courland Bay, hunting targeted mammals such as agoutis, pacas, nine-banded armadillos, black-eared opossums, collared peccaries, rice rats, tree rats, and pocket mice, next to reptiles such as sea turtles and iguanas. The overexploitation of collared peccaries in Early Ceramic times, when peccaries represented the most highly ranked prey, now resulted in reduced yields. The fish remains found reflect the exploitation of the extensive coral reefs and eelgrass beds offshore southwest Tobago, targeting snappers, parrotfishes, groupers and seabasses, grunts, jacks, surgeonfishes, and sharks. Here, too, the catch of parrotfishes was less than that in the Saladoid era. Besides, the shallow-water, sandy-bottom lagoonal habitat beyond the area's sandy beaches yielded species such as jacks, snooks, porgies, drums, and needlefishes. Finally, flyingfishes and tunas were caught in the shallow-inshore and oceanic environments. Scrapers made of thick lucinas may have been used for peeling cassava tubers or for scaling fish. Obviously, a bipointed bone projectile point, found at Great Courland Bay, originally tipped a fish spear. Crab and shell collecting took place in the lagoons, mangrove swamps, rocky shores, and coral reefs, yielding blue crabs, cross-barred venus clams, thick lucinas, West Indian crown conchs, 'Coon oysters, Atlantic pearl oysters, queen conchs, and West Indian top shells. Sea urchins were gathered at the coral reefs and eelgrass beds.

Analysis of the ground stone tools and rock debris found at the Troumassoid sites of Tobago has shown that the island's Amerindians utilized all of the various rock categories locally available for manufacturing implements, ornaments and ritual artifacts. In fact, they appear to have had all the raw materials at their disposal required for making the entire spectrum of utilitarian tools they employed, notably implements for cutting, grinding, pounding, rubbing and polishing, each of which needed distinct technological qualities. Clearly, the Indians were fully aware of the mechanical properties of the various rock types and utilized this information in choosing the raw materials for making specific stone implements. In this way metamorphic rocks such as greenstones, greenschists and quartzites, as well as igneous (volcanic) rocks including andesites and basalts, were primarily used for manufacturing cutting tools, while igneous and sedimentary

Figure 32. Two quartz crystal beads, a turquoise pendant, and a pottery bead, found at Great Courland Bay (TOB-23), Tobago. Diameter largest quartz crystal bead 1.1 cm; height turquoise pendant 0.8 cm. Troumassoid series, Late Ceramic Age, ca. AD 1150-1400. Coll. THM.

rocks as sandstones and mudstones served as the raw materials of grinding, polishing and pounding tools. All of this suggests that the Troumassoid Amerindians either had free access to all parts of Tobago or had established exchange relationships with the local communities dominating the source areas of the rock types that were exploited. Obviously, the various raw materials were collected at localities where they could be picked up from the surface, for instance, in river valleys and mountain gullies, or from coastal cliffs where the rock boulders being sought after had been exposed by erosion due to water or wind.

Besides, throughout Troumassoid times Tobago continued to form a major centre of manufacturing diorite beads, thus continuing the tradition established in late Saladoid times. Button- as well as barrel-shaped examples were produced at various workshops, apparently in order to be exchanged as social valuables with the other Amerindian communities in the region. Many of the barrel-shaped beads encountered are blanks in the sense of being unperforated, though showing well-polished sides. Rasps made of fossil coral and a channeled stone found at Golden Grove (II) may have been used for smoothing the beads. Other local bodily accoutrements found at the Troumassoid sites of Tobago include greenschist and ochre beads and pendants, bone, shell and pottery beads, geometrical and bird-shaped pendants, shell and pottery ear plugs, and, finally, perforated peccary tusks, the latter typically representing male adornments symbolizing prowess in hunting and warring. The Troumassoid sites also yielded stone ornaments made of materials which are clearly exotic to the island, i.e. biconical beads made of quartz crystal, a turquoise pendant and a jet ear plug (Fig. 32). These ornaments probably originated from the South American mainland. Clearly, although from the onset of Troumassoid times Trinidad and Tobago became incorporated into separate major interaction networks, contacts between the two islands and the mainland did not cease. This is suggested also by the rare presence of shell- and *cauíxi*-tempered pottery at the Troumassoid sites of Tobago, while apparently diorite beads as well as greenstone and greenschist axe heads were exported from the smaller island to Trinidad as in Saladoid/Barrancoid times.

Most likely Tobago played a mediating role in terms of cultural exchange between Trinidad and the mainland on the one hand and the Windward Islands and Barbados on the other. Indeed, specific vessel shapes and several modes of incised or gouged and modelled decoration, notably rim modifications such as the bat-shaped triangular and trapezoidal lugs, shown by the high-quality Troumassoid ceramics of the entire Windward Islands, Barbados and Tobago, seem to duplicate examples on the Bontour earthenware of Trinidad.[15] In the Lesser Antilles these designs have often been seen as local simplifications of decorative modes dating back to Saladoid times, but the present evidence suggests that the transformation from Saladoid to Troumassoid may have taken place at least partly under the stimulus of the inception of the Arauquinoid series in Trinidad. Similarly, the human face designs on the Plymouth earthenware of Tobago resemble the anthropomorphic imagery characterizing the Arauquinoid pottery of the mainland and Trinidad. Direct contacts between the Troumassoid communities of Tobago and the Lesser Antilles are suggested, for instance, by a biconical bowl decorated with incised arches and a necked jar showing an anthropomorphic face design, both found in contemporary contexts on Barbados. Moreover, the Great Courland Bay site yielded some potsherds showing black-on-red or buff painted designs, most likely exemplifying exchange pieces or somewhat crude imitations of the so-called Caliviny Polychrome ware known from the Troumassoid tradition in the Windward Islands and Barbados.

A few Troumassoid artifacts from Tobago relate to the animistic religious convictions of the local Amerindians. They comprise a single threepointed stone with hollow base, recovered from the surface of the Golden Grove settlement site, thus perhaps associated originally with the upper levels of this site which yielded Troumassoid pottery. A most interesting stone artefact found at the Great Courland Bay site is formed by a relatively large and heavy boulder of local volcanic rock, showing a group of three cup-shaped cavities on one face, while a fragmentary specimen of this same type of rock is provided with a series of five similar pits. A comparable boulder without known provenance, exhibited in the Tobago Museum, Scarborough, shows a group of ten such cavities on one face and another group of two pits on another side. The function of these small hollows is unknown, although it is noteworthy that petroglyphs showing groups of small, cup-shaped cavities are known from the South American mainland. Perhaps they were used for grinding pigments or hallucinogenic substances. Ceramic figurines may have functioned in particular shamanic rituals. Part of a female figurine, showing arms, legs and prominent breasts, and a zoomorphic specimen in the shape of a shark, were found at Great Courland Bay, while a less naturalistically modelled figurine with pregnant belly was encountered at the Lovers' Retreat site. Moreover, two

15 The bats may have symbolized ancestor spirits as they did in contact-period religion throughout the West Indies.

horizontally perforated pottery artifacts resembling pestles have been encountered at Great Courland Bay, one of which is decorated with an anthropomorphic face design showing arching eyebrows on its upper portion. Similar pestle-like objects from contemporary sites in the Windward Islands and Barbados have been interpreted as 'loomweights'. More likely, they represent pestles used for pulverizing plant foods or perhaps hallucinatory substances, and may have belonged to the local shaman's religious/ceremonial paraphernalia. Finally, clearly ritual vessels are represented by high-quality wide jars showing pedestal-like lower portions, which were possibly used for burning hallucinogenic drugs, and nostril or sniffing bowls for inhaling tobacco or pepper juice through the nose, similarly employed during shamanic healing ceremonies.

On the brink of the Historic Age: Mayoid in Trinidad and Cayo (?) in Tobago

The final Amerindian pottery series of Trinidad, the Mayoid tradition, is characteristic of the Amerindian–European contact period. It may have emerged shortly before the time of Columbus' encounter with the inhabitants of the island in 1498, perhaps as the result of the immigration of Amerindians from the mainland, probably the coastal zone of the Guianas, into Trinidad (Fig. 9). At some sites in south Trinidad sparse amounts of Mayoid pottery have been found associated with Bontour ceramics, suggesting a certain period of overlap between the latter and the Mayoid tradition. Mayoid ceramics typify the indigenous pottery encountered at St. Joseph 2, the site of the first Spanish settlement of the island, and those of the Capuchin missions established from 1687 onward in central and west Trinidad. It may have been made until the mid-eighteenth century. In St. Joseph (*San José de Oruña*), which was founded in 1592, it was encountered in association with sparse amounts of Spanish *majolica* and other wheel-made historic ceramics, suggesting that Mayoid pottery formed the Spanish kitchen ware, obtained from 'loyal' Amerindians on the island. The present evidence suggests that several of Trinidad's Amerindian ethnic groups manufactured and used Mayoid ceramics, including at least the Nepoio and Arawak (Lokóno). Apart from St. Joseph 2 and seven Spanish–Amerindian mission sites, in all seven indigenous settlement and camp sites have yielded Mayoid pottery. They are distributed all over Trinidad, suggesting that Mayoid formed the dominant ceramic complex of the island at the time of the Amerindian–European encounter and long after. Some of these indigenous Mayoid settlement sites yielded Spanish chevron beads dating from the sixteenth century.

Mayoid pottery is perhaps the thinnest (on average 4–6 mm) and strongest ceramics of pre-Columbian Trinidad and Tobago. It is made by coiling and was fired in an open fire, resulting in incompletely oxidized vessel surfaces. The latter were generally well smoothed. Mayoid pottery is invariably tempered with *caraipé*, the ash of the quartz-rich bark of small trees belonging to the *Licania* genus. This is known among the Amerindians of the Guianas and Amazonia as *couepia* (*kwepi*, *kwep*) or *kauta*. At present it is the only material the Amerindians of the coastal part of the Guianas use for tempering their pottery clay. The bark is burned, removing most organic components, and afterwards pounded. *Licania* trees were once indigenous in Trinidad's Northern Basin, as specimens of this genus have been collected in the O'Meara and Aripo savannahs in 1861 and 1913, respectively. The most characteristic Mayoid vessel shapes include jars showing sharply everted, straight or slightly outcurving necks, which closely resemble the so-called Arawak cooking vessels or 'buck pots' of the Guianas. In colonial times these jars were adopted as vessels to cook the famous pepperpot at many plantations in the region. The Mayoid complex is further characterized by open serving bowls, bottles and huge vessels which undoubtedly served as cassava beer-brewing containers. A rare necked vessel shape, found at Icacos, is identical to a major form typical of the late-prehistoric to historic Cayo and Koriabo pottery of the Windward Islands and Guianas, respectively, of which the former represents the earthenware of the Island Caribs. Decoration is reduced to a minimum on Mayoid ceramics, being restricted to a few nicked or undecorated wall or rim knobs and occasionally some all-over red painting or black painted zones along the vessel rims.

The contention that the Troumassoid pottery represents the ceramics of the Island Caribs, who are known to have occupied the Windward Islands in the contact period and still inhabit small parts of Dominica, St. Vincent and Trinidad, has been proven to be unsound. Ethnohistorical reconstruction of the Island Carib pottery complex has shown this to be closely related to that of the present Kali'na (Mainland Caribs) of the Guianas and its precursor, the late-prehistoric Koriabo complex. This has been confirmed by archaeological research at sites throughout the Windward Islands yielding pottery of the Cayo complex which can be taken to represent the Island Carib earthenware. Apart from showing its derivation from the Koriabo complex, Cayo appears to have been influenced to a certain extent by the ceramics of the 'Taíno' Indians of the Greater Antilles while, similarly, some interaction and amalgamation appear to have taken place with the domestic ware of the Troumassoid tradition. Although sites exclusively yielding Cayo pottery are unknown from Tobago, individual potsherds perhaps resembling this assemblage have been encountered at a few sites. Thus far reconnaissance surveys to identify Amerindian sites shown on various historic maps of Tobago, dating from the seventeenth and eighteenth centuries, have remained unsuccessful. However, eventually intensified searching in the field should be rewarding, as it has been in the Windward Islands in the past few years.

5. Amerindian culture and society in Trinidad and Tobago at the time of the encounter and thereafter

With Columbus' third voyage to the West Indies (1498) the first sketchy documentary evidence on the Amerindian societies of Trinidad and Tobago emerged, providing a completely different source of information on the indigenous peoples of the two islands than the archaeological evidence discussed thus far. More written data soon followed, as in the wake of the Admiral's small fleet numerous other discoverers, fortune hunters, sailors and/or merchants passed by, or indeed set foot on, one or both of the twin islands. Besides, the Spanish colonization of the Greater Antilles and the rapid decline of the Amerindian population in those islands induced adventurers to attempt capturing Amerindian slaves in the Lesser Antilles and on the mainland coast. Ship's journals or governmental reports on all of these journeys provide scattered bits of information on the various indigenous societies of the region. The sixteenth-century Spanish efforts to conquer Trinidad and explore the Orinoco River added more detailed knowledge, written down by the participants in these events and the official colonial chroniclers. When in the course of the sixteenth century numerous merchants/privateers of the other European nations started to traverse the Caribbean, trading with the Amerindians and the Spanish colonists or attacking the latter, even more documentary sources became available. Unfortunately, the definite Spanish settlement in Trinidad (1592), and the establishment of Amerindian–Spanish mission sites in the island (1687), did not lead to extensively detailed descriptions of local Amerindian society and culture such as those from the Lesser Antilles. Neither would the seventeenth-century Spanish, English, Courlander (Latvian), and Dutch attempts at colonizing Tobago yield such accounts. Nevertheless, a reasonably comprehensive picture of the traditional lifeways and world view of the Amerindians occupying the two islands can be reconstructed, if only the ethnocentric lens through which the Europeans viewed the indigenous peoples of Trinidad and Tobago is continually readjusted and their (often hidden) objectives and motives behind the portrayal of Amerindian society and culture are sharply kept in mind.

Population and settlement patterns

Although several sixteenth-century assessments of the indigenous population size in Trinidad were recorded, none can be accepted without hesitation. After a short visit in 1519, the Spanish traveller Fernández de Enciso called the island 'highly populated', and this is repeated by several other chroniclers. Estimates of Trinidad's indigenous population range from 200,000 Amerindians in 1534 and 100,000 in 1570 to 50,000 in 1589, 35,000 in 1593, and 40,000 in 1595. Whether this descending series reflects the declining numbers of Amerindians throughout the sixteenth century, or the lessening exaggeration of the recording Spanish *conquistadores* involved, or both, is open to discussion. The first exploration of Trinidad and what was claimed to be a full count of the Amerindians of the island was undertaken by its first Spanish governor, Antonio de Berrío, in 1593. Berrío wished to have an accurate estimate of the Amerindian population of Trinidad as he intended to establish an *encomienda* system and allocate the existing indigenous villages and their inhabitants to his soldiers. Berrío arrived at a number of 7000 warriors and estimated the total number of natives on the island at 35,000 persons. However, it can be assumed that this figure is slightly exaggerated.[16] If the contact-period population of Trinidad would be put at a conservative estimate of 20,000 persons, this would point to in all 40–80 Amerindian villages, each counting 250–500 inhabitants. It would mean an overall population density of 4.1 persons per km^2. Unfortunately, early population estimates of Tobago have not been recorded.

Often the southern coastal zone of Trinidad is mentioned as the densest occupied part of the island. In 1498 Columbus reported to have seen many gardens and villages along the south shore and one year afterwards Amerigo Vespucci visited a 'large village' in this part of the island. Columbus also found freshly-dug wells on the beach of Icacos Point (present Columbus Bay). The description of the building of a dwelling on probably the western shore of Trinidad in 1516 suggests that at least some Amerindians of the island lived in large, bell-shaped communal (multi-family) houses capable of sheltering up to 100 people. This house reportedly had a roof of palm leaves and was apparently closed entirely. Although such a single dwelling could have made up an entire village, the documentary evidence indicates that most likely the Amerindian settlement in which this particular house was built comprised several communal dwellings and may have had up to 400–500 inhabitants. Similar multi-family houses are described by Columbus' crew as characterizing the Amerindian villages on the west coast of the Gulf of Paria in 1498. According to Columbus, this region seemed to be well cultivated, showing 'innumerable houses and people'. Pedro Mártir noted that the Spanish were entertained in a round house situated on a large square. During this visit the men stayed in one part of the dwelling, the women in the opposite one. Finally, in 1499 Amerigo Vespucci reported he visited 'a large village standing beside the sea' at the mouth of a sizeable river, probably the Caño Manamó, just across the Serpent's Mouth. The descriptions of the Trinidad and Paria dwellings suggest that they resembled closely the traditional multi-family houses or *malocas* of many present-day Amerindian peoples in the Upper Orinoco Valley. At the time of the

16 Berrío's count took place nearly a century after the first encounter and, consequently, the possibility of a local demographic decline due to Spanish slave raids and imported diseases, comparable to the one that decimated the Amerindian population of the Greater Antilles, cannot be excluded. On the other hand, some exaggeration by Berrío of the number of Trinidad's Amerindians, most of whom opposed him, remains likely. Actually, in 1595 Berrío's lieutenant, Domingo de Vera, estimated the population of Trinidad at not more than 14,000 Amerindians.

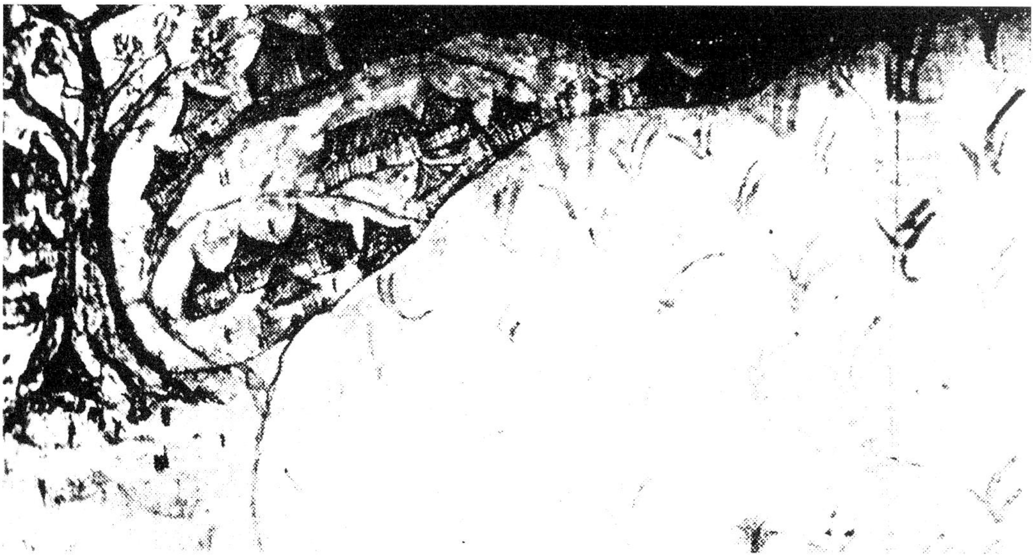

Figure 33. Part of an ink and watercolour manuscript map, probably drawn by Willem Mollens in 1654, showing an Amerindian village situated northwest of the Courlander fort Jekabs (here not shown) at present Plymouth, Tobago. Adapted from a photographic reproduction; original destroyed during the Second World War.

encounter such communal round houses characterized a number of the Amerindian communities on the Lower Orinoco River as well.

The traditional settlement pattern of the Caribs (Kali'na/Kali'nago/Carinepagoto) Amerindians of the coastal zone of the mainland, north Trinidad, Tobago, and the Windward Islands, which is well known from the seventeenth-century documentary evidence, was quite different. The single reliable representation of a Carib village is shown on a unique ink and watercolour manuscript map depicting the Courlander (Latvian) fortress Jekabs (Jacob) on the leeward coast of Tobago in 1656. This map was probably drawn by Willem Mollens, the Dutch governor of the Courlander settlement, and shows an Amerindian village at the back of the fortification, approximately at the site of present-day Plymouth (Fig. 33). According to the map, this settlement consisted of a series of (perhaps originally about twenty) round (family) houses with conical, thatched roofs, encircling an open square (plaza), the centre of which was occupied by a rectangular building with thatched roof, apparently a men's (assembly) house such as those described in numerous accounts on the Lesser Antilles throughout the seventeenth century. Such an assembly house served as a meeting place for the men of the village, as an arms depot, a place to receive and accommodate guests, to hold communal feasts, and to bury deceased (male) members of the community. Mollens' drawing suggests that the walls of both the assembly house and family huts were made of closely-set poles or reeds. The structures are overshadowed by a tree of considerable size. Dark-skinned, sparingly clad Amerindians, holding spears in their hands, are shown inside the village. (Unfortunately, the original drawing, which was kept in the Berlin archives, was lost during the Second World War.) It is noteworthy that an Amerindian village consisting of fifty houses is mentioned in Tobago in 1667. By the end of the seventeenth century the traditional Carib settlement pattern was slowly abandoned and replaced by villages consisting of one or a few extended-family houses. In 1792 such a one-roomed house at Louis d'Or, Tobago, was described by Sir William Young as 'scarcely weather-tight, being wattled and thatched, crowded with [...] a great variety of nets for fishing, hammocks for sleeping in, and different sorts of provision, stores, &c &c'.

Subsistence and food processing

Horticulture, hunting, fishing, and the collecting of invertebrates and wild vegetable foods formed the mainstay of the Amerindian subsistence economy in the contact period, as it had throughout much of the twin islands' pre-Columbian past. Many food crops were raised in the indigenous kitchen gardens and swidden fields (or *conucos* as they are called in Trinidadian Spanish), which gradually developed into the African/European 'provision grounds' of historic times. The latter are often still made by simple slash-and-burn techniques. After 3–5 harvests plots are generally abandoned, often when the land 'is losing she fat' according to the Tobagonian expression. The post-Columbian introduction of metal cutlasses and hatchets simplified essentially garden clearance work and many other activities. Indeed, European tools became highly desired objects in contact-period Amerindian society. Four crops are allotted most space in modern West Indian provision grounds such as those of Tobago, including cassava (*yuca*), maize and sweet potatoes, all originally cultivated by the Amerindians, and pigeon peas, deriving from Africa. They are often complemented with other indigenous crops such as tannia and kidney beans, and dasheen, an African tuber species. In Tobago cassava and sweet potatoes are typically planted in small mounds which provide loose, well-aerated soil for cultivation. Charles Kingsley's description of a Trinidadian provision ground in the 1870s forms the most elaborate account of the variety of food crops, fruits and useful plants raised in traditional West Indian *conucos*. Apart from tubers and cereals such as cassava, arrowroot, Indian yam, tannia, and maize, he lists fruit trees, including avocados, guavas, mammee apples, papaws, sapodillas, star apples, sweetsop, bananas, mangoes, and oranges, as well as legumes such as pigeon peas and vegetables, including pumpkins, breadfruit, okras, and plantains. Of course, part of these domesticates, notably bananas, mangoes, oranges, breadfruit, okras, plantains, and pigeon peas, are post-Columbian introductions. The same applies to sugar cane, ginger and pineapples which, together with an indigenous variety of food crops, fruits and vegetables, are mentioned as grown by the Amerindians of Trinidad and Tobago in the documentary sources of the sixteenth and seventeenth centuries. Similarly, American domesticates such as cocoa, tomatoes and christophines, that did not reach the twin islands in prehistory, were now introduced due to Spanish interaction.

Apart from cultivated food plants, the indigenous peoples of the twin islands consumed many wild (or tended) fruits and vegetables. The seeds of various palm species and trees such as sea grapes, wild-chestnuts, cashimas, coco plums (fat pork or *hicáco*), wild amaranths (*bledos*), and locust berries are mentioned among the fruits collected by the Amerindians of Trinidad in the sixteenth century, while as early as 1498 Columbus noted the consumption of hog plums and sea grapes among the inhabitants of Paria. The introduction of European metal implements in the contact period substantially transformed the processing techniques of the cultivated food plants, notably those of ground provisions such as cassava. Iron knives replaced the sharpened bivalve shells or flint flakes of pre-Columbian times as peeling instruments, while iron graters rather than wooden boards inlayed with sharp stone chips were used for grating tubers.[17] The subsequent stages in the processing of (bitter) cassava remained the same: by placing the cassava pulp into a press made of twilled basketry (*matapee*), known as the *sebucán* or *coulebre* (*coulev*) in colonial Trinidad, the poisonous juice could be expelled from the pulp. The juice or 'cassava milk' (*casareep*), now detoxicated, was thickened over a slow fire and formed an essential ingredient of the pepperpot, while the pulp could be passed through a sieve and the resulting flour (*cazábi*) fried on a (metal) platter (*aripo*, *platine*), known as the 'baking-stone' (later 'baking-iron') in Trinidad, placed on three stones (*topias*), in order to bake huge, flat discs of unleavened bread (*arepas*). Alternatively, a crumbly grainy flour (*farine*) was produced by crushing the grated and dried cassava in a mortar. The pepperpot stew was kept by simmering on the fireplace in a large, open earthenware pot, known as *canari* or *conari*, a term afterwards used for a similarly employed, round-bottomed iron basin. A mildly intoxicating Amerindian drink, called *paiwari* in the Guianas, was made by fermenting burnt cassava with grated sweet potatoes and some sugar cane juice. It formed a favourite beverage among the African slaves. Another alcoholic drink, *mábi*, was made from sweet potatoes which, following boiling, were beaten to a mash, mixed with water and left fermenting for a few days. In the seventeenth century it was called the 'universal' drink of Tobago. Ethnographic evidence from the Guianas and Lesser Antilles suggests that wooden mortars and stone pestles continued to be used for processing root crops other than (bitter) cassava and for moist or leafy vegetable foods. Grinding stones, encountered at the site of the eighteenth-century Montserrate (Mayo) mission, were undoubtedly used for processing seed crops, most likely maize.

In addition to food crops, useful plants such as gourds (*totúmo*) and cotton trees, shrubs for obtaining red pigment and food colouring/flavouring (*anatto* or *roucou*), and medicinal and/or hallucinogenic species, including tobacco, were grown in contact-period Amerindian provision grounds and kitchen gardens. Cotton twine was used for the weaving of hammocks, waistbands, girdles, and fishing lines on large looms. As in pre-Columbian times, spinning whorls served for spinning cotton twine. Such a small, flattish, calabash spinning whorl, attached to a thin wooden shank, forms the oldest ethnographic object known from Trinidad. It was

17 According to a mid-seventeenth-century Dutch source, the Amerindians of Tobago used coral knives.

Figure 34. Watercolour painting, showing an Amerindian from Trinidad capturing parrots, using the cries of a captive parrot to lure other birds into a wickerwork cage, ca. 1586. After *Histoire Naturelle des Indes*, The Drake Manuscript, f. 83. Courtesy The Pierpont Morgan Library, New York.

reportedly collected by the Swede Samuel Fahlberg among the Caribs living on the island in 1786 and is still kept in the Museum of Ethnography in Stockholm, Sweden. Apart from cotton twine, the Amerindians used fibres of wild silk grass for the making of hammocks, fish lines and bow strings. Silk grass hammocks are referred to with respect to the Island Caribs living on Tobago in the late seventeenth and eighteenth centuries. Similarly, throughout historic times wild fibres were used in Trinidad as the raw materials of basketry: rectangular, two-piece storage baskets were manufactured of tirite and mamuri (*mamoo*) bush ropes and larger baskets of the leaves of the cocorite, moriche and awara palms. Amerindian-styled basketry, silk grass fish lines and cotton hammocks were soon adopted by the African slave population of the twin islands and continued to be made until recently. In Trinidad the African slaves and free blacks bought baskets, back-packs and cassava strainers, skillfully woven by the Caribs of Arima from the ribs of tirite (*larouman*) leaves. In the early nineteenth century such 'Charaib' or 'Injun' baskets were preferred by hucksters to display their wares on the roadsides of Tobago.

Both the contact-period hunting strategies and captured fauna differed little from those in the prehistoric period. Setting fire in the dry season to the grassy plains of Trinidad's Northern Basin was common practice throughout colonial times, in order to facilitate the hunting of especially red brocket or white-tailed ('savanna') deer. In the contact period deer was invariably listed as good hunting game in Trinidad. Interestingly, as late as the seventeenth century the Arawaks (Lokóno) of the Guianas went specially to Trinidad in order to catch parrots for their feathers. A Trinidad Amerindian capturing parrots, using the cries of a trapped parrot to lure other birds into a wickerwork cage, is shown on a unique sixteenth-century painting (Fig. 34). Besides, the Trinidad Amerindians of colonial times were accustomed to exploit the colonies of oil birds (*guácharo*) in the Northern Range and on the islet of Huevas in the Bocas by collecting hundreds of young birds at the peak of their fatness, in order to boil them down to produce cooking and lighting oil. The eighteenth-century mission Amerindians of Savana Grande (present Princes Town) and Montserrate (Mayo) in south-central Trinidad specialized in training dogs for hunting collared peccaries and nine-banded armadillos, respectively. The animal bone materials encountered at Montserrate indicate that the Amerindians of this mission hunted also for red howler monkeys, agoutis, opossums, and deer, as well as porcupines and pacas. Hunting dogs formed a valuable article of trade in the island, and throughout British colonial times Warao from the Orinoco delta supplied the inhabitants of Trinidad with excellent hunting dogs, raised on the mainland, on their annual visits to the market of San Fernando. These dogs, a short-legged breed, were known as '*Warahoon* (*Guaraoon*) dogs' after the ethnic name. Until recently it was customary in Toco to bathe hunting dogs with tobacco, rum and particular herbs prior to a hunting party in order 'to sharpen their scent'.[18] In 1499 Vespucci described the Amerindians of south Trinidad as 'excellent archers', and the year before Columbus had met

18 An anonymous visitor of the Amerindian–Spanish missions of Trinidad noted in 1780 that their indigenous inhabitants love their hunting dogs 'blindly; they speak to them and treat them as friends, singing songs to them in praise of their skills and the captures they make'.

a group of them who carried wooden shields, bows and feathered arrows 'at the top of which there is a sharp bone with a thorn, like a fishhook', as the Admiral noted. Manatees (*lamentins*) and sea turtles were caught in aquatic environments in both Trinidad and Tobago, while in 1595 the Trinidad Amerindians supplied the Spanish with land tortoises (*morocoys*). Finally, domesticated European animals such as horses, cattle, pigs, goat, and sheep were taken to Trinidad and Tobago by various Spanish explorers and by the end of the sixteenth century turkeys, European chickens, donkeys, and mules as well as African guinea fowl had been introduced to the larger island.

The colonial period fishing methods duplicate those of pre-Columbian times. The hook-and-line technique was (and is) typically used offshore in shallow-water (banks) areas and inshore in rivers, ponds and ravines. In the Gulf of Paria kingfishes and mackerels were caught traditionally with the hook-and-line method from stationary boats. At present sharks, groupers and snappers are caught with long, baited lines on the banks off Tobago, as they were probably in the prehistoric era. Seine fishing is still practised daily in Tobago. It is adapted to inshore-estuarine areas with smooth bottoms and calm seas, typically catching mullets, jacks and snooks. Cone-shaped creels or fishpots were and are widely used both in riverine situations and offshore in reef areas. In the nineteenth century the Trinidad fishpots, employed for catching freshwater fish in the island's rivers, were made of bamboo or arrow reed (*white roseau*). Fish poisoning is a technique which was formerly widespread both in Trinidad and Tobago. Usually a stream or pool was fenced off, after which a vegetable fish poison, often *haiari* roots, was added to the water. Of course, chunks of fish and meat formed major ingredients of the pepperpot which, together with casareep and some water, were boiled into a thick soup into which cassava bread was dipped. Baking on a barbecue (*boucan*), smoking, salting, and drying were further means of meat and fish processing. In the late eighteenth century the Amerindians of the Guayria mission (present San Fernando) reportedly preserved fish especially by drying.

Although badly documented, the sea-shore and riverine collecting of land crabs, crayfish, mollusks, sea urchins, and turtle eggs provided excellent substitutes for or supplements to the sources of protein-rich food obtained by hunting and fishing in the two islands. The only historic account of shellfish exploitation in Trinidad dates from 1803, when an English naval officer refers to Island Carib women at Toco gathering mollusks (probably whelks) 'from the rocks', using 'great baskets [...] supported upon their backs by a band pressing over their foreheads'. In the late seventeenth century the quality of the shellfish collected on the shores of Tobago was praised, while in 1766 the gathering of oysters from the mangrove swamps stretching along the shore of Bon Accord Lagoon, and that of queen conchs from the reefs and eelgrass beds of Buccoo Reef, by the Island Caribs of Tobago was recorded.

Social organization and life cycle

The documentary evidence on the structure of Amerindian society in Trinidad in the contact period is vague and scanty. The earliest information is to be found in the Spanish sources on the resistance of the Trinidadian Amerindians against the attempts of Antonio Sedeño to settle on the island in the 1530s. The conflict evolved from an alliance concluded between the Spanish and Maluana (Maruana), an Arawak (Lokóno) chief and 'lord of many people' who headed the 'province' of Chacomar (Chacomare, Chacomari), encompassing most of south and southwest Trinidad. An Arawak village called Carao (Cayao, Carowa) is mentioned as situated on the south coast, close to Punta Curao, from as early as 1582 until well into the seventeenth century. Assisted by Maluana, the Spanish attempted to get a foothold in another part of the island, the country of a chief called Baucunar who headed a 'province' called Cumucurapo (Camorocabo, Camocorabo), situated on the northeastern shore of the Gulf of Paria. A village with this name is recorded in the documentary sources throughout the sixteenth and seventeenth centuries. The Cariban toponym Cumucurapo, meaning 'place of the silk cotton tree', still exists as Mucurapo, the name of a residential quarter in Port-of-Spain, close to the mouth of the Maraval River. Apparently, Baucunar was the chief of the Carinepagoto (Mainland Caribs) inhabiting this part of the island. He is recorded as a 'lord of many people and a valiant person' and succeeded in concluding an alliance with various other Amerindian chiefs of Trinidad and Paria in order to fight off Sedeño. The Spanish sources suggest that at the time Maluana and Baucunar represented Trinidad's most important Amerindian chiefs or headmen (*acarewana*, *aquirivano*). Probably they should be seen as tribal 'great men' in the process of evolving into the leaders of small chiefdoms ('rank societies'), in which leadership would become hereditary. At any rate, Baucunar allied himself with other village chieftains of equal status, thus forming a temporary military confederacy against the Spanish under his command. Baucunar's 'province' reportedly was densely populated and had two large villages situated on the Gulf of Paria, and even more towards the interior. It was ruled by three or four local chiefs (*caciques*) of which Baucunar was paramount. His ascendancy might have originated from his dominant personal qualities in war and trade, as a result of which he was able to attract a large following through gift giving. To a certain extent his leadership may have been hereditary, as it is recorded that during one of the skirmishes an Amerindian captain, a nephew of Baucunar and 'the heir to all of his lands', was killed. This suggests matrilineal inheritance although it is unclear whether this nephew was a sister's or a brother's son.

Little is known about the socio-political organization of the other Amerindian peoples, the Nepoio, Shebaio, Chaguanes, and Yaio, living in Trinidad at the time of the encounter. Most likely, the structure of their societies would not have deviated markedly from those of the Arawaks (Lokóno) and Carinepagoto. All chieftains apparently attempted to enlarge their following by contracting marriages with many wives, as each new marriage created a another set of affinal relatives from which support could be exacted. By public display and distribution of gifts, often exotic goods obtained during war and/or trade expeditions, these 'great men' were able to build their influence and bind their following. Chiefs could boost their prestige by holding drinking parties at initiation rituals of young warriors, burials of chiefs, war councils, the settlement of disputes between neighbouring villages, boat launchings, and marriage ceremonies. Indeed, a retinue was created by amassing goods and distributing them during large public feasts. All this led to a decidedly dynamic political landscape in which leadership was highly competitive. This kind of socio-political organization was typical also of Kali'na/Kali'nago society in the Guianas, Tobago and the Lesser Antilles. According to Charles de Rochefort, the Island Caribs of the 1650s had two grades of war chiefs; the 'admirals' (*ubutú*), commanding an entire fleet, were especially respected. These 'great men' had the right of virilocal residence for themselves and their sons, simultaneously receiving services from their sons-in-law. The war chief himself did not have to serve his in-laws. Arawak (Lokóno) social structure was more formally integrated than that of the Caribs as their traditional system of blood relationship was based on exogamous, matrilineal clans (prescribed kinship groupings).[19] Prospective Arawak chiefs (*adumasi*) had to undergo painful initiation rituals during community fêtes, like the Caribs. Chiefs were typically polygynous. According to a seventeenth-century Spanish source, Arawak *caciques* had six or seven wives, ordinary Arawaks only two or three. One of these Arawak 'great men', Aracoraima, who lived in Carao village on the south Trinidad coast in the early 1600s, once went to the Spanish settlement on Margarita with six war canoes in order to barter not less than 24 of his women for the sum of 6000 pesos worth of axes, knives and other trade goods. The alteration of the Amerindian burial customs under European (Christian) influence was expressed by Louis, an Island Carib living with his family on Tobago in 1792. He noted that formerly a deceased male was buried in sitting posture, holding his bow and arrows, but now he is interred *au long et 'droit'* ('stretched on the back').

The Amerindian division of labour was based on sex and age; semi-specialists operated only on the community level. Subsistence activities such as the clearing of *conucos*, hunting and fishing were typically masculine tasks in Amerindian society, as was house building, basketry making, wood carving, as well as bone and stone working for tools, weapons and furniture. Heavy labour such as clearing gardens, boat construction, pulling the seine to shore, and house building was often communal work in which a group of male in-laws, neighbours and friends collaborated, being rewarded with food and drinks after completion of the task, and of course the reciprocal commitment of future assistance by the beneficiary. This form of teamwork is still found in the twin islands, known in Trinidad as *gayap* (*gaiappe*), a term derived from Cariban *gayapo*, and in Tobago as *lend-hand*. Planting, weeding and harvesting were typically female occupations, as well as food preparation, spinning and weaving cotton, and pottery making. Collecting wild vegetable foodstuffs and invertebrates were tasks of both women and children. It is noteworthy that among the present-day peasantry of Trinidad and Tobago, as well as elsewhere in the West Indies, the traditional division of labour between

19 The present Arawak Sabáiono clan of the Guianas may have emanated from the Shebaio (Sapaio, Suppaye, Sepoye), an distinct ethnic group which originally lived in the Orinoco Valley and on the coast of south Trinidad.

men and women, especially for subsistence activities, closely resembles that of past Amerindian society.

Amerindian ethnic and status distinctions were expressed by bodily ornamentation, painting, tattooing, hair style and dress. According to Columbus' ship's journal, at the time of the encounter the warriors of both south Trinidad and Paria wore their hair 'long and smooth', parted in the middle and down to the shoulders.[20] They bound their head with a multi-coloured cotton scarf. The ordinary dress of both men and women was restricted to loincloths or (bead) aprons. The sixteenth-century south Trinidad males wore a small loin cloth (*guayuco*) tied on both sides by a string encircling the waist. The appearance of great chiefs such as Baucunar was impressive. The latter is described as entirely painted red and black, attired with an elaborate feather headdress as well as an eagle-like breast ornament made of *caraculí* (an exotic gold/copper alloy also known as *guanín*), and armed with a bow and two quivers. (He had some unspecified Spanish weapons as well.) In the 1530s other chiefs opposing the Spanish were clad in jaguar skins with the animal mouth placed over the head. Subordinate warriors reportedly sported cotton head-bands. And in 1595 Sir Robert Dudley noted that the Trinidad Amerindians were 'a fine shaped and a gentle people, al naked and painted red, their commanders wearing crownes of feathers'. Throughout historic times Carib women typically wore tight cotton bandages on shanks and upper arms, in this way producing abnormally bulging calves and biceps. Distinctions in rank were typically expressed in lavish bodily decoration which reflected the wearer's ability in war and exchange. Male warriors wore jaguar claws or necklaces made of teeth and bones of slain enemies and/or teeth of jaguars, peccaries or caimans, all in order to show prowess. Some Island Carib men had flutes cut from a dead enemy's bone dangling from the neck. The Amerindians of Paria reportedly wore necklaces containing *caraculí* discs and pearls. Typically female ornaments included pins stuck into the lower lips and necklaces of stone and shell beads as well as animal-shaped pendants, predominantly frogs, made of green-coloured stone, as in pre-Columbian times.

Interaction: war and exchange

Chronic small-scale warfare between 'traditional enemies', involving surprise raids on target villages and limited open-air battles, characterized the region throughout the contact period. Such hit-and-run attacks were motivated by revenge, the acquisition of prestige and human trophies, as well as by the wish to loot valuables, exact tribute and abduct young women and boys to be used as concubines and/or slaves. The conscription of their labour was necessary to produce enough food and cassava beer for communal feasts and dancing parties serving the status rivalry

---

20 As late as 1825 the Amerindians of the Savana Grande mission (present Princes Town) were described as 'short in nature, […] yellow in complexion, their eyes dark, their hair long, lank and glossy as a raven's wing'.

Figure 35. Watercolour painting, showing a fight between pirogues from Trinidad and Margarita, ca. 1586. After *Histoire Naturelle des Indes*, The Drake Manuscript, f. 56. Courtesy The Pierpont Morgan Library, New York.

among the local 'great men'.[21] Indeed, Ralegh noted that the Amerindians 'warre more for women, the[n] eyther for gold or dominion'. Competition for trade routes formed another cause of war. In the 1590s the Orinoco Arawak war chief Aramaia (Armago, Armaio), a nephew of chief Aracoraima of south Trinidad, fought with the Warao of the Caño Manamó, who threatened the monopoly of Arawak trade between the Lower Orinoco River and Trinidad by selling canoes for tobacco in the latter island. On the other hand, at the same time trade and ceremonial exchange persisted uninterruptedly between antagonistic neighbouring peoples or conglomerates of ethnic groups such as the Arawaks (Lokóno), who were allied with the Shebaio and Nepoio, and the Kali'na/Kali'nago/Carinepagoto, forming each other's 'favourite enemies and formal partners'. Indeed, in 1628 Dutch sailors met Island Caribs from Grenada who were on an apparent raiding/trading expedition in Nepoio country in east Trinidad. Such raids took place as late as the 1640s when the French governor of Guadeloupe sent a musqueteer to Captain Baron of the Island Caribs of Dominica in order to support the latter during an attack on the Arawaks of Trinidad. The traditional weaponry consisted of wooden clubs, still known in Trinidad as *boutou* (from Cariban *aputu*), bows and poisoned arrows, kept in quivers, spear-throwers, sling-stones, wooden spears, and round or squarish shields (bucklers). In 1499 Vespucci described the Amerindians of south Trinidad as 'very valiant and energetic people' who were 'excellent archers'. Spears and arrows showing points made of shark's teeth and spinray spines are mentioned among the weapons employed by the Trinidad Indians during the various battles they fought against the Spanish in the 1530s. In addition, the Amerindians of Trinidad, Paria and beyond had poisoned arrows both for hunting monkeys and for warfare. The Trinidad warriors may have used the juice of the manchineel tree to poison their arrows like the Island Caribs.

In order to fight their overseas enemies, the Amerindians of Trinidad built large war canoes or pirogues (*piraguas*) consisting of a hollowed-out log to which planks had been added to increase the freeboard. In 1498 Columbus saw 'a large canoe' with 25 men offshore southwest Trinidad, while one year later Vespucci reported a pirogue of 26 'paces' in length off the island's west coast. A unique painting shows a fight between such a Trinidadian pirogue and a war canoe from Margarita in the late sixteenth century (Fig. 35).[22] The Arawaks of Trinidad and the coastal zone of the Guianas considered it 'the greatest glory to wage war' with the *caribes*, with whom they are 'in the uttermost enmity', as a Spanish observer from Margarita noted in the 1550s. On the approach of the dry season they would form a fleet of thirty to forty pirogues, each capable of holding thirty to fifty men. After long preparations and deliberations they would sail along the coast and enter the rivers of the Guianas in order to look for hostile fleets of dugouts or villages to raid. If the Lokóno met a fleet of Kali'na (Mainland Carib) pirogues, a naval

21 Preparations for a raid began when an old war leader invited his associate village headmen to take part in an intended raid by sending them knotted cords or notched sticks for reckoning the number of days remaining until a communal council and feast initiating the foray would be held. Such strings with knots for reckoning time were still used by the mission Indians of Trinidad in the 1780s.

22 Small types of dugout canoes ('corials'), typically showing pointed stems and sterns, were used for fishing.

battle followed. Such an engagement between fleets of Kali'na, led by a chief called Tocaurama, and Arawaks under Aramaia took place at the mouth of the Waini River in northwest Guyana in 1596. The Arawak won, and afterwards Tocaurama had to send a pirogue with hammocks, cassava, cotton, and six female slaves as an annual tribute to Aramaia who lived on the south bank of the Río Grande, the easternmost outlet of the Orinoco.

Raids of enemy villages invariably led to their destruction by burning. Older inhabitants were usually killed during these raids, but young men and women were often captured and taken home as slaves (*poitos*). The Arawaks cut the hair of their Carib slaves so as to show their status. The captives often married to Arawak men or women and, according to a sixteenth-century Spanish observer, in this way became Arawaks themselves. He added that the Caribs treated the Arawak similarly. A few male captives were killed ceremonially during communal feasts. Skulls of defeated enemies were curated as trophies while flageolets were made out of the long bones. According to a seventeenth-century source, the Island Caribs of Grenada celebrated a victory on the Amerindians of the mainland and Trinidad with a drinking and dancing party, during which they 'eat part of the prisoners of war, [...] which they rather did out of malice, chewing only one mouthful and spitting it out again [...] rather as a religious injunction'. Comparable sixteenth- and seventeenth-century reports on the cannibalistic practices abound in the documentary records on the Caribs as well as the Arawak and other peoples of the region. Their form of ritual cannibalism may have been connected with the notion of gaining the power and strength of the enemy one has slain. However, whether all of these reports are indeed trustworthy is difficult to decide. No doubt, many accusations of cannibalism can be seen as Spanish imperial propaganda, serving the purpose of Amerindian enslavement.

Long-distance exchange between the Amerindian communities of Trinidad and those of the mainland and the Lesser Antilles continued without cessation in spite of the otherwise hostile relationships among the ethnic groups in question. The ritualized exchange of luxury articles ('social valuables'), at the occasion of events such as the formation of political alliances associated with marriage pacts and ritual services, was invariably accompanied by trade in utilitarian articles. The social mechanism through which most exchanges were made took the form of formal trade partnerships between prominent members of the ethnic groups or trading communities concerned, who by exchanging names became each other's *guatiaos* ('friends, allies'), linked by ('classificatory') kinship. The major social valuables exchanged in the area throughout the contact period include *caracolí* ear, nose and breast ornaments, frog-shaped pendants and beads made of green-coloured rock and huge strings of flat shell beads, known as *uruebe* or *quiripá*. All derived from the mainland and found their way up the islands through Trinidad and/or Tobago. Adornments made of thinly hammered plates of *caracolí*, shaped as 'eagles' (birds of prey) and 'crescents', occasionally set in frames of polished black wood, were especially prestigious objects. Manufactured in the Colombian Andes, they reached the twin islands by exchange through the Orinoco Valley or the Venezuelan coast

Figure 36. Postcard picture, showing Naparima Hill (prior to quarrying) and High Street, San Fernando, Trinidad, 1890s.

and the Gulf of Paria.[23] Animal-shaped pendants, predominantly representing frog-shaped creatures, and beads made of green-coloured rock materials, occasionally nephrite, reached the Orinoco River and Lesser Antilles from the Guianas and Amazonia. They formed major exchange items as a means of alliance formation, death compensation and bride wealth. It is likely that Tobago played a role in the exchange of these frog-shaped pendants and beads, as for the Caribs this island formed a half-way station between the Windward Islands and the Guianas. In 1654 the governor of the Courlander colony on the island noted that 'many savages arrive here with canoes from St Vincent, who proceed from here to the mainland, and from the mainland they come here as well'. Finally, *quiripá* shell beads reached Trinidad, the Lesser Antilles and the Guiana coastal zone from the Orinoco Valley. Huge quantities were worn by Amerindian women throughout the region as ostentatious displays of wealth. In Spanish times these strings of shell beads became standardized in length and size, now developing into a form of 'commodity money' of which the value increased with distance from the manufacturing centres in the Venezuelan llanos: in the eighteenth century one string long enough

23 When visiting Trinidad in 1594, Sir Robert Dudley picked up the rumour that an Amerindian called Braio, who lived in the Arawak village of Carao on the island's south coast, was 'very expert in the melting of [...] ore into the metal of *calcurie*'. Wishful thinking obviously interfered with Dudley's search for the local gold which would have been processed by this Braio, as the so-called gold samples he collected from Trinidad all turned out to be fool's gold (iron pyrites).

to encircle a man's girth was worth four gold *reales* on the Orinoco and eight on Trinidad. They can be compared with the uniform rolls of chewing tobacco which were used as a monetary standard by the Island Caribs in the Lesser Antilles.

Numerous other products were transmitted via Trinidad and/or Tobago between the mainland and the islands. In the 1570s it was observed that the Amerindians of Trinidad visited the Orinoco Valley in order to exchange conch trumpets (*botutos*), pearls, salt and (metal) axes with the indigenous peoples of the mainland, some of which had travelled more than 300 'leagues' in their canoes to this end. The conch trumpets, deriving from Tobago or Trinidad's north coast, were used for signalling during war expeditions. Pearls were valuables which were obtained at the pearl oyster beds of the islands of Cubagua and Margarita. Columbus saw pearls among the inhabitants of the Paria Peninsula. When asked where they came from, the Amerindians pointed to the west and north. Salt, produced by evaporating sea water, was traded in the form of bricks from the Venezuelan coast, notably the Araya Peninsula, to Trinidad and the Orinoco Valley. Besides, mainland articles such as jaguar pelts and claws as well as feather headdresses found their way up to Trinidad and the Lesser Antilles. The Arawak of the Guiana coastal zone, Trinidad and the Lower Orinoco were especially noted for the long-distance trade journeys they undertook, paddling on the rivers of the mainland and along the Atlantic and Caribbean coasts. From at least the 1510s onwards the Arawak, Yaio and Nepoio carried out a lively trade with the Spanish on the pearl islands, exchanging foodstuffs, mainly cassava bread, and indigenous slaves, for iron implements. In the 1550s a Spaniard of Margarita joined the Arawak on a trading journey, lasting in all eleven months, which went from Margarita via Trinidad to the Orinoco Valley and llanos and then to the Essequibo in the Guianas. The Arawak village Carao (Carowa) on the south coast of Trinidad and the Yaio settlement of Parico (Paracoa, Paracowe, Parracow), situated perhaps at the mouth of the Guapo River south of present-day San Fernando, formed indispensable hinges in this Amerindian trading system between the mainland and the pearl islands. By this time the Arawak already used pirogues with sails, like Spanish *bergantines*.

Throughout colonial times Warao Amerindians of the Orinoco delta annually visited south Trinidad on a pilgrimage to Naparima Hill, which forms the abode of their major culture hero Haburi, the inventor of the canoe and the paddle, thereby reenacting the route taken by him, his mother and her sister during their mythical flight from the mainland to Trinidad.[24] Indeed, most likely the name Naparima, originally Anaparima (first recorded in 1596), is of Waraoan derivation, meaning in their language 'guardian of the waves' (Fig. 36). Naparima Hill is sacred to the Warao, who see it as a petrified world tree, which assumed the shape of an isolated mountain and landmark serving as the home of their northern 'earth spirit', the 'Butterfly Grandfather', which became Haburi's port of refuge. On their voyages to Naparima Hill, which was declared a national landmark in 1986, the Warao collected quartz crystals and pieces of quartzite for their shaman's rattles,

24 In the 1940s the Venezuelan government imposed restrictions on travel to Trinidad and forbade these periodic visits by the Warao. Nevertheless, irregular canoe trips of Warao to Trinidad are made until at present.

considered to form the embodiments of the latter's guardian spirits. Simultaneously, they traded monkeys, beeswax, baskets, parrots, hunting dogs, and hammocks for tobacco, roucou, mirrors, cotton cloth, clothing, and household goods at the market of San Fernando. Tobacco, which cannot be grown in the delta, is essential to the Warao as their entire shamanic system is based on it. Indeed, as Sir Walter Ralegh noted in the 1590s, in his time the Warao obtained tobacco by exchange for canoes from the Amerindians of Trinidad. In the mid-eighteenth century it was during one of these trips to Trinidad that the Warao adopted the violin, now their most important musical instrument, from the Spanish. Clearly, for the Warao the crossing of the Columbus Channel meant a highly spiritual pilgrimage to an island with a mythical aura, which features prominently in their tales of primordial times. They call Trinidad *burojo*, simply meaning 'island', suggesting that to the Warao Trinidad was the prototypical island, *the* island. Similarly, the other Amerindian peoples of Trinidad referred to it as *kairi*, Arawakan for 'island', implying a comparable perspective.[25]

Religion: cosmology and shamanism

Although the Spanish from the onset of their settlement in Trinidad attempted to introduce the Christian faith among the indigenous peoples under their control, in 1629 the parish priest of St. Joseph complained that most Amerindians of the island were 'living like barbarians using their false idolatries and their medicine men speaking with the devils'. This last expression was no doubt inspired by the supposedly spirit-induced voice alterations the indigenous shaman (*peai*-man, *piaye*) used during his curing rituals. And indeed, the animistic belief in the total spirituality of the universe coupled with shamanic ceremonialism remained the axis of Amerindian religion in Trinidad and Tobago until well into the nineteenth century. Functioning as a curer, advisor and diviner, also directing the ceremonies of the life cycle and performing rituals to promote the growing of food crops and acting as a game-keeper by magically controlling the availability and fertility of wild game, the village shaman represented the local group in taking defensive or aggressive magical action against its enemies. It is recorded that in the 1530s shamans performed magical rites to ensure a successful outcome of Baucunar's raids on the Spanish led by Sedeño, taking tobacco or sniffing powder of crushed *yopa* (*cohoba*) seeds 'in order to know the future'. The shaman's eyesight was felt to be amplified by visionary power due to his copious use of hallucinogenic drugs. Accordingly, Warao shamans were referred to as 'lookmen' in the Toco community of the 1940s. As illness is seen as a symptom of social and cosmic disharmony, the shaman's curing approach is based on getting the assistance of his guardian spirits by shaking his rattle (*marac*, *maraca*) during a nocturnal session in which he visits the spirit world in order to dispel the spirit causing the sickness.[26] Until recently

25 There exists an ineradicable but mistaken belief in Trinidad that *kaíri* or *kaéri* means 'land of the hummingbird', a misconception that was started by E.L. Joseph in the 1830s.

26 In the past few centuries the Amerindian shaman's rattle has become a popular secular musical instrument (*shac-shac*), used in Trinidad by parang and calypso musicians.

comparable ideas were still alive among rural folk in Trinidad where ill health was ascribed to evil *jumbies*, which could be expelled only by the personal spirits of the local practitioner of magic.

As a game-keeper the shaman has to mediate on behalf of his people with the Master of Animals, a bush spirit controlling the number of animals killed by humans. In order to compensate for the game taken from the forest by hunting, souls of deceased humans have to be pledged by the shaman to the Master of Animals who acts as both the protector and the procreator of game in the high woods. A similar spirit personage living in deep pools, the Master of Fish, governs the underwater world and comparable negotiations have to be made with him in exchange for a good fishing season. The shaman has to journey spiritually to both of them in order to mediate. The humans whose souls are offered to these 'masters' are thought to have been taken by accident or disease. The Master of Animals is known as *Papa-Bois* (Creole French for 'father of the forest') in the folklore of Trinidad, Tobago and the Lesser Antilles. He is imagined as a short, bearded and hairy creature with a human body, an animal-like, horned head, and cloven hoofs. Leaves are supposed to grow from his beard. *Papa-Bois* carries a hunting horn in his hand which he sounds whenever he rescues one of the animals under his protection from hunters. He cures wounded animals and takes vengeance on hunters who kill but take home only part of the game by making them lose their way. He is supposed to be capable of transforming into a deer. The Master of Fish is known as the *Mait-source* (Creole French for 'master of the spring') in Trinidad folklore. The French Creole names of these spirit characters reflect their origin in Island Carib culture and their introduction to Trinidad by the slave population from the French West Indies who came to the island with the French immigration of the 1780s and 1790s. The Spanish *mestizos* and African slaves of Trinidad and Tobago were profoundly influenced by the religious views and cosmological concepts of the local indigenous peoples, leading to numerous forms of syncretism between elements of the European, African and Amerindian belief systems.

Another Amerindian otherworldly character, which became assimilated with the spirit pantheon of the African slaves in the West Indies, is *Maman-Dlo* (Creole French for 'mother of the waters') of present Trinidad and Tobago folklore. Known as the *watramama* among the rural population of the Guianas, she is generally imagined as a beautiful, long-haired woman, the lower body of which resembles a snake, who lives in pools and rivers. She is believed to protect the waters of the streams from those who pollute them. In the Amerindian mythology of the mainland *Maman-Dlo* acts as a major fertility spirit and as a protectress of women in childbirth. She has no navel, reflecting that she was never born, and is believed to rule the heavenly waters with the caiman as her guardian spirit. The mermaids and fairymaids of Tobagonian folklore represent related characters. Mermaids, who live in the sea, are considered to be male, showing a human upper portion and a lower half in the form of a fish. They are supposed to mate with fairymaids who inhabit caves behind waterfalls, rivers and secret mountain pools. Fairymaids have one foot in the shape of a deer's hoof, hinting at their diabolical disposition, and always try to lure men in order to take 'he shadow'. Caves and pools or lakes are invariably seen as entries to the 'Other World'. Ancestral spirits are believed to inhabit especially caves which they leave only at night. As a result, in Trinidad and Tobago bats are often assumed to embody the ghosts of the deceased, notably the white or *jumbie* bat. The nocturnal behaviour of the ferruginous pygmy-owl (or *jumbie* bird) and the oilbird (*guácharo*), locally known as the *diablotin* ('little devil'), which inhabits caves throughout the Northern Range, place them into the same category. The pygmy-owl is regarded as a bird of ill omen. According to a Warao myth, the owl and the bat are affines and hunt together. The habit of roosting in hollow trees such as the silk-cotton tree (*fromagier*) adds to the supernatural qualities ascribed to bats. Folk belief attributes the sometimes noisy eruptions of mud volcanoes such as The Devil's Woodyard in south Trinidad to the activities of the many *jumbies* that 'come out here at night'. In Toco it was formerly customary to offer the first fruits of a harvest to the ancestral protector *jumbies*.[27]

The syncretic Amerindian–African spirit pantheon is invariably linked to the silk-cotton (kapok) tree (Arawakan: *ceiba*; Cariban: *kumaka*), which represents one of the tallest trees in the tropical forest. Throughout the West Indies the massive branches of this tree are believed to be inhabited by numerous, often malevolent, *jumbies*, notably ghosts of the deceased (ancestral spirits). To the Amerindians the silk cotton tree is symbolic of the world tree, the so-called *axis mundi*, which represents the central structural element that connects the various spheres of the cosmos by being rooted in the underworld and spreading its crown into the celestial (heavenly) world. The tree may have acquired these associations as it invades open spots in the forest, for instance abandoned villages and cemeteries. Mountains are often believed to represent petrified world trees; to the Warao of the Orinoco delta this applies to Naparima Hill, the northernmost site of their universe. Both in Trinidad and Tobago silk-cotton trees are treated with respect and credited with numerous medicinal properties. They figure in various tales with supernatural associations such as the story of *Gang-gang* ('old woman, granny') Sarah, a respected and wise witch with tremendous power once living at Golden Lane, Tobago. Wishing to fly back to Africa after the death of her husband, she climbed into a silk-cotton tree but found that she had lost the art of flying as a result of having eaten salt. Indeed, slaves who refrained from eating salt were believed to be able to fly back to their home in Africa. Abstaining from salt goes back to the Island Caribs, who believed that the salinity of the sea is caused by the fact that rain forms the urine and sweat of a huge, dangerous anaconda-jaguar spirit associated with the rainbow.[28] According to Tobago folklore, eating salt leads to the loss of magical powers, and some fifty years ago salt was still taboo among the villagers of the Toco area, many of whom originated in Tobago.

---

27 In the 1650s Tobago was called *Aloubaéra* by the Island Caribs, suggesting that the contour of the island reminded them of the monstrous 'bejewelled' snake, known as *alloüebéra*, the Master Boa (*Maître Tête-Chien*), which was formerly assumed to live in a cave on the east coast of Dominica.

28 This malevolent jaguar-snake hybrid is sometimes imagined as having two heads, both of which are buried in the earth, just as the rainbow.

Although Trinidad is referred to in several mythical tales of the Warao and Arawak of the Orinoco delta and the coastal zone of the Guianas, only one myth is known which was documented among the Amerindians formerly living on the island. This tradition explains the origin of the Pitch Lake, which was known as *pichen* ('flow, stream') in local Arawakan. (It has nothing to do with English 'pitch'.) The myth was recorded by E.L. Joseph in 1838, but perhaps was alluded to as early as the 1720s. According to Joseph's account, formerly the area of the lake was dry land inhabited by Amerindians of the Chaima tribe. They had chosen this spot to build their village as the land abounded in pineapples, while on the coast numerous oysters and other edible shells were to be found and here the finest turtles and fish could be caught. There were countless birds as well. However, the Chaima offended the Good Spirit by killing many hummingbirds, which were actually animated by the souls of their dead ancestors. One night the Good Spirit punished them for this misconduct by having the whole village sink beneath the earth and the next morning nothing remained of it, but, in its place, the Pitch Lake had sprung up. Joseph heard the tale from an old man of partly Amerindian descent, called Señor Trinidada, who was born and bred in the village of La Brea, close to the Pitch Lake. Until well into the nineteenth century La Brea had a relatively large Amerindian population: an 1815 census estimated their number at 129. Another tale related to the Pitch Lake was recorded in the 1890s. According to this tradition, the lake forms the entry to the world of the dead. In order to visit their descendants, the souls of deceased Amerindians who had been virtuous throughout their earthly existence would occasionally leave it in the shape of hummingbirds, but the souls of bad Amerindians would take the shape of vultures. Comparison of the Pitch Lake myth with those of the mainland Amerindians shows that it is closely related to a mythological cycle told by the Arawak of the coastal zone of the Guianas, which narrates the vicissitudes of Arawanili, the first Arawak shaman. According to this tale, originally the Arawak lived on an island, *kairi*, which indeed may refer to Trinidad. After Arawanili had obtained his first sacred rattle from a female water spirit and learned the use of tobacco for curing, his brother commits adultery with the shaman's wife. Arawanili now changed into a hummingbird, singing as if calling his brother's name. The latter shoots at the bird, but is not able to kill it, and looking behind now sees that where his house once stood, a big lake has formed and he is on a small island in the middle of this lake. In one version of the tale subsequently Arawanili's brother is imprisoned by an evil spirit, but is finally rescued by the shaman who forgives him his adulterous behaviour.

The key element of the Trinidadian version of the myth is, of course, the killing of the hummingbirds. This little bird forms a common element in many Amerindian mythical tales on the mainland. It is a celestial bird which is closely associated with the Sun, the male principle, tobacco, and the shaman. The association of the hummingbird (*colibri*, *quilibee*) with tobacco originates from its habit of nestling in tobacco plants and sucking the tobacco flowers which are rich in nectar. According to a Warao myth, the first Warao shaman sent the hummingbird overseas to get seeds of the tobacco plant from the only place where this was supposed to grow, an island which was identified by the Warao as Trinidad. The fact that a particular Amerindian people, the Chaima, appears in the Trinidadian version of an originally Arawak myth as the violators of the universally accepted laws of culture, legitimized by the spirit world, perhaps reflects the animosity which seems to have existed between the Chaima and the other Amerindians of Trinidad in historic times. In fact, Chaima Amerindians did not take up residence in Trinidad until the early eighteenth century. Originally they lived on the Paria Peninsula and in the Cumaná region of eastern Venezuela, but fled from here due to the efforts of Aragonese Capuchin priests to concentrate them in mission villages. In Trinidad they settled especially in the area of the Northern Range, as far as Cumana and Toco, as well as the west-central part of the island. The toponym Carapichaima still reminds of their presence in the latter area. They moved to Tobago as well. With respect to the late nineteenth-century tale on the Pitch Lake, it is noteworthy that in Amerindian thought birds with dark and dull plumage such as vultures are considered to be associated with the underworld, a connection which is strengthened by their habit of eating carrion. Finally, it is likely that the Good Spirit represents a Christian element in the myth.

In Amerindian belief the hummingbird is seen as a celestial bird, representing a messenger of the Sun and acting as a close helper of the shaman (the 'doctor'). It is, consequently, known as the 'doctor bird' among the Arawak and Warao as well as in Trinidadian folklore. Other animal and bird species are similarly considered to be symbolic of particular cosmological principles and associations. The frog, for instance, is typically associated with water, female fecundity and the underworld. Its croaking is an unfailing sign of rain and the beginning of the wet season. As we have seen, frog-shaped pendants, made of green-coloured rock, were exchanged from the Guianas to the Lesser Antilles, the Orinoco Valley and Trinidad and Tobago well into historic times. They were believed to guard against snake bites and prevent illnesses like epilepsy, bloody flux and kidney stones. As such they were valued items of trade between the Amerindians and European sailors. Besides, the Island Caribs used these pendants for assisting women in childbirth. This is confirmed by the general notions associated with the colour green which, as a positive category, fulfills the female function of nurturing fecundity. In Amerindian mythology these frog-shaped pendants were thought to have been manufactured by the 'women-without-men', waterspirits like *Maman-Dlo* who exchanged them for golden objects with humans. They would have formed the materialization of water and its virtues. For this reason these frog-shaped pendants were thought to be protective against illnesses which led to a stiffening or hardening inside the body by promoting fluidity and softness. Belief in the healing qualities of specific rock types was observed as early as the 1590s when Sir Robert Dudley noted that the Arawak of Trinidad had a stone, known as *harowa*, which was 'good for the head ache'. Throughout historic times ideas like these were commonly shared among Amerindians, Europeans and Africans alike.

6. The Amerindian–European struggle for Trinidad and Tobago (1498–1592)

The narrative of the early Amerindian–European relationship in the twin islands is one of originally peaceful encounters which soon changed into violent clashes, and of amicable meetings and trade activities as well as violent slave raids. The first Spanish attempts at settlement in Trinidad were repulsed successfully. In the first century of European–Amerindian contact the indigenous opposition to Spanish colonial ambitions was personified by a major Amerindian chieftain, Baucunar, who in the 1530s successfully sought ways and means to ensure local Amerindian independence by confronting the invaders. Although in Tobago actual attempts at European settlement did not commence until the early seventeenth century, the island's indigenous population was decimated by slave raiders (*indieros*) from the first decades of Spanish presence in the Caribbean.

The first European–Amerindian encounters in Trinidad and Tobago

It was during Columbus' short reconnaissance of Trinidad in August 1498 that the first (fleeting) meeting between the Amerindians of the island and European explorers took place. After having passed Galeota Point the Admiral sailed quickly along Trinidad's south coast, only taking in water just west of Erin Point.[29] Although no Amerindians showed up, the area seemed well populated, 'carefully cultivated, high and beautiful'. After having entered the Gulf of Paria, Columbus anchored his three-vessel fleet for some days beyond Icacos Point at what is now called Columbus Bay. Here the Admiral noticed the approach of a large pirogue with 25 young indigenous warriors. Apparently wishing to make contact, they rested their oars at a short distance, shouting to the Spanish. To attract them to come closer, Columbus now had his sailors playing on a tambourine and a kettle-drum while the ships' boys danced to the rhythm. This, however, was taken by the Amerindians as a sign of war and they sent the Spanish a shower of arrows which the latter answered with some cross-bow shooting. The skirmish ended when the Amerindians sought shelter behind one of the other vessels of Columbus' fleet, whose pilot jumped into the pirogue and handed its presumed captain a cap and a coat. This settled the matter, but there was no sequel as Columbus forbade his

29 Columbus' arrival in Trinidad is reenacted annually on Emancipation Day (formerly Discovery Day) by the villagers of Grand Chemin at Moruga. However, it is certain that water was taken in by members of the Admiral's crew much further to the west, beyond Erin Point, while Columbus himself did not go ashore anywhere on the island.

crew to follow the Amerindians, who went ashore and signed the Spanish to come along. Instead, the Admiral raised anchor and continued his journey by crossing the Gulf of Paria as far as the Dragon's Mouths, from where he sighted an island 'with very high ground', clearly Tobago. He called it *Belaforme*, 'because from a distance it seemed beautiful'. Subsequently Columbus reconnoitred the coast of Paria where his crew visited some Amerindian villages, whose inhabitants seemed friendly and entertained the Europeans. The latter noticed with interest that the Amerindians were adorned with collars and bracelets of *guanín* and ornaments of pearls. The Spanish obtained a modest amount of these pearls by exchange. On moving out of the Gulf through the Bocas, Columbus anchored for a while at Chacachacare and sent a boat to Huevos where his crew found some fishermen's huts. Taking a wide circle on sailing out, which enabled him to sight Grenada as well as Tobago, the Admiral now proceeded west into the Caribbean Sea, passing without anchoring the rich pearling grounds of Margarita and Cubagua where the indigenous inhabitants of Paria obtained the pearls they wore as adornments.

The news about Columbus' discovery of pearls among the Amerindians of the Gulf of Paria soon reached Spain, and within one year several private expeditions were equipped and licensed to follow in the wake of the Admiral and obtain more pearls than the latter's crew had been able to gather. These authorized journeys of exploration, most of which entered the Caribbean by way of Trinidad and the Gulf of Paria, soon led to the discovery of the pearl islands and the area along the Venezuelan coast where pearls could be obtained by barter with the Amerindians. It consequently became known as the Pearl Coast. Sadly, trade and peaceful reconnaissance soon turned to pillage, destruction and slave-taking. The pearl islands were first visited in 1499 by Niño and Guerra, followed by Ojeda and de la Cosa. Amerigo Vespucci, who for a time sailed with the latter two explorers, initially reconnoitred the coast of the Guianas and Brazil, then changed his course and followed Ojeda's trajectory by passing along Trinidad's south coast into the Gulf of Paria. Going ashore in south Trinidad in 1499, Vespucci went to see an Amerindian village two leagues inland for a day. He describes its inhabitants as being of 'courteous disposition and fine stature', noting that 'they go about completely naked'. Continuing his voyage, Vespucci anchored near a large settlement at the mouth of a large mainland river, possibly the Río Manamó. He was kindly hosted by its inhabitants, receiving pearls and parrots as gifts. These Amerindians reportedly assured him that the island people he first visited were cannibals. Not all encounters during these early Spanish voyages were as peaceful: Niño and Guerra, who amassed a fortune of pearls on the Venezuelan coast, got into a fight with a fleet of 18 pirogues in the Gulf of Paria, close to the Serpent's Mouth. The Spanish were able to seize a canoe with two Amerindians, one apparently a captive. In 1500 another adventurer, Pinzón, explored south Trinidad and the west coast of the Gulf of Paria, noting that the Amerindians who treated Columbus and Vespucci so well had become quite hostile, taking refuge in the forests and mountains as soon as they spotted his ships. He reported deserted and destroyed villages, suggesting violent encounters with previous Spanish sailors, probably Niño and Guerra.

While during the first decade of the sixteenth century the Spanish trade with the Pearl Coast continued unabated, gold mining, based on forced labour of the 'Taíno' under the so-called *repartimiento* system, peaked in the young colony of Hispaniola, giving way to sugar cane cultivation from 1515 onwards. Here the demand for slave labour increased strongly due to the drastic demographic decline of the local Amerindians, as the result of imported European diseases against which the indigenous population had no natural resistance, such as smallpox, measles, and influenza, and harsh labour demands as well as open slaughter. Besides, the discovery of the pearl oyster beds near Cubagua (1509), and the subsequent Spanish settlement of this island, led to a similar demand for forced labour, notably Amerindian divers. As a result, slave raiding (*rescate*) intensified especially in the 'useless islands' of the Bahamas where the local population was ruthlessly captured, since the Lucayans of this archipelago 'were extraordinary swimmers', experienced in diving for queen conchs. Indeed, by the 1510s the Bahamas were largely depopulated. Simultaneously the first African slaves were transported to the Greater Antilles. In these years the Spanish Crown was concerned to develop peaceful trade relationships with the indigenous population of the Venezuelan coast, as the Spanish settlers of Cubagua, a quite barren island, depended for water, foodstuffs and firewood on these Amerindians. Moreover, when in the 1520s Margarita was settled by the Spanish, the local Guaiquerí Indians were exempted from enslavement, a status they kept throughout colonial times. As a corollary, in 1510 slaving on Trinidad was forbidden so as not to disturb the trade in pearls between the Amerindians of Trinidad, considered to be 'peaceful', and those of the Pearl Coast. Also, it was rumoured that there was gold in Trinidad, and the Spanish Crown urged the officials in Hispaniola to check whether this 'secret of Trinidad' was true or not, by sending an expedition taking along Amerindians from Trinidad, kept as slaves on Hispaniola, as interpreters.

Soon, however, capture of the Trinidad Amerindians was officially allowed. In a royal order of 1511 the citizens of Hispaniola were given permission to wage war upon, and to enslave, the Amerindians 'who are called *caribes*'. These natives were accused of resisting the Spanish and fighting Amerindians favourably disposed to the latter, taking them prisoner and eating them 'as they really do'. The decree, which was repeated in the following year, specified the settlement area of these *caribes* as all of the Windward Islands, Barbados, Trinidad and Tobago, as well as parts of the mainland.[30] In fact this royal order confirmed and elaborated decrees of 1503 and 1505, authorizing the enslavement of Amerindians 'that are called *canyvales*' (cannibals). Probably it was the massive rebellion in Puerto Rico of

30 This is the first time Tobago is mentioned in the Spanish documentary sources under its present name. Most likely the island was called as such by a Spanish sailor, possibly a slaver from Hispaniola, who named it *Tabaco* (originally also spelled as *Cabaco*, *Tavaco* or *Tabacho*) since Tobago's elongated contour, if seen from the ocean, reminded him of a long, fat cigar. Cigars such as the 'Taíno' Amerindians of the Greater Antilles were accustomed to smoke were called *tabacos* by the Spanish. It is a term derived from an Arabic expression. The Mainland Caribs were, like the Spanish, struck by the characteristic contour of Tobago, calling the island *Urupaina*, 'meaning big snail' as a Spanish chronicler noted. Apparently they compared it with the outline of the large marine gastropods found in the Caribbean.

1510, which was believed to be supported by *caribes* from the smaller islands, that led the Crown to urge the local Spanish colonists to fight the latter. The Puerto Rican revolt also led to an exodus of 'Taíno' Amerindians from there to the smaller islands, indeed as far south as Trinidad. Clearly, the term *caribes* had no specific ethnic significance: it just lumped all Amerindian groups who fiercely opposed the Spanish, justifying their enslavement by accusing them of eating human flesh. Although the Spanish sailors who visited Trinidad and the Gulf of Paria region no doubt also often bartered peacefully with the Amerindians of the region for foodstuffs, pearls, *guanín* objects, salt, exotic woods, pigments, etc., slaving now became the most frequently occurring phenomenon of European–Amerindian interaction. In this respect the designation *caribes* was interpreted freely: in 1519 a slaver from Hispaniola obtained 70 or 80 slaves in the Gulf of Paria region who were war captives of Amerindians considered to be *guatiaos* ('friends, allies') of the Spanish and, consequently, their indigenous enemies could be seen as *caribes*, whatever ethnic or linguistic affiliation they may have had. Obtaining indigenous slaves in this way became common practice, obviously intensifying the mutual warfare among the Amerindians. Another Spaniard declared that although Trinidad was inhabited by *guatiaos*, malicious persons did not hesitate to call them *caribes*.[31]

The atrocities of the most notorious slaver who operated in and around Trinidad, a Basque called Juan Bono de Quejo, were recorded with disgust by the 'Defender of the Indians', Father Bartolomé de Las Casas. In 1516 Bono and his crew of sixty men were well received by the Amerindians of a village on Trinidad whom they told that they wished to live with them. While the Spanish were treated daily with fish, cassava bread and fruits, the Amerindians built a house for them. This, a large, bell-shaped dwelling, could easily accommodate some one hundred people or even more. It had walls of twice a man's height, made of closely-set wickerwork so that it was impossible to see from the outside what was going on inside. When the Amerindians were busy putting palm leaves as thatching on the wooden rafters, Bono requested as many as possible Amerindians to enter the house who thought that some festivities would be held. While part of the Spanish now lined up around the dwelling so as to prevent anybody to leave it again, others captured the Amerindians who were inside. A number of the latter were able to escape, however, and together with those who had remained outside the dwelling fled into another house in the village. This was put on fire by Bono's men as a result of which some one or two hundred Amerindians were burned alive. Subsequently, Bono and his crew sailed away with 185 enslaved Trinidadians. They were sold in Puerto Rico and Hispaniola. Other Spanish slavers repeated this mean trick the following year. Reportedly received by the Trinidad Amerindians yelling '*Juan Bono, malo, Juan Bono, malo*', the Spanish assured them that Bono was not among them as he had been hanged for his crimes and that they had come with good intentions. Lured with promises of gifts, the Amerindians accepted the Spanish hospitably, entertaining them in their village. After a few days, however, the latter

31 In these years it is reported that the name for Trinidad was Amacarabi. However, it is more likely that this term was the name of an Amerindian village on the island.

suddenly drew their weapons and captured a large number of Amerindians who were carried away as slaves and sold in Hispaniola.

In these years the originally relatively peaceful conditions on the Venezuelan coast were definitely disturbed by intermittent slave expeditions. As an Italian traveller noted, the Spanish of Cumaná were 'rapacious for pearls, licentious to the women, and doing many other wanton violences'. The appalling living conditions of the indigenous divers on Cubagua led to a continuous demand for forced labour, and since the supply from the Bahamas had dried up, the mainland coastal area was now raided for slaves, frequently also making use of local indigenous allies. All this resulted in a strongly increased warlike spirit among the Amerindians, leading to major revolts during which the newly founded Spanish settlements and monasteries were destroyed (1519). The area was reconquered by the Spanish, now reportedly waging a deadly war 'by fire and blood', three years afterwards. Meanwhile much of the confusion which existed among the Spanish about exactly which Amerindians of the islands and mainland were indeed *caribes* (and could 'legitimately' be enslaved) and which of them were *guatiaos* (and should be appeased), had been resolved by an official report written by magistrate Rodrigo de Figueroa of Hispaniola (1520). Following intervention by Las Casas, Trinidad was included in Figueroa's listing of islands and mainland areas inhabited by *guatiaos*, like Barbados and Margarita. (Another document of 1520 refers to Barbados as depopulated already.) Although Tobago was not specifically mentioned in Figueroa's report, the island was considered as settled by *caribes*. Finally, in 1521 an expedition to Trinidad, led by Rodrigo de Bastidas, made it obvious that in spite of all rumours gold was definitely not to be found there. Amerindians from Trinidad, who were kept as slaves in Hispaniola, sailed along as interpreters.

The long-standing acquaintance of the indigenous peoples of Trinidad and the Gulf of Paria area considered to be *guatiaos* with the Spanish settlements in the pearl islands and Cumaná led to increasingly profound changes in local Amerindian culture and society. Redirection of many of the indigenous long-distance exchange patterns as the result of the availability of much desired European trade wares, such as metal tools, fine textiles, beads, and other goods in the pearl islands, formed the most obvious of these alterations in the Amerindian way of life. The Arawak (Aruac) of south Trinidad, the Lower Orinoco Valley and the coastal zone of the Guianas from the 1520s onwards established a long-lasting trade relationship with the Spanish of the pearl islands, exchanging foodstuffs and slaves for European manufactures. It would eventually develop into a pact of mutual assistance. The name Arawak (*aruacos*) was recorded for the first time in 1518 in the instruction given to Rodrigo de Figueroa, which two years afterwards would lead to his report classifying the Amerindians of the West Indies into *guatiaos* and *caribes*. The report speaks of a province *que dize de Aruaca*, situated beyond the Gulf of Paria. It is quite obvious that Arawak formed a generic term incorporating a number of (not necessarily Arawakan-speaking) ethnic groups in the area, all 'friendly' to the Spanish, including the Lokóno, Nepoio, Shebaio, and perhaps others as well. A Spanish royal order of 1532 speaks of the *río e probinçia Aruaca*, and eighteen years later a Spanish traveller mentions this same river. According to a contemporary

Spanish manuscript map of the area, Río Aruaca is an obsolete name of the present Río Grande, the easternmost outlet of the Orinoco. It is likely that as early as the time of Figueroa Arawaks already occasionally visited Cubagua in order to barter European tools and ornaments for their own products. (In 1520 some Arawaks took part in a short rebellion in Cubagua, protesting against the execution of a local Amerindian chief called Melchor.) The name Arawak may have been the result of the culture-contact situation. Most likely it is derived from a major settlement on the Lower Orinoco, Aruacay (Arowacai), which, as the Spanish understood, was 'a famous place, praised by the Indians of the coast'. The name Arawak must have been adopted by various Amerindian ethnic groups as it protected them against Spanish slave raids following Figueroa's report.

Attempts at Spanish settlement in Trinidad and slave raids in Tobago

After Bastidas' expedition to Trinidad, it became obvious to the Spanish Council of the Indies that the necessity of preserving a large labour force in Trinidad for hypothetical future work at gold placers had evaporated. Nevertheless, when in 1530 the request by Antonio Sedeño, the *contador* (auditor) of Puerto Rico, to colonize the island was granted, he was forbidden to enslave the indigenous population, all of this in accordance with Figueroa's ruling of ten years previously. In fact, the development of Trinidad into a supplier of Amerindian slaves was actually what Sedeño, a quite unruly character, had at the back of his mind. His efforts to establish a foothold in the island, lasting four years, finally turned out to be unsuccessful, predominantly because of the fierce opposition which various Amerindian peoples of Trinidad and Paria, unified under chief Baucunar, a Carinepagoto 'great man' living at Cumucurapo, were able to put up. Sedeño attempted to take advantage of the ethnic division among the Amerindians of Trinidad by allying himself with Maluana (Maruana), the chief of the densely populated Chacomare 'province' of south Trinidad, and Turipari (Turpiari, Tiropiari, Turuquiare), another major chief who occupied a mainland village not far from the mouth of the Río Manamó (Huyapari), the western outlet of the Orinoco. The latter was soon baptized as Don Diego. Maluana probably had a village in southwest Trinidad, facing the Gulf of Paria. Both Maluana and Turipari may have been of Arawak ethnic affiliation and as such traditionally opposed to the Carinepagoto of Baucunar, who, in the words of the poet/chronicler Castellanos who accompanied Sedeño in Trinidad, 'were bellicose to the extreme'. Sedeño's failure to occupy Trinidad was due as well to his conflicts with other, similarly ruthless, *conquistadores* such as Diego de Ordás, the first Spanish explorer of the Orinoco, and the officials of Cubagua and Margarita, who feared that Sedeño's actions would cause lasting disturbance of their precarious relationship with the indigenous peoples of the Venezuelan coast and Gulf of Paria on whom they largely depended for food, water and slaves.

Most likely Sedeño obtained information from traders and slavers in Puerto Rico about which indigenous groups in Trinidad were accustomed to co-operate with the Spanish. At any rate, on arriving at Trinidad by passing Galeota Point and formally taking possession of the island in November 1530, he went directly to meet Turipari, who subsequently took him to Maluana, presenting both chiefs numerous gifts such as polished ornaments, textiles, Castilian wine, and iron implements. In return, Maluana handed Sedeño an indigenous war captive. Accompanied by Maluana, Sedeño now went to the area he wished to settle, the *Gran Bahía de las Sierras*, no doubt the coastal zone of the Gulf of Paria around present Port-of-Spain which, of course, formed the territory of chief Baucunar. The latter received the Spanish less than wholeheartedly, and Sedeño quickly judged the Amerindians of northwest Trinidad to be 'suspicious, unfriendly, and untrustworthy'. Returning to the mainland, Sedeño now built a modest mud-walled fortress close to the village of Turipari, assisted by the latter's people and those of Maluana. Afterwards, while Sedeño was away in Puerto Rico to enlist new men and collect supplies, this stronghold was taken over by the newly arrived Diego de Ordás (February 1531), who left afterwards for his ascension of the Orinoco. Unaware of these events, Sedeño sent a caravel with new recruits as well as horses, mares, calves, sheep and pigs from Puerto Rico to Trinidad. They anchored at Cumucurapo, where Baucunar first received the Spanish well, but then attacked those ashore by surprise after a week, killing 24 of them. The ship and the rest of Sedeño's men escaped to Cubagua.

It was a year before Sedeño again attempted to get a foothold in Trinidad. Gathering men in Cubagua and Margarita, in late 1532 he sailed to Trinidad and crept at night down the coast with his men in six pirogues in order to take Cumucurapo by surprise. An Amerindian guide led the Spanish through the forest to the rear of the village. In spite of the fact that Baucunar had fortified his village and kept constant watch, the night attack by the Spanish was successful. The Amerindians defended themselves, 'fighting to the point as if their souls left their bodies', and several Spanish died because of poisoned arrows. The Spanish burned the village and few Carinepagoto survived the massacre. Subsequently Sedeño took possession of the village, cleared the land by felling many trees around it, put up a double stockade of prickly palms surrounded by a ditch for defence, and built some thirty huts for his men. Guns from Sedeño's ships were placed at two bastions. Fields near the settlement were planted with maize and vegetables. Undeterred, the Amerindians attacked the Spanish outpost by surprise in June 1533, when 'the air was full of countless arrows'. They killed two Spaniards and wounded 25 of them, also killing five horses. Nevertheless, Sedeño held the upper hand. Three months later Baucunar's force returned, now enlarged with numerous warriors from Trinidad and Paria, led by chiefs such as Guyma (Guaimá), Pamacoa, Diamaná (Diamaimá), Amanatey, Paraguaní, and the gigantic Utuyaney who, according to Castellanos, wore a jaguar skin with its mouth placed over his head. Surrounding the fortified village, the Amerindians were able to wound several Spaniards, but fled into the foothills of the Northern Range when Sedeño sent out his men mounted on the horses he had left. Thirty Amerindians were killed. By now the Council of the Indies declared that the Amerindians of Trinidad were worthy of enslavement 'for their savagery', and urged fighting the *caribes* of Trinidad and Tobago. Altogether it was a narrow victory for the Spanish and by early 1534 Sedeño had completely run out of supplies, only Maruana and Turipari still sending him some provisions. Forced by a mutiny among his hungry men, Sedeño had to leave Trinidad for good in August 1534. He left two horses with Maluana which were collected half a year later by Jerónimo de Ortal, heir to Ordás' governorship, who used Trinidad temporarily as a stopover and supply base for a mainland explorative expedition (*entrada*), searching for treasure. Relations with Maluana deteriorated rapidly, however, probably due to excessive demands of food by the Spanish on the Amerindians, and Ortal left in July 1535.

Nevertheless, the overall connection between the Arawak and the Spanish of the pearl islands remained friendly. By the late 1530s overexploitation had exhausted the pearl beds of Cubagua and its population gradually moved to Margarita, where new pearling grounds were discovered as well as near Coche. It was on the initiative of the Arawak that in 1545 the exchange relationship with the Spanish got a fresh impetus when fifty pirogues with Arawak 'chiefs' arrived in Margarita, accompanied by a *morisco*, a slave who had fled from one of the ships of Ordás during his journey up the Orinoco and spent twelve years among the Amerindians. The Arawak were treated well and from now onwards they brought annual loads of cassava to Margarita. According to an account written in 1557 by Rodrigo Pérez de Navarrete, the *escribano* (notary) of Margarita and an old captain of the *rescatadores* (traders with Amerindians), the Arawak headmen were accustomed to send their sons to Margarita in order to learn the Spanish language. When due to the absence of rain there was a great need of foodstuffs in the island, such a boy would be sent home, and after one month numerous Arawak pirogues with 2,000 loads of cassava would arrive in Margarita. For each load, approximately 24 kilograms, one iron knife would be paid by the Spanish. The crew members of some of these convoys stayed for a year on Margarita. Apart from cassava bread, they supplied the Spanish with products of the tropical forest such as timber, processed dyes, jaguar pelts, birds, gums, and resins. Navarrete compared the Arawak with the gypsies because of their eagerness to travel for trading purposes, making expeditions of more than 200 miles to the east and west, along the coasts and up the rivers. 'They sail or go wherever they like, as people who have no fear or dread of any other nation of *indios*'. In 1554 the Arawak of Trinidad were anxious to intensify their relationship with the Spanish. A chief called Ocharayma (Acharaima) first sent some messengers to Margarita and after receiving presents from Navarrete, he came himself. In these years Navarrete's interest in deepening the Spanish–Arawak relationship even led to a grand scheme by the Black Friars to evangelize the Arawak of Trinidad and the Guiana coastal zone. A secular plan to establish a Spanish colony in Trinidad was abandoned in favour of the Dominican project. Apart from a short visit to the Arawak of Trinidad by the Bishop of Cartagena (1556), for the time being nothing came of this, however. Exchange between the Trinidad Amerindians and the Spanish is shown by the recovery of red, white and blue 'layered' chevron beads, also known as 'star' or 'rosette' beads, dating to the sixteenth century. Such faceted Venetian glass beads have been found in south Trinidad in the context of Mayoid sites at Mamoral and Moruga Road/Esmeralda (Fig. 37). In addition, individual finds of chevron beads have been encountered

Figure 37. Red, white and blue European 'chevron' bead, dating to the sixteenth century, found at Mamoral (CAR-12), Trinidad, associated with ceramics of the Mayoid series, Historic Age. Harris Coll., WFT.

at Golden Grove in central Trinidad and on Carrera Island in the Dragon's Mouths.

From the 1550s onwards Trinidad and the Gulf of Paria region were increasingly frequented by French 'corsairs' (privateers), intent on plundering the Spanish settlements in the West Indies as they had been doing for several decades, but now entering the archipelago by the Lesser Antilles. The pearl fisheries of Cubagua, for instance, were regularly raided by the French beginning in the 1520s. The French Crown handed privateers letters of *marque*, giving them the legal right to capture Spanish ships and attack ports in wartime. While the Franco–Spanish war ended in 1559, a common understanding ruled that there would be 'no peace beyond the line' (west of the Azores), and French privateering as well as 'contraband' trade continued to flourish. A short stay on the coast of south Trinidad by André Thevet, who was on his way from the Brazilian coast to the Caribbean, is the first recorded French visit to the island (1556). Thevet made a crude map of Trinidad (Fig. 38) and noted that it had many guaiacum (*lignum vitae*) trees, then much sought in Europe as timber, while a

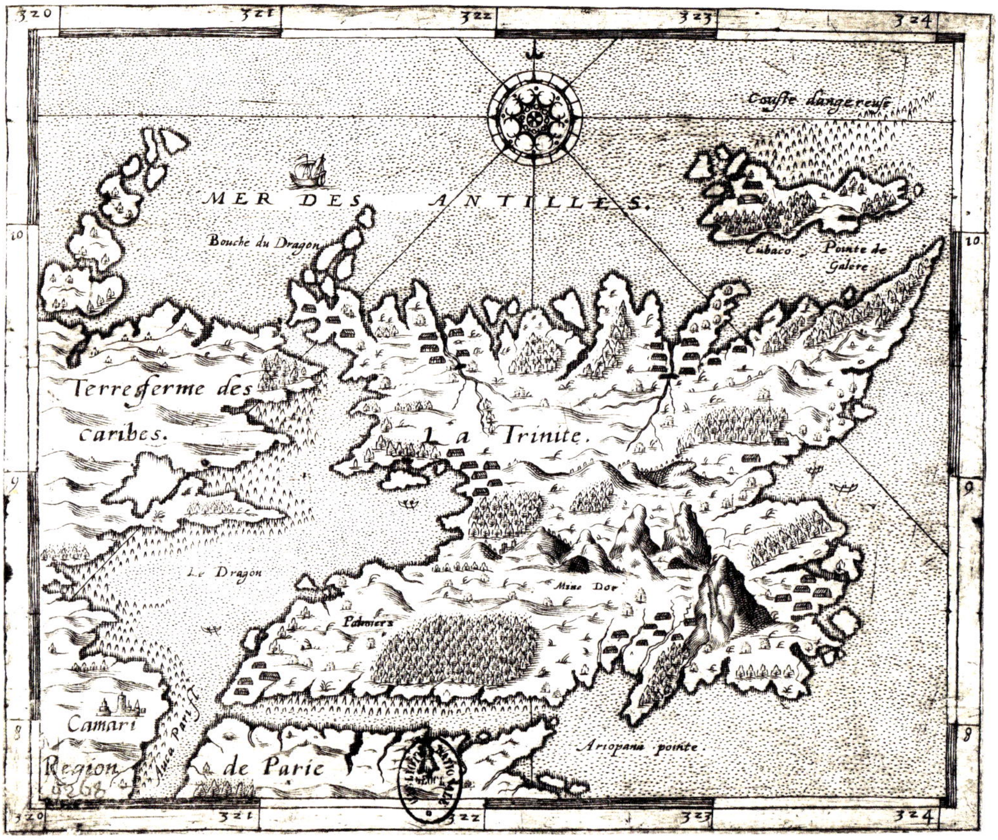

Figure 38. Manuscript map of Trinidad and Tobago, drawn by André Thevet, 1556. Original in the Bibliothèque Nationale de Paris, France.

gum deriving from the wood was believed to be a cure for syphilis. Trinidad became a favourite port of call for the French, like Thevet, on their way from Brazil to the West Indies and was used by them for victualing, watering and careening their vessels, as well as trading with the Amerindians especially in the southern part of the island. In 1562 two French ships spent some time on Trinidad's south coast, after which part of their crew ascended the Orinoco in some sloops, exchanging axes, knives and other European goods for bird-shaped ornaments of *guanín* and crescents (*caraculís*) with the Amerindians. French predation on Spanish ports and shipping induced the Crown to initiate a convoy system for ships going from Spain to the West Indies. From 1562 onwards annually two fleets of merchant vessels with accompanying warships were dispatched to the Caribbean: the *flota* ('fleet'), destined for the Greater Antilles and beyond, and the *tierra firme* ('mainland') fleet, also called the *galeones* as six to eight galleons escorted it, sailing from the Canaries to the mainland. The latter occasionally entered the West Indies through the Tobago Sound or Galleons' Passage between Trinidad and Tobago, a name which has remained until the present.[32]

The French privateer activities in the region convinced the Council of the Indies that new attempts would have to be made to colonize Trinidad. Besides, rumours that beds of pearl oysters were to be found in the waters of Tobago and Grenada, which first circulated in the 1530s, now cropped up again. The local Amerindians used these pearls as ear ornaments and inserted them in bead aprons. Apparently, the Arawak trade partners of the citizens of Margarita kept repeating this information, which was noted in various documents and on Spanish manuscript maps dating from this period. (Although devoid of any truth, references to Tobago's presumed pearl beds are to be found in the literature until the early eighteenth century.) Intrigued by these reports, the Spanish Crown now incorporated Tobago in contracts made with adventurers intent on colonizing Trinidad. A further argument to settle the island (and Tobago) were regular complaints by the Spanish of Margarita about attacks made by *caribes* on this island and on the 'friendly' Amerindians of Trinidad. Indeed, sixteen pirogues with *caribes* from Dominica and Trinidad attacked the pearl fisheries of Margarita in 1563. Just previously the Arawak–Spanish relationship was dealt a serious blow. In 1558 a small commercial expedition from Margarita, led by Father Francisco de Ayala and guided by Arawaks from Trinidad, had run into difficulties in the Orinoco Valley when the Spanish attempted to kidnap an indigenous girl, whereupon the whole party was killed by the Amerindians. The Arawak brought the story to Margarita in 1560, and it was not until 1562 that they re-established their trade relationship with the Spanish of the pearl islands. The importance of the Arawak deliveries of foodstuffs to Margarita cannot be overestimated: as a result of the temporary stop in the supply famine promptly struck in the island. A royal order of 1562 urged continuation of the attempts to convert the Arawak. Five years afterwards this led to a short-lived mission among the Arawak of Trinidad which achieved little.

Clearly intrigued by the rumour of the Tobago pearl beds, the next Spanish *conquistador* who attempted to colonize Trinidad, Juan Troche Ponce de León from Puerto Rico, deliberately had Tobago included in his concession. Arriving at Trinidad's south coast with some 600 men, including soldiers, farmers and a few clerics, by December 1569, he was approached by a pirogue with some 15–20 Amerindians with food for bartering. After entering the Gulf of Paria, León met two large pirogues with a chief called Mayroa who reportedly just came back from a fight with *caribes*. Together with four other Amerindians, including a certain Manuel who spoke some Spanish, he went on board León's ship, conversing amicably with the crew. The name Mayroa is sufficiently close to that of Mayaro for the southeastern coastal stretch of Trinidad, still called Mayaroa by Spanish-speaking Trinidadians, to suggest a connection. Trinidad Arawaks, possibly

32 Documentary evidence suggesting that sometimes the galleons of the *tierra firme* fleet watered and refreshed at Tobago following the crossing of the Atlantic is lacking. However, the still existing name Cape *Gracias-a-dios* (Cape 'God-be-thanked') for one of the easternmost promontories of northeast Tobago may represent a navigational term related to at least the irregular passing of galleons belonging to the *tierra firme* fleet, or sailing apart from it, a practice which from 1575 onwards was quite regular.

Mayroa's people, carrying foodstuffs to Margarita, informed its settlers of León's arrival. After visiting a number of indigenous villages, León decided to build a fort and settlement 'apart from the *indios*' in an area just north of the Caroni River, probably at Laventille, and was able to establish relatively peaceful relationships with the Amerindians (Carinepagoto) of the area. However, after spending all the 'goods from Castile' as exchange gifts with the local inhabitants, he had to get provisions from the Arawak of south Trinidad. During a visit to an Arawak village to this purpose, León's son García was kidnapped by Island Caribs who had just carried out a raid on this settlement. García was taken to Dominica where he reportedly still lived as a Carib prisoner ten years afterwards. Disease, hunger and desertion decimated the Spanish population, and within less than a year after arrival León and his remaining men left Trinidad again. Besides, although Tobago was explicitly included in his concession, no attempt by León to visit this island has been recorded. Nevertheless, it is likely that occasionally slave raids were carried out by the Spanish on Tobago as it was assumed to be inhabited by *caribes*.

Meanwhile Spanish interest in the country of the Arawak had grown further due to the regular visits the latter paid to Margarita, allowing its citizens to collect much, though somewhat embellished, information on the Orinoco region and Guiana. One of these, Juan de Salas, learned from the Arawak that beyond their territory Amerindians lived in a country, situated near a lake, where much gold was to be found. In 1576 Juan Martín de Albujar, a fugitive from a long-forgotten and ill-fated Spanish expedition into the Orinoco Valley, arrived in Margarita. Albujar, who had lived among the Amerindians of interior Guiana for seven years, finally travelled with Arawak traders to the Atlantic coast and afterwards to Trinidad. When he told people in Margarita that he had seen Arawaks trading golden objects with other Amerindians in Guiana, the legend that the gold-land El Dorado was to be found near a lake in the mountainous hinterland of Guiana was born. Soon it led to increased voyaging by Spanish traders and adventurers from Margarita into the Orinoco Valley, exchanging machetes and knives for *guanín* objects. Guided by Arawak pilots, in 1582 the Griego brothers made such a trip, on the way calling at the Trinidad ports of Paracoa (Parico), the settlement of the Yaio Amerindians, and the Arawak village of Carao on the south coast. By now English corsairs had joined the French in their predation on Spanish shipping, sacking settlements and looting the pearl islands. In 1576 one of them, Andrew Barker of Bristol, spent a week in Trinidad, trafficking for victuals and having 'conference with certaine Indians inhabitants' who gave him 'very friendly and courteous entertainement'. Afterwards he sailed to Margarita. The English intrusion would reach epidemic proportions during the Anglo–Spanish war which finally broke out in 1585. However, plundering the Spanish colonies by French and English would increasingly go hand in hand with peaceful exchange with the colonists. More often than not this 'contraband trade' would be welcomed by the local settlers as the mother country, lacking men, ships and money to back her vast responsibilities and claims, was completely unable to meet their needs.

While interacting peacefully with the French and English privateers or corsairs who visited the Gulf of Paria area prior to sailing to the pearl islands for trade or plunder, the Arawak of Trinidad and Guiana continued supplying the citizens of Margarita with maize as well as cassava bread and flour. Moreover, from the 1570s the Arawak–Spanish trade relationship gradually became a pact of mutual assistance: the Arawak supplied Margarita with provisions and indigenous slaves from the mainland, while the Spanish, in turn, provided them with iron tools and weapons, and assisted the Arawak in raiding the villages of hostile Amerindian groups, notably the Kali'na. Ultimately this development would permanently disturb the traditional equilibrium between war and exchange among the local Amerindians. By now both the French and English began to leave men as resident trade factors in south Trinidad, to facilitate the exchange and stimulate the Amerindians growing or searching for the desired trade wares. Accordingly, a Frenchman disembarked some of his compatriots on the island in order to 'learn the local language' in 1585, while two years afterwards the French Captain Jean Retud from Le Havre left two young Englishmen on Trinidad 'under the care of an Indian chief' for this same reason, together with a load of gifts including metal axes, knives, jew's harps (small musical instruments held against the teeth or lips), blue and white beads, and coloured cloths, all much desired by the Amerindians. Two others were left on the Lower Orinoco. In 1591 another French privateer, Captain Boutillier of Sherbourg (Cherbourg), exchanged a knife for a piece of 'gold' weighing a quarter pound at the port of Paracoa in southwest Trinidad. Indeed, it is recorded that in these years Amerindians from Trinidad went to the Orinoco region in order to obtain hardwood used for shipbuilding, dye wood and *guanín* objects, which were afterwards traded with the French. The English as well as the French considered south Trinidad as a major way-station for trafficking with the Amerindians, refurbishing their ships, taking in provisions, if necessary recovering crew members' health, and collecting information about the pearl islands. Indeed, the Arawak of Trinidad were paid by the Spanish of Margarita to warn them when a privateer arrived on the coast of Trinidad. In 1590 one of these sentinels reported that six English ships had landed men in Trinidad asking the Amerindians about Margarita. According to Sir Walter Ralegh, the latter now called their chiefs or 'great men' by the term 'Capitaynes', thus replacing the indigenous expression *acarewana*, 'because they perceiue that the chiefest of euery ship is called by that name'. Understandably, the Spanish of Margarita kept pressing the Council of the Indies for the speedily settling of Trinidad both for commercial and strategic reasons. It was not until 1592, however, that this was effected, and not by the citizens of Margarita.

7. The Spanish–Amerindian frontier in Trinidad (1592–1686)

The gradually lessening resistance to and ultimate acceptance of restricted European colonization by the Trinidad Amerindians did not mean that the indigenous peoples of the island were fully subjugated, although it led to the emigration of several groupings to the coastal zone of the mainland and to Tobago. In fact, throughout the seventeenth century (and thereafter) the remaining Amerindians continued to represent an important and, for the weak Spanish community, uneasy political factor, being the largest population group of the island. The fierce and independent character of the Trinidad Amerindians is personified in this period by a major indigenous chieftain, Hierreyma, who by seeking an alliance with the Dutch unsuccessfully attempted to evict the Spanish from the island.

Spanish settlement and Amerindian reaction

Traditional indigenous society was definitely disrupted after the Spanish got a permanent foothold on Trinidad. In 1592 Domingo de Vera took possession of the island in the name of Antonio de Berrío y Oruña, an old *conquistador* who led several expeditions on the mainland to discover the mythical goldland El Dorado, and had become convinced that this was to be found in the interior of Guiana. When during his journey of 1590-1591 Berrío decided to descend the Orinoco, his party arrived sick and almost starved to death in the village of the Nepoio chief Carapana (Caripana, Caepan, Garrapana) on the lower Orinoco. The latter received Berrío in a friendly manner and the Spanish stayed for six weeks in his village. Carapana was an expert in trading with the Spanish and Sir Walter Ralegh describes him as 'a man very wise, subtill, and of great experience'. In his youth Carapana had been sent by his father to Trinidad 'by reason of ciuill warre' among the Nepoio. When staying in the village of Parico in southwest Trinidad, he went several times with the Yaio Amerindians to Margarita and Cumaná in order to deliver foodstuffs. Guided by Carapana's pilots, Berrío arrived in the Gulf of Paria, surveyed Trinidad for three weeks, and decided to settle in the island as soon as possible, using it as a springboard to the mainland in order to continue his search for El Dorado. Afterwards he left for Margarita in order to obtain reinforcements, sending his lieutenant Vera, who had been successful in getting troops and supplies in Caracas, to Trinidad in order to occupy the island. Vera arrived in Trinidad in May 1592, officially taking possession at Cumucurapo where he met two (local?) Amerindian chieftains, Maycay and Pareco, to whom he handed military sashes, declaring that he had come to christianize them, protect them against the *caribes*, fight the English and French trading visits to the island, and prevent the selling

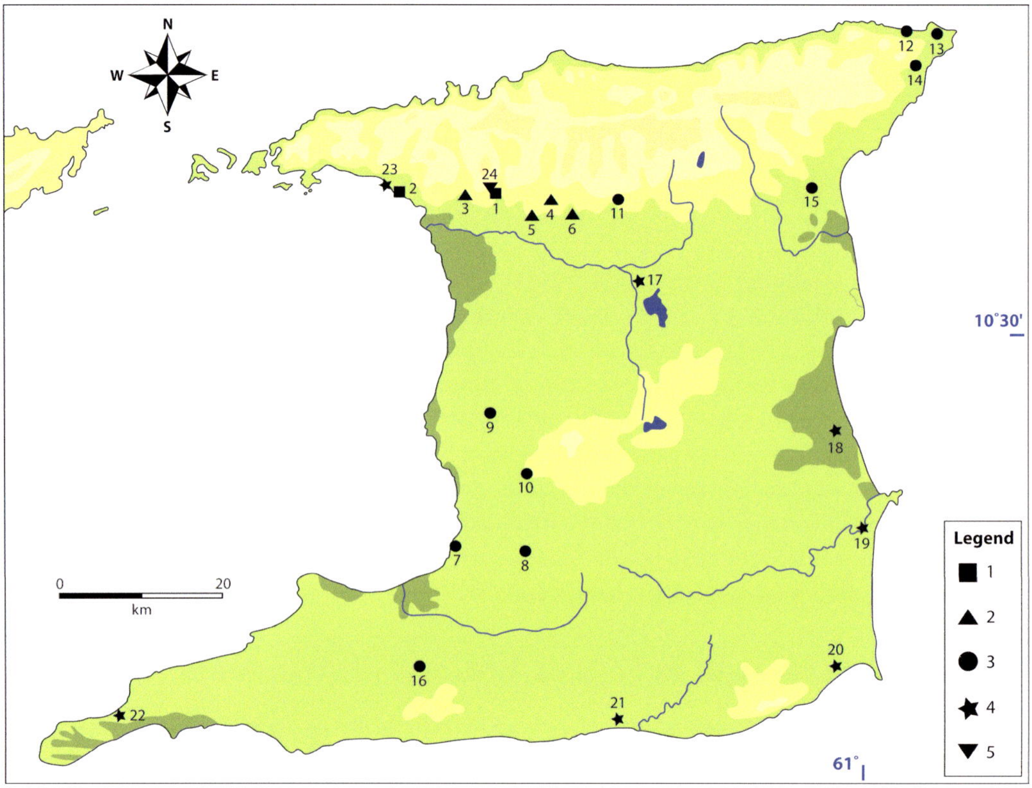

Figure 39. Map of Trinidad, showing the locations of Spanish towns, *encomiendas*, and Capuchin missions, 1592–1797. Legend: (1) Spanish towns; (2) *encomiendas* (after 1716 missions); (3) missions (long-lasting); (4) missions (short-lived; most locations approximate); (5) other Amerindian villages. Key to towns and villages: (1) St. Joseph (1592–present); Port-of-Spain (1592–present); (3) Aricagua (San Juan) (1595–1716); (4) Tacarigua (1595–[1716]–1786); (5) Cuara (Caura) (1595–[1716]–1786); (6) Arauca (Arouca) (1595–[1716]–1786); (7) Guayria (San Fernando) (1687–1784); (8) Savana Grande (Princes Town) (1687–1849); (9) Savaneta (1687–1794); (10) Montserrate (Mayo) (1700/1705–1797); (11) Arima (1749–1754, 1786–1849); (12) Toco (The Mission) (1758/1759–1849); (13) Arrecifes (Salybia) (1758/1759–1849); (14) Cumana (1758/1759–1849); (15) Matura (1758/1759–before 1784); (16) Siparia (1759, 1784–1849); (17) Arenales (1688–1699); (18) Los Cocos (Nariva?) (1689); (19) Mayaro (St. Joseph?) (1691–1698); (20) Careiro (Guayaguayare?) (1691–1698); (21) Moruga (1691–before 1706); (22) Cedros (1691); (23) Mucurapo (1749–1751, 1754); (24) Buenavista (1689–1786).

of Amerindians as slaves to Margarita.[33] (Whether the purport of this was fully understood by both Amerindians is open to doubt, of course.) At any rate, Vera now founded *San José de Oruña* (St. Joseph) in the foothills of the Northern Range, some 12 km east of Port-of-Spain, determining the sites of the *cabildo* (council) building, the governor's residence and the prison around the new town's central *plaza* (the present savannah), and that of the church at some distance south of it.

33 By the end of the sixteenth century the Spanish of the pearl islands were accustomed to join the Arawaks and buy female slaves from the Caribs of the mainland for three to four hatchets each, selling them in Margarita with great profit. While making the crossing from Trinidad to the Orinoco delta, Ralegh took a canoe which came from the mainland 'loden from thence with people to be sold' in Margarita.

St. Joseph occupies a low hill on the right bank of a tributary of the Caroni, the St. Joseph (Maracas) river, which allowed pirogues to sail upriver as far as half a league from the town (Fig. 39). It would remain the only Spanish settlement in the island for a long time, and Trinidad's (modest) capital until as late as 1757. It was a local Carinepagoto chief, Goanagoanare (Guanaguanare, Wannawanare), who, probably appeased with Spanish gifts, 'granted' Vera the St. Joseph area (his own village?) and afterwards 'with his men withdrew to another part of the island', most likely the San Juan area, between St. Joseph and Port-of-Spain. Uneasy about the future Amerindian disposition, Vera forbade selling weapons to them.

Antonio de Berrío came to Trinidad less than a year afterwards. His ruthless behaviour towards the Amerindians of the island inevitably led to resistance and in 1593 Berrío reported to the Spanish Crown that he was surrounded by hostile Indians 'who have tried to destroy this Island [...] I have only 70 men, yet in this Island are more than 6000 war Indians, the major part of them by no means peaceable'. The traditional Amerindian trading with the steadily increasing numbers of English and French *contrabandistas*, from now onwards joined by Dutch smugglers, formed a major bone of contention. While Vera reportedly prevented four English ships from provisioning, Berrío found two English ships trading for tobacco with the Amerindians. This indicates that, like the Island Caribs of the Windward Islands, the Amerindians of Trinidad had begun producing tobacco for the European market, reacting to the meteoric rise of smoking and the rapidly growing demand for tobacco in the 1590s. Besides, some of the Arawaks of Trinidad may have been reluctant to accept Berrío because of their trading relationship with the Spanish of the pearl islands. The latter and those of Cumaná, the governor of which had been granted with Trinidad, Tobago and Grenada by the Spanish Crown in 1592, attempted to frustrate Berrío's plans as far as possible. In order to counteract the hostile attitude of the Trinidad Amerindians, Berrío now attempted to blow up the traditional interethnic differences between the Carinepagoto and the Arawaks, which, according to an English source, he did 'by the accommedacion of a Fryer [Friar], that had lived at the Island Margaritta and had some Judgment in their Language and Manners'. Also, he sent Vera to combat the *caribes*. Most importantly, Berrío tried to balance the numerous hostile Amerindians in Trinidad by having many Nepoio, followers of Carapana, come over from the mainland, thus adding to the Nepoio already living on the island. Or, as Ralegh put it, he encouraged the settling in Trinidad of Amerindians 'of other countries, & planted there to eat out & wast those that were natural to the place'. All of this enhanced the status of Carapana tremendously, being able to build up an impressive retinue. Numerous European manufactures now became available to him. Indeed, when Berrío sent Vera on a reconnoitring expedition to Guiana in 1593, the latter first went to Carapana's village, unloading numerous gifts such as red bonnets, glass beads, knives, cutlasses, combs, and flutes. Originally being a 'Lorde of no other than ordinarie power', as Ralegh's lieutenant Keymis expressed it, after 'hee had entered into friendshippe with Berreo [...] the Indians on all sides left some their habitations, and manie their commanders to become his subjectes, that they might have the privilege to trade with the Spaniardes for hachets and knives, which are jewels of great price amongst them'. Clearly, Carapana had become a 'great man', using his contacts with the Spanish to (temporarily) dominate the lower Orinoco area.[34]

Meanwhile, Berrío attempted to prevent the privateers, who kept calling at Trinidad, from watering, victualing and loading tobacco or other tropical goods, using Amerindian auxiliaries ('ethnic soldiers') to assist the Spanish in ambushing them. In this way in 1593 eight crew members of the vessel of Jacob Whidden, one of Ralegh's scouts, were lured ashore for a deer hunt by Amerindians in a canoe while their captain was absent, after which they were killed by Berrío's soldiers. Two natives of Trinidad and two from Cumaná sailed with Whidden to England. Berrío successfully avoided an encounter with the much larger party of Sir Robert Dudley, who arrived with two major vessels at Curiapan (present Columbus Bay) in January 1595. Trading with the Arawaks (from whom he collected word lists), Dudley exchanged hatchets, knives, fish hooks, bells, and glass buttons for 'hennes, hogs, plantans, potatos, pinos, tabacco, and manie other prettie commodities'. Afterwards, he visited the Pitch Lake, sailed to Parico where he made a small redoubt ashore, and marched 'through a most monstrous thicke wood' to the Arawak village of Carao on the south coast, finding, however, that all of its inhabitants had fled. Besides, he sent a boat to explore the Orinoco, using Balthasar, an Arawak from Curiapan who could speak some Spanish, as its pilot. The latter escaped on the way back to Trinidad (Fig. 40).

Immediately after Dudley had left the island in March 1595, Berrío sent a troop of soldiers to punish the Amerindians of the south coast and others for trading with the English. Two of them were hanged and quartered while headmen from all over the island were taken prisoner, including Carroari, Maquarima, Tarroopanama, Aterima, and Goanagoanare, the Carinepagoto chief of northwest Trinidad. Ralegh relates how Berrío 'kept them in chains, & dropped their naked bodies with burning bacon, & such other torments'. Understandably, when Ralegh arrived in Trinidad in April 1595, claiming that he would save the Amerindians from 'the intollerable tirrany of the Spaniards', he was received with approval by many indigenous residents of the island.

Ralegh's sojourn on Trinidad was actually part of a search on the mainland for El Dorado, which, apart from making his own fortune, was meant as a means of recovering royal favour. As one of the most active promoters of privateering, he realized that an alliance with the indigenous peoples of Trinidad and the Orinoco would be vital for defeating the Spanish in this endeavour. In order to contact the local Amerindians, he had on board the four natives who had joined Whidden on the latter's home journey. One of these may have been Ralegh's interpreter, afterwards

34 Carapana's ascendancy was short-lived. His friendship with the Spanish cooled down and turned into enmity since the latter used his followers for rowing their canoes, as guides and porters, and, moreover, took many Nepoio women. Now Carapana even had a hand in a successful plot by Kali'na of the mainland to kill a party of roving Spaniards. This cut him off from his source of valuable trade goods. In 1596 Carapana was reported by an English traveler to be 'sicke, olde, and weake', and left with only a 'choise guarde of men' as by far most of his subjects had deserted him. He had died by 1610.

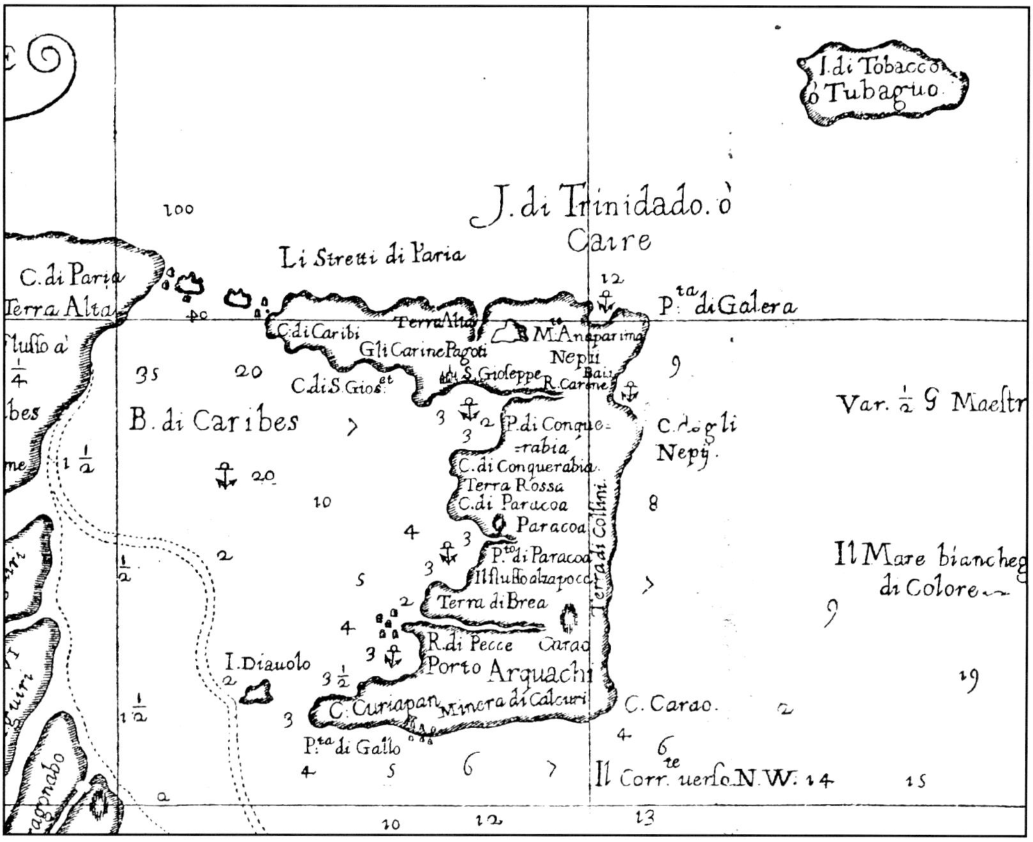

Figure 40. Map of Trinidad and Tobago, drawn by Sir Robert Dudley, published in his *Dell'Arcano del Mare* at Florence in 1645/1646.

called John of Trinidad (or John Provost), probably a Yaio.[35] First dropping anchor at Curiapan, Ralegh immediately contacted the local Amerindians. Finding the Yaio on his side, he had to concede that at least some of the Arawaks were still assisting the Spanish, judging them to be 'a vagabond, poore, and small people'. Indeed, reportedly induced by 'gifts and bribes', some Arawaks, who went aboard Ralegh's ships, actually acted as spies for the governor of Margarita. After some coastal surveying, Ralegh sailed to Cumucurapo where he rapidly befriended several Amerindians, including an Arawak called Cantyman who was an acquaintance of Whidden. Informed about the situation in the island, Ralegh now killed a small party of Spaniards sent by Berrío, together with 25 Amerindian auxiliaries, to meet him, referring to the fate of Whidden's crew as a justification. Subsequently, guided by the Amerindians in a single file, Ralegh marched with a hundred soldiers towards St. Joseph over a forest path, undoubtedly the present Old St Joseph Road and Eastern

35 When accompanying Ralegh's lieutenant Laurence Keymis as a pilot on his reconnaissance journey of the Guiana coastal zone, in April 1596, John of Trinidad was unwilling to contact the Amerindians of northeast Trinidad, as 'he knewe no part of that side of the Island'.

Figure 41. Sir Walter Ralegh sets free five Amerindian chiefs, chained in St. Joseph, Trinidad, by Antonio de Berrio, 1595. Eighteenth-century fantasy engraving, published in Edward Cavendish Drake's *A new universal collection of authentic and entertaining voyages and travels* [...], London, 1768. Courtesy Gérard A. Besson.

Main Road. Spending the night in the Carinepagoto village of the imprisoned Goanagoanare, situated halfway to St. Joseph (probably in the San Juan area), at dawn he attacked the Spanish town, killing 37 Spaniards and taking Berrío prisoner. Before burning the town (reportedly at the instigation of the Amerindians), Ralegh freed the five 'Lords or litle kings' whom he found 'in one chaine almost dead of famine, and wasted with torments' (Fig. 41). Some Spaniards were able to escape to La Brea where they found some friendly Amerindians and fled to Margarita. The Carinepagoto resettled St. Joseph. Before leaving Cumucurapo, Ralegh assembled as many Amerindians as possible for a great conference, announcing the end of the Spanish empire in glowing terms and placing Trinidad under the English Queen. Subsequently, he returned to Curiapan where he erected a small fortification. Provisioned by the local Amerindians, he now left for his search of gold mines on the mainland, keeping Berrío as a prisoner. While crossing over to the Orinoco delta, he picked up an Arawak, called Ferdinando, as a pilot, who together with his wife was on his way to Margarita with cassava bread and cotton hammocks. Returning from the mainland following visits to major Amerindian chiefs of the Orinoco in June 1595, Ralegh continued his expedition by privateering in the West Indies, joined by various Amerindians from the mainland and Trinidad, including one called by a French traveller the 'Son to the King of the Island of Trinidad'.

Berrío, who accompanied Ralegh on his Orinoco journey, was put ashore by the latter in Cumaná. He immediately went to Margarita, gathering the remnants of his troops, and returned to Trinidad, afterwards moving to the mainland where he founded a Spanish town, *Santo Tomé de Guayana*, at the confluence of the Orinoco and the Caroní, considered to be the entrance to El Dorado, in December 1595. His absence from Trinidad was used by the governor of Cumaná, Francisco de Vides, to occupy the island. This was an exceptionally corrupt character who, however, had a legal claim to Trinidad. In April 1596, Domingo de Vera, who had been sent to Spain in order to recruit colonists and get the backing of the Council of the Indies for Berrío's endeavours, returned on Trinidad with no less than 1500 settlers, including many women and children. The fate of Vera's expedition was dramatic. First he chased away Vides' followers from Trinidad. Finding St. Joseph in shambles, he built some huts in Port-of-Spain after having appeased the local Amerindians by distributing trade wares. Simultaneously, Vera succeeded in chasing away some Dutch ships ('Flemings') who called at Trinidad for trade. However, soon all food was exhausted and nothing could be obtained from the region's Amerindians who had all withdrawn. Ships with soldiers and colonists sent to the Orinoco fled to Caracas, while other settlers, mainly married couples and children, who went in pirogues to the mainland, got into a storm on the Gulf of Paria and were drowned. Still others were killed while the women and children were taken by Island Caribs from Dominica who were on their way to visit a Kali'na settlement on the Guarapiche River of the west coast. Finally, many of those who were able to reach Santo Tomé died of hunger or disease. Antonio de Berrío himself passed away soon afterwards, being succeeded by his young son Ferdinand (1597).

At the beginning of the seventeenth century the relationship between the Spanish and most Trinidad Amerindians was at an all-time low. Indeed, as a Dutch explorer, Cabeliau, explained in 1599, 'whosoever are enemies, and bear enmity to the Spaniards, are friends with the Indians'. Partially this was due to Ralegh's intervention, but primarily this deterioration resulted from Antonio de Berrio's attempts to prevent Amerindian trading with the privateers, and, moreover, his efforts to introduce a *repartimiento* system in the island such as that of Hispaniola and Puerto Rico. In 1595 it was reported that Berrío had divided the entire island and given out seventy *encomiendas* to his soldiers as a reward for their services. According to Spanish law, e*ncomiendas* ('commands') were land grants incorporating the resident Amerindians, made to Spanish settlers (*encomenderos*) who were permitted to exact both tribute in the form of foodstuffs or money and labour service from the Amerindians. In return the Spanish were theoretically responsible for teaching them the principles of Christianity, generally instructing them in European ways of life, and rendering military service, thus protecting the Amerindians from foreign assaults. Besides, the Amerindians could be rented out by the settlers for seasonal work on public work projects such as road construction under the *mita* ('work party') scheme. Compulsory labour by the Amerindians was the overall purpose, of course. Although legally they were not required to work for more than three days a week, abuse of the system was simple, all the more because a *corregidor*, an official responsible for protecting the Amerindians from exploitation by the settlers, overseeing the *mita* as well as supervising the trade between the Amerindians and the Spanish, was not appointed in Trinidad throughout the seventeenth century. Similarly, providing priests (*curas doctrineros*) to the *encomienda* villages was largely neglected as well. It is noteworthy that the employment of Amerindians in personal service was officially forbidden although this law was often disregarded. The whole system rested on the assumed political authority of the indigenous leaders, who controlled nominally the day-to-day activities of the *encomienda* workforce. The chief of a vilage and his oldest son were exempted from paying tribute.

Only a small fraction of the indigenous population of the island was involved in the *encomienda* system, as only four *encomienda* villages are reported in the seventeenth century (Fig. 39). Undoubtedly this illustrates the limited political control of the island by the Spanish and the hostile attitude of most Trinidad Amerindians to the colonizers. All the *encomiendas* were situated on the banks of rivers in the Northern Basin, at a distance of at most 10 km, as the crow flies, from St. Joseph, and connected with the Spanish town by the present Eastern Main Road, then a bridle path which, as a 'Royal Road', was kept open by the Amerindians. At present three of these *encomienda* villages are still centres of population: *San Juan de Aricagua* (present San Juan), *San Pablo de Tacarigua* (Tacaribe, Tacarima; present Tacarigua) and *San Agustín de Arauca* (Aruaca, Aracao; present Arouca). A fourth *encomienda* village, Cuara (Caura, Quare), was situated south of Tacarigua, perhaps at present Orange Grove. It is the only one which did not develop into a modern community, although the name still exists as that of a river and a valley. Most villages were reportedly occupied by Nepoio, which is illustrated by the fact that their names are typically Cariban such as was formerly spoken in the Venezuelan coastal zone. These Nepoio were probably the followers of Carapana, Berrío had come over from the mainland. Arauca (Aruaca) forms an exception; its name clearly indicates that its inhabitants were Arawaks. All the village names duplicate those of rivers. The Amerindians in the *encomiendas* typically cultivated tobacco for contraband trading while growing food crops such as maize, cassava, beans and cocoa, and raising chicken for consumption by the *encomenderos* and for selling to the Spanish settlers in St. Joseph and Port-of-Spain.

The attempts by father and son Berrío to establish an *encomienda* system all over the island and to suppress all Amerindian independence, aggravated by unlimited slave taking, led to an increasing flight of Amerindians from Trinidad to the mainland, especially the Guiana coastal zone, and to Tobago. The mainland exodus of many Amerindians, including Yaio, Shebaio and some Arawaks, was preceded in the 1590s by a generally eastern movement along the coast of the Guianas as the result of slave raids by mainland Arawaks, together with Spaniards from Margarita and Caracas. It first affected Yaio who had settled near the Moruka river on the coast of present Guyana. In 1596 a Yaio chief called Wareo told

Ralegh's lieutenant Keymis that he formerly lived on the Moruka, but that two or three years previously a Spanish party, guided by the Arawak chief Aramaia of the lower Orinoco, had come to his village in order to kidnap 'his best wife', but that he had killed half of them. Nevertheless, they had taken many Yaio women and children, and when half a year before another mainland Arawak had led the Spanish to his village again, he had burnt his houses, destroyed his fields, and fled to the east, leaving his country 'to be possessed by the Arawaccas'. Wareo told Keymis that the Yaio were a 'mightie people' and that they 'of late time were Lordes of all the sea coast so farre as Trinidado, which they likewise possessed'. Several similar stories of Yaio who fled from the west have been recorded, for instance that of Weepackea on the Maroni (Marowijne) river between present Suriname and French Guiana, who told an English visitor around 1610 that he had been born on the Orinoco, was captured and tortured by the Spaniards, but escaped and ran away to the east. Similarly, the Yaio and Shebaio of southwest Trinidad moved to the Guiana coastal zone. While in 1598 Cabeliau and other Dutch sailors carefully charted these parts of the island's coast, trading with the local Amerindians and composing Arawak, Yaio and Shebaio wordlists, this was the last time that the two latter ethnic groups are mentioned in the documentary sources with reference to Trinidad. (Cabeliau was joined by two Yaio from Trinidad on his home journey to the Dutch Republic.) Significantly, throughout the seventeenth century Yaio and Shebaio are mentioned as living interspersed with the Arawaks and Kali'na especially in the eastern portion of the Guiana coastal zone. In the early 1600s the Yaio, Arawaks, and Shebaio are listed by Robert Harcourt and other English explorers as among the Amerindian peoples living in this region that 'haue beene chased away from Trinidado, and the borders of Orenoque', while Keymis notes that many of the Arawaks 'doth also hate' the Spanish. Indeed, in the 1620s a Spanish chronicler observed that the Arawaks 'who were always friendly disposed to the Spaniards, [...] have been in a state of rebellion for over 10 years'. All in all, in 1612 it was estimated that only some 4000 'heathen' Amerindians were left in Trinidad, with 300 'civilised' ones, the latter living in the *encomiendas*.

Meanwhile, following a series of attempts to discover the mysterious goldland his father had sought, Ferdinand de Berrío turned to promoting the cultivation of tobacco in Trinidad and on the lower Orinoco, which soon proved to be a financially more rewarding, albeit insecure economic base, founded as it was on the contraband trade with Spain's enemies, notably English, French and Dutch interlopers, since registered ships from Spain rarely called at Port-of-Spain or Santo Tomé. In Trinidad most tobacco was grown around St. Joseph (with some sugar cane and ginger) and the *encomiendas* of Aricagua and Aruaca. In fact, the growing demand for tobacco in Europe stimulated its growth in the entire Venezuelan coastal zone, and the Spanish colonies of this region came to depend entirely upon the *rescate* (illicit trade) in tobacco. As early as 1595 'Trinidado' and 'tobacco' had become interchangeable in English common usage even though at this time most tobacco was still obtained by the privateers from the local Amerindians. Ten to fifteen years later the plantations of Trinidad and the lower Orinoco produced some 200,000 pounds of tobacco each year and twenty to thirty ships of *contrabandistas*, mainly English and Dutch, called at Trinidad alone.[36] As an English chronicler observed, the 'Tobacco of Trinidada is ye best in the knowne World'. Indeed, tobacco had become 'one of the chief factors these coasts to be so much frequented by pirates', the governor of Cumaná complained in 1607. Unable to exercise sufficient military control, the Spanish government decided to halt the contraband trade by prohibiting tobacco cultivation and depopulating its chief production centres. This suicidal policy was successfully pursued on the Venezuelan littoral and Margarita, but Ferdinand de Berrío chose to ignore the metropolitan orders, and the illicit trade now concentrated at Trinidad and the lower Orinoco. Besides, Trinidad became the outlet not only of the tobacco grown on the island itself, but also tobacco produced illegally in the Venezuelan coastal zone. It was the flourishing tobacco trade that allowed Berrío in 1606 to purchase in all 470 African slaves from a Dutch merchant for rebuilding St. Joseph and work on the tobacco fields. This slaver, Isaac Duverne, subsequently reconnoitred Trinidad for the States General of the Dutch Republic and reportedly 'did Converse much with the Indians' of the island.

Apart from black slaves, Berrío obtained cheap labour for the tobacco plantations by undertaking slave raiding expeditions in Trinidad as well as Tobago. According to a report of 1605, ill-treatment had caused the death of more than 1000 Amerindians in the island, and an eye-witness account from this very year states that ten to twelve canoe loads with Amerindians from the *encomiendas* had departed from Trinidad to be sold as slaves in Margarita. In 1609 an old companion of Antonio de Berrío complained to the Crown that 'all the Indians and other articles of barter are brought to this Island of Margarita for sale', an accusation that was confirmed by a special commissioner. The next year Ferdinand de Berrío sent 32 Amerindians to Margarita who were sold for thirty ducats each. The Spanish blamed the Amerindian emigration to the Guiana coastal zone, largely caused by Berrío's slave raids, on attacks by the *caribes*. In 1604 it was declared that as the result of 'the injuries and crimes which the *caribes* effect' more than 10,000 Amerindians had left Trinidad for the mainland, and an account of 1609 refers to an assault on St. Joseph which led to the death of seven or eight Spaniards while many others were wounded. Indeed, it was noted by an English observer that the Spanish 'knew not by any meanes to suppresse them'. Four years later a Spaniard complained that Trinidad was 'surrounded by the Flemings and *caribes* both by sea and land [...] The *caribes* even come as far as the City to rob and ill-treat' its inhabitants. Indeed, it is recorded that in 1613 a party of Island Caribs from Grenada, Martinique and Dominica attacked the Spanish settlers of Trinidad. In spite of all these reports, one should hardly accept the Spanish view that these raids were the main reason for the flight to the mainland by many of the Trinidad Amerindians rather than the Spanish slave raids. In fact, Ferdinand de Berrío officially allowed buying Amerindian slaves from the *caribes* (probably Kali'na) of the mainland. Clearly, it is not surprising that in 1608 Berrío's followers were characterized as 'in general a seminary of rascals'.

36 The contraband traders were allowed as well to cut pitch at the Pitch Lake for caulking their vessels.

Hierreyma and the great Amerindian rebellion

While the Trinidad Yaio, Shebaio and numerous Arawaks fled to the mainland, in the first decades of the seventeenth century many Carinepagoto took refuge in Tobago. In the 1630s it was noted that at Maracas Bay there was a supply of plantains 'from the old plantations of the Caribs who were driven from the [...] island by the Spanish and still come here every year in their canoes to lay provisions'. Occasionally, the Spanish sent small expeditions to the mainland in order to fight the Kali'na, for instance on the request of Warao of the Orinoco delta in 1603, and ten years later on that of Arawaks from the littoral zone of present Guyana. In the latter case the Spanish, assisted by 300 'friendly Indians', destroyed a Dutch/Kali'na tobacco plantation on the Corentine (Corantijn) river between Suriname and Guyana. Slave taking was behind many if not all of these activities, as it is noted that the Amerindian women captured during the latter attack were kept as involuntary servants in the houses of the citizens of St. Joseph. Many Trinidad Amerindians, not living in the *encomiendas*, now withdrew as far as possible from the centre of Spanish habitation. In 1612 a royal commissioner complained that no *encomienda* had more than thirty Amerindians, while boats were not to be found in St. Joseph and when they were found, Indian rowers were not to be got as they had retired inland and did not come to St. Joseph 'unless they are fetched'. Clearly, many Amerindians had 'hidden themselves and moved well inland'. Nevertheless, in 1611 others, no doubt induced by gifts of European manufactures, kept up some form of communication with St. Joseph, including the inhabitants of a village situated five leagues from Galeota Point, who warned the Spanish about ships which passed by the south coast. Similarly, during Ralegh's last voyage to the region (1617), he exposed seven Nepoio who came as spies for the Spanish to his ship, but subsequently were quite willing to provide him with cassava bread and oranges. (Fearing an attack, the citizens of St. Joseph now blocked the Eastern Main Road with forest trees.) Ralegh 'raised in rebellion all the Indians who dwell on the sea coast', as the Council of the Indies recorded, while in 1624 the governor of Trinidad complained that all the Indians of the island were revolting, trading 'freely and openly' with the English and the Dutch. A Spanish chronicler blamed Amerindian hostility on mistreatment by the Spanish as well as 'foreign instigation'.

By this time the contraband tobacco trade had definitely ended. Following the boom years between 1604 and 1612, gradually fewer Dutch and English vessels still called at Trinidad for loading tobacco. (For the latter the contraband trade had become quite insecure, since after the Anglo–Spanish peace treaty of 1604 privateering lacked official backing.) They were occasionally joined by a French ship taking in tropical hardwood. A single visit to Port-of-Spain by warships conveying the *tierra firme* fleet (1612), in order to chase away the contraband traders, remained without much effect. Accused of trading with the enemy and selling Amerindian slaves, Berrío reacted by arranging sporadic and brutal attacks upon the foreigners to prove his loyalty, but meanwhile continued trading with them until the last possible moment, even after the arrival of an investigating judge. An English visitor, Sir Thomas Roe, judged the situation quite sharply when he wrote in 1611 that the Spanish were 'equally proud, insolent, yet needy and weake: theyr force is reputation, and theyr safety opinion'. When in 1614, after repeated requests, finally a registered Spanish ship arrived in Trinidad, it was the first in 19 years. Another one called at the island in 1617. Found guilty of trading with the enemy, Berrío was temporarily deprived of his post but later reinstated again. He died in 1622. Throughout his governorship and long thereafter, St. Joseph remained a poor town inhabited by at most some 30-40 *vecinos* ('householders'). Apart from the public buildings, the town consisted of small wattle-and-daub houses 'made of earth stamped solid, which they call *tapias*, and roofed with thatch or other combustible material', as a Dutchman observed in 1637. Actually, *tapia*, which was applied to a stick framework, consisted of clay mixed with long grasses. The earthen floors were plastered with a mixture of clay, dung and dried grass.[37] A watch house was kept at the confluence of the St. Joseph river and the Caroni in order to prevent foreign pirogues from ascending the river to the town, while an Amerindian kept watch on the mountain of El Tucuche overseeing Maracas Bay. Archaeologically, the poverty of the Spanish settlers is illustrated by the recovery of only relatively small amounts of the finest, colourful (blue, white, cream, yellowish, and orange) Spanish tableware available at the time, the tin-enamel glazed *majolica*, at excavations carried out in the centre of St. Joseph by John M. Goggin of the Florida State Museum and Irving Rouse of Yale University in 1953. The first Spanish inhabitants of the town used *majolica* that was shipped directly from Seville, Andalusia, while from the 1640s onwards it was imported from Mexico. As noted above (Chapter 4), the ordinary kitchen ware used by the Spanish in St. Joseph consisted of Mayoid pottery, obtained from the loyal Amerindians on the island, probably those of the *encomiendas*. Further archaeological finds encountered at St. Joseph include fragments of olive jars (*botijas*), pipe bowls, glass, and metal, all of which are difficult to date. Dutch and English influences are shown by a single delft potsherd, a Rhenish saucer plate (1659-1750), a German stoneware bottle or flask, and a decorated English pipe bowl dating to the 1650s.

Spain's self-imposed destruction of the tobacco trade ushered in an extended period of poverty and occasionally despair among the Spanish settlers of Trinidad. From now onwards the island was considered as a remote outpost by the mother country, an unpromising frontier colony. Although freedom of trading and custom dues had been granted on all tobacco that was shipped to Spain from as early as 1616, registered vessels to collect the produce rarely called at Trinidad. Indeed, by 1633 conditions had worsened so much that there was a grave shortage of clothing and other necessities of life. Wine was in such short supply that it was impossible to celebrate mass in St. Joseph. Understandably, several *vecinos* considered vacating the island. Besides, the Spanish lived in constant fear of attacks by Dutch or

37 These traditional Spanish houses are known as *ajoupas* in Trinidad. This is a term derived from the Tupi language of coastal Brazil which was adopted by the French in the early sixteenth century and introduced to the West Indies afterwards. It may have reached Trinidad with the French immigration of the 1780s. By no means is this type of wattle-and-daub houses originally Amerindian, as is often thought.

English forces. Indeed, in 1626 Thomas Warner arrived with three ships intent on plundering the island, but left empty-handed as it 'proued bootless'. Spanish fear of the external enemy was as deep as of the internal enemy: only a few Amerindians outside the *encomiendas* still kept up a friendly relationship with the citizens of St. Joseph.[38] Even most of the some 300 Amerindians in the *encomiendas* remained unconverted as there was no priest available to take care of them. Apart from some Carinepagoto distributed on the north coast, Arawaks and Nepoio formed the indigenous ethnic groups still living on the island. Spanish concern was further increased when, during the 1630s and 1640s, no doubt encouraged by the restricted Spanish presence on the island, English and Dutch settlers established small colonies on Trinidad's east and south coasts primarily in order to trade with the Amerindians and to grow tobacco for the home market, thereby encouraging local indigenous hostility towards the Spanish. The first of these was Sir Henry Colt who settled with a small group of English in northeast Trinidad, constructing a small fortification at Toco near Galera Point late in 1632. Subsequently, he entered trade contacts with the Amerindians of this part of the island. Warned by Portuguese vessels which called at Toco for watering and refreshing, the following year the governor of Margarita sent three companies of Spanish soldiers assisted by fifty Guaiquerí archers in three pirogues along Trinidad's north coast. They were able to surprise Colt's men who were subsequently put to death on Margarita.

A major challenge to the Spanish control of the island was presented by an alliance between the Dutch and the Nepoio of east and central Trinidad.[39] In 1628 settlers from the province of Zealand in the Dutch Republic founded a tobacco plantation, defended by a major fortification and a smaller one, on the leeward coast of Tobago. It was probably abandoned in 1630 due to raids by Island Caribs from St. Vincent and Grenada. New settlers were sent to the island in 1633 who reoccupied the old settlement and, moreover, established friendly contacts with the Nepoio of Trinidad. Indeed, a number of young boys were sent to the Amerindian villages in order to learn 'the Indian language'. In February 1636 the Nepoio chief and 'great man' Hierreyma (also spelt Hyarima) visited Tobago, offering to trade with the colonists and suggesting an alliance in order to dislodge the Spanish from Trinidad. Hierreyma had been 'a slave' on a Spanish *encomienda* eleven years previously, but had run away and 'more than once' joined raids on them. As he had killed two Spaniards in some encounter, he was 'the most famous and powerful' amongst the Nepoio 'and considered the chief by the others' (Fig. 42). To be sure, Hierreyma would turn out to be the most formidable opponent the Spanish had to face since the time of Baucunar, one century previously. His name is remarkably similar to that of the later mission village of Arima, first mentioned in the documentary sources in 1699. Identification of Arima as Hierreyma's settlement

38 In 1629 a 'friendly' Arawak chief called Aramaia is mentioned who had just been baptized. He reportedly expressed strong feelings of enmity to the *caribes*. However, it is unknown whether he lived in an *encomienda* (Aruaca?) or not.

39 According to the Spanish, the Amerindians 'embrace the Dutch because they imitate the barbarians in their lives and allow them full liberty without constraint of tribute or labour or the sweet yoke of the Gospel, heavy in their opinion'. Besides, the Dutch would be 'so mixed with the Indians that they marry with the Carib women as well as with those of other tribes'.

Figure 42. Statue of Hierreyma, Hollis Avenue, Arima, Trinidad. Steel frame with concrete, finished in bronze paint by Selwyn Borneo, 1993.

is strengthened by a Dutch testimony stating that the Nepoio chief's village was situated 3.5 leagues (one day's walking) from St. Joseph. At any rate, Hierreyma offered the Dutch as hostages all the old men, women and children of his tribe in return for the assistance of eighty men with arquebuses. The Dutch estimated the total strength of the Nepoio and Arawaks at 'over 600 able men', considering the Nepoio to be 'deadly enemies to the Spanish', but stating of the Arawaks that they 'occasionally serve the Spaniards by rowing their canoes and cannot be relied upon so well'. Apart from providing foodstuffs to the Tobago colony, which the Dutch needed very much, the Nepoio started to grow tobacco for them. (Trinidad tobacco was esteemed much higher in Holland than that cultivated in Tobago.) In order to facilitate trade relations with the Nepoio, the Dutch established small fortifications in east Trinidad, one at Galera Point in the northeast, possibly close to Colt's old dwelling at Toco, and another one at Moruga or Quinam in the eastern portion of the south coast.

Although it is questionable whether the Dutch had any intention to dislodge the Spaniards from Trinidad, and most likely only wished to establish trade centres without provoking them, the Spanish did not lose time to remove the Dutch from both Trinidad and Tobago. Action was taken when a new governor, Don Diego Lopez de Escobar, arrived in Trinidad. In November 1636 Escobar reported to the Spanish Crown that all Amerindians of Trinidad were in rebellion. He learned about the Dutch trading stations from an Arawak 'who had run away on account of the bad treatment he had received at the hands of the rebels who wanted to kill him'. The latter told Escobar of an imminent attack on St. Joseph by the Dutch of Tobago, assisted by the 'rebel Indians more than a thousand strong'. When five other Arawaks, including a chief called Curiguao, came to St. Joseph as spies for the rebels, they were detained and forced to betray the locations of the Dutch settlements. Reinforced by a group of fifty Amerindian auxiliaries[40] and Spanish soldiers from Santo Tomé as well as Margarita, Escobar sailed to the east with four pirogues, following the north coast, while another troop marched overland, guided by two Arawak 'spies' and Curiguao. Meeting at Galera Point, both forces overwhelmed the few defenders of the Dutch fortification. Next Escobar and his men followed unnoticed a Dutch vessel which had wanted to anchor at the fort in order to load the produce the Nepoio had delivered to the Dutch, but, noticing that it had been taken, subsequently sailed to the small Dutch stronghold on the south coast. Escobar was able to conquer this outpost as well, taking captive practically all the Dutchmen. The Nepoio allies of the Dutch all escaped, subsequently trying to ambush the Spanish troops which marched back to St. Joseph overland after destroying many Amerindian supplies and ravaging their provision grounds.

Following a rest of three months in St. Joseph, in December 1636 Escobar made the crossing to Tobago in eight pirogues with 90 soldiers but no Amerindian auxiliaries (employed as oarsmen), as all of them had run away. After conquering the Dutch colony of Tobago by tricking the Dutch into surrender (see Chapter 8), Escobar sent all captives to Margarita, keeping only the two principal ones, the son of the colony's patron ('owner'), Cornelis de Moor, and its secretary. All prisoners except some boys were hanged in Cumaná, a gross violation of the surrender conditions. Their deaths were revenged the following year by Groenewegen, the factor of the Dutch colony of Essequibo on the mainland. Together with Carib, Arawak and Warao auxiliaries, he first moved to the Orinoco, where he burned Santo Tomé in June 1637, freeing Cornelis de Moor, who had been taken to the mainland by Escobar and was kept prisoner here. While refitting close to the Orinoco delta, Groenewegen's small army was strengthened by Hierreyma and a group of Nepoio warriors from east Trinidad. In October 1637 a multi-ethnic indigenous force consisting of twenty pirogues with Nepoio, Arawaks, Caribs, and Warao sailed up the Caroni and then the St. Joseph river, sacking the Spanish town. One Spaniard was killed and others wounded while some black slaves joined the Amerindians in fighting the Spanish.[41] The events had a sequel when, one year later, a relief expedition was sent to Escobar with food, munitions, clothing, and provisions while a fresh troop of soldiers arrived from Caracas in 1639. Reinforced, Escobar was now able to rebuild St. Joseph to a certain extent and punish the

40 These 'ethnic soldiers' included a troop of so-called Chacomar Indians. These were most likely Arawaks from Trinidad's south coast, the central part of it was called the Chacomare 'province' in the 1530s (see Chapter 6).

41 The present Indigenous (First) Peoples Day of Trinidad and Tobago is the anniversary of the destruction of St. Joseph on October 14, 1637.

Nepoio and their allies, capturing thirty Amerindians whom he sent to Margarita and Cumaná for sale as slaves. Hierreyma's fate is unknown.

Following this disaster, the Spanish carefully refrained from attacking the small English colonies which were subsequently founded on Trinidad's south and northeast coasts under the patronage of the earl of Warwick. The first was established at Toco in 1640 by a group of settlers under Captain Robert Masham, who had been chased from Tobago by Island Caribs of St. Vincent. It was shortlived. Masham was reportedly murdered by Caribs who believed that the English would ally themselves with the Arawaks and Nepoio. Also in 1640, an attempt to raid St. Joseph by English corsairs, aided by Trinidad Amerindians, turned out to be unsuccessful as they tried to attack from the north coast. The survivors of Warwick's Toco outpost amalgamated with another group of settlers, experienced planters from Barbados and St. Kitts, who established a new colony under Major Jeremiah Hartley 'near a river' on Trinidad's 'leeward side', possibly the southwest coast. Regularly receiving provisions and ammunition, this community flourished for five years, keeping up a friendly relationship with the Arawaks and Nepoio of the region. Another settlement, founded possibly at Moruga on the south coast in 1644, was abandoned after a year due to a virulent illness which took the lives of many colonists. Fear that the epidemic would strike their community as well, Hartley's group returned to Barbados this very year. Meanwhile, the Spanish relationship to the local Amerindians remained problematic. In 1645 the just founded Santa Hermandad in St. Joseph, a religious society for laymen established to enforce law and order, claimed to have assisted in converting some 250 *encomienda* Amerindians. This may have been the total number of inhabitants of these villages, as in this very year the actual number of their householders was at an all-time low: the largest of the four *encomiendas* had not more than twenty of them and the smallest one only five.

All of this is quite understandable in view of the continuing poverty of the Spanish town and its inhabitants. In 1640 the governor of Trinidad complained to Madrid that he went around St. Joseph practically naked and did not own a single pair of shoes. In all there were not more than 30 Spanish settlers and three priests. Licensed Spanish vessels hardly ever called at the island due to the high costs of shipping from Spain, and only illicit trade (especially by the Dutch) was attractive. In these years the production of cocoa slowly took the place of tobacco on the Spanish plantations around St. Joseph. In fact, the cocoa grown in Trinidad was soon renowned as being 'the best of the sort in all the Indies'. Domestic livestock remained rare. Many Amerindian slaves, primarily captured Kali'na, were now imported from the Orinoco region. Nevertheless, no proper market could be found for the cocoa and other tropical crops cultivated on the island. As a result, European manufactures and clothes remained in great demand. In 1662 the governor of Trinidad reported to the Spanish Crown that the colony was in a 'miserable state': the colonists were lacking knives, hatchets, cutlasses and agricultural tools, while the Amerindians of the *encomiendas*, now counting only 80-90 individuals, rendered 'very indifferent service' as the *vecinos* were unable to pay them for their labour with iron tools and other products. In fact, 'all the rest' of the Amerindians 'had gone back to liberty', and indeed all of those outside the *encomiendas* were in rebellion. Nevertheless, the governor could inform Madrid that he had pacified the latter with the aid of friendly natives, 'reducing some by kindness and the rebellious by force of arms'.

Things did not improve in the 1670s and 1680s. They even worsened, as now English and French corsairs or regular forces, occasionally joined by Island Caribs, at regular intervals raided the destitute Spanish colony. Only Dutch traders and slavers still called at the island at times. In 1670 the governor reported that St. Joseph was virtually deserted as most residents had left Trinidad for Cumaná and Caracas, while the following year money to pay the garrison of St. Joseph, counting not more than 47 men, was lacking as a result of which many soldiers deserted the island. The Council of State did not consider it worthwhile to assist the outpost colony as in their opinion, Trinidad defended itself 'by its bad climate and the barrenness of its soil, for which reason the French had not occupied it'. The town presented a vision of abject poverty. Indeed, in 1681 the church of St. Joseph is described as an 'old and [...] threatened ruin' which was 'made of *tapias* covered with palms and all [...] rough and unadorned and indecent'. Port-of-Spain had not more than ten houses, a church and a watch house. By the 1680s there were some 120 Spanish colonists, including whites, *mestizos* and *mulatos*, in the island and in all a hundred African slaves. In these years the official Spanish attitude towards the local Amerindians outside the *encomiendas* gradually began to change, since now the understanding began to take root that rather than as a rule approaching them aggressively, the best method to 'pacify' the Trinidad Amerindians would be by appeasing, converting and Hispanicizing them. In 1678 the governor claimed to have called together some 500 chiefs, encouraging them to settle in the coastal zone of the island so as to be able to better defend the colony, and also to be assimilated more easily to Spanish society (and thus to be controlled with less effort). Some Amerindians reportedly followed his request. A grand scheme to bring the Amerindians of Trinidad definitely under Spanish political control through a *conquista de almas* ('conquest of the souls'), proclaimed to be the official policy of the Spanish Crown in 1652, would be initiated in the second half of the 1680s by founding Capuchin missions on the island.

8. European settlement and Amerindian response in Tobago (1592–ca. 1810)

After more than a hundred years of occasional slave raids but no attempts at European settlement, the seventeenth-century Amerindians of Tobago were confronted with a series of not less than probably fourteen intermittent colonization efforts by the Spanish (1614), Dutch (1628–1677), English (1637–1646), and Courlanders (1639–1693). Apart from the rivalry among the European nations themselves, it was due to the fierce resistance against foreign settlement by the joined forces of the Tobagonian Amerindians and their allies in the Windward Islands that all of these European endeavours at colonization of the smaller island were eventually fruitless. Indigenous power waned only as a result of the sharp demographic decline of the Amerindian population in the entire Lesser Antilles and the coastal zone of the mainland towards the end of the seventeenth century. Being contested between France and Britain but left unoccupied by both, Tobago became a refuge area for Amerindians from the mainland and the Lesser Antilles in the first half of the eighteenth century. They became gradually gallicized by adopting the French language and much of its culture due to the seasonal influx of especially turtlers from the French West Indies to the island. After being ceded by France to Britain in 1763, the massive influx of white planters and African slaves led to the rapid marginalization of the remaining Amerindians and their inevitable decline. In the early nineteenth century the last survivors disappeared from the island by migrating to Trinidad.

Slave raids and the first European attempts at settlement

Throughout the sixteenth century Spanish interest in Tobago was only as a rich source of slave labour. Indeed, when Laurence Keymis called at Tobago in 1596, he noted that the governor of Margarita 'went lately in a Pinesse [light sailing ship] to viewe this Island'. This must have been Pedro de Salazar who is reported to have been accustomed to capture indigenous slaves in Trinidad before Berrío settled on this island. Keymis was perhaps induced to visit Tobago by his pilot Gilbert, possibly a Nepoio, who 'sometime lived there'. Gilbert told Keymis that Tobago 'is plentifull of all things, and a very good soyle'. Indeed, he 'noteth it for the best and fruitfullest ground that hee knoweth'. A few years later it was especially Ferdinand de Berrío who organised slave raiding expeditions to the island although once he nearly lost all of his pirogues half-way between Trinidad and Tobago due to bad weather. Berrío reportedly contemplated a 'punishing expedition' against the Kali'na of Tobago as early as 1602 which was effectuated two years later. Another assault of this kind took place in 1606 when the Spanish settlers of Trinidad, 'unable to tolerate such dangerous neighbours any longer', raided Tobago's Amerindians who were 'exterminated and destroyed', although the Spanish claim that Tobago was depopulated seems exaggerated. At least some women and children were carried to Trinidad as slaves. The first and only Spanish effort to found a colony in Tobago was undertaken by one Juan Rodríguez from Spain in 1614. In view of the hostile relationship between the island's indigenous settlers and the Spanish, it is not surprising that he proved to be unsuccessful in 'Courting the Indians to a Trade'. Forced by mutiny and disease among his soldiers, Rodríguez left the island after four months, sailing for Trinidad 'where landing in that weake Condition' most of his followers died. The Spanish slave raids continued well into the 1620s. After such an incursion from Margarita in 1616, the *caribes* of Tobago attacked the Spanish on the islands of Los Testigos northeast of Margarita with 'numerous' dugouts the following year. Finally, in 1623 six Spanish pirogues from the latter island made a stop-over in Trinidad on their way to Tobago for what undoubtedly must have been another slave raid.

Amerindian resistance against the various seventeenth-century European attempts at settlement on Tobago was induced at least partially by the island's function as a half-way station between the Windward Islands and the coastal zone of the mainland. As such it formed an indispensable link in the pattern of long-distance trade and communication between the Island Caribs (Kali'nago) of the Lesser Antilles and their allies, the Kali'na of the Guianas and the Venezuelan coastal zone (see Chapter 5). In this respect it is noteworthy that in the 1630s Tobago reportedly was inhabited by Kali'na, while Grenada was shared between Kali'na and Kali'nago. As early as 1599 Keymis explained the fact that Tobago was 'not nowe inhabited' (by the Spanish) 'because the Charibes of Dominica are evill neighbours unto it' while, similarly, in the 1620s Sir Thomas Warner, the English governor of St. Kitts, considered Tobago unsuitable for settlement as it was too close to the Spanish of Trinidad and too much Carib traffic was passing by. Indeed, it is recorded that in this period Kali'na from the mainland regularly visited the Windward Islands while Island Caribs travelled to the Guianas and the Venezuelan coastal zone in order to join the Kali'na for war and trade expeditions to the Arawak. Interestingly, various seventeenth-century narratives recorded among the Island Caribs of St. Vincent on their origins mention Tobago as one of the first islands they settled on their mythical movement from the Guianas into the Windward Islands. These tales clearly reflect the island's position intermediate between the South American mainland and the Lesser Antilles.

It were the Dutch who, induced by the soaring price of tobacco on the home market, were the first who attempted to establish an European settlement on Tobago based on the cultivation of tobacco (1628). The Dutch were attracted to Tobago by its excellent natural harbours and, above all, its crucial geographical situation between the Caribbean islands and the Dutch possessions on the coast of the Guianas and Brazil. Besides, the belief that tobacco would grow better in *Tabaco* island than anywhere else in the tropics may have formed part of Tobago's appeal to the European powers in these years. The Dutch colony of Tobago was financed by an enterprising merchant and burgomaster ('mayor') of Flushing (*Vlissingen*) in the province of Zeeland, Jan de Moor, who had already established a series of trading posts along the coast of the Guianas and the Lower Amazon, and acquired the exclusive right to become the patron of a colony of free settlers on Tobago from the Dutch West India Company (WIC) of which he was a participant. While the principal crop to be grown was tobacco, the colonists had the right to carry on 'the inland trade', i.e., with the indigenous Tobagonians. The WIC stipulated that the settlers had to behave properly towards the Amerindians, 'not to rob them and especially not to commit adultery' with the indigenous women. In all a hundred settlers established themselves at Great Courland Bay on Tobago's leeward coast. A major fortification was constructed on top of a steep cliff in present-day Plymouth, Fort *Nieuw Vlissingen* ('New Flushing'), just north of the mouth of the Courland River, while a second, minor stronghold was built at Black Rock. On the flat land along the shore of the bay, in between both forts, a small settlement developed. The area around it was cleared of vegetation and brought under tobacco cultivation. The colony was called *Nieuw Walcheren* after the Zeeland island on which Flushing is situated.

Most likely, the relationship between the Dutch colonists and the Tobago Amerindians was strained. Drawings of the fortifications show guns protecting against approaches from the sea as well as from the interior of the island, i.e., by the local Amerindians. Labour on the tobacco fields was organized in military fashion and continually 'a very good watch' was kept, especially at night, obviously to prevent being surprised by indigenous attacks. Still in 1628 an especially hostile encounter took place somewhere on Tobago's windward coast when a Zeeland warship, which called at the island for watering and refreshing, lost 54 men of its crew after skirmishes with unnamed Amerindians. Besides, apparently the colony was regularly attacked by Island Caribs from Grenada and St. Vincent. This may even have led to a temporary abandonment of the settlement in 1630. Two years later Dutch sailors encountered two enslaved men and a woman on Dominica who had been kidnapped on Tobago by the Island Caribs. *Nieuw Vlissingen* was occupied by a group of some 200 new settlers in 1633. As has been noted above (Chapter 7), the Dutch now affiliated themselves with Hierreyma, the famous leader of the Nepoio of east Trinidad, and established small fortifications here for the shipment to Holland of tobacco grown for them by the Amerindians. Feeling threatened by the Dutch–Nepoio alliance, Escobar, the Spanish governor of Trinidad, decided to strike first by conquering the Dutch trading posts in east Trinidad. In December 1636 he made the crossing to Tobago with a force of 90 Spanish soldiers. Landing at Canoe Bay, they marched overland to Great Courland Bay and surprised the garrison of the small fort at Black Rock. Afterwards the Spanish surrounded Fort *Nieuw Vlissingen*, cutting off Dutch access to the Courland River. By making much noise and stationing groups of soldiers at wide distances around the fortress, Escobar was able to make its garrison believe that it was surrounded by superior forces. The Dutch surrendered on the condition of a free passage to St. Kitts. As we have seen, the Spanish grossly violated the peace agreements, ultimately leading to the sacking of St. Joseph by a multi-ethnic force of Amerindians, including Nepoio under Hierreyma, and the Dutch, in 1637.

Probably still in 1637 a short-lived English attempt at settlement in Tobago was made by a Puritan clergyman from Barbados. However, shortly after anchoring at the island, an exploring party was attacked by (local?) Caribs whereupon the survivors took off. Two years afterwards the Duke of Courland initiated the first of several seventeenth-century efforts his people made to occupy Tobago. At the time Courland, now part of Latvia, was a growing maritime power on the Baltic Sea, commanding a considerable merchant fleet and navy. Probably backed by Dutch bankers, Duke Friedrich of Courland sent a ship to Tobago 'accomodated with trade to buy it of the Indians, and to take possession on it in his Right'. The Duke reportedly concluded a 'Sinister Contract [...] with ye Indians' and the latter 'gaue him a cleare possession' of the island, but the few hundred Courlander settlers soon 'mouldred to nothing', probably due to disease. This same year the first of a series of English efforts to settle on Tobago was made under the patronage of the Earl of Warwick. Most of them were short-lived. A few hundred people led by Captain Masham established a colony in an unknown part of the island in 1639, but had to abandon their settlement due to attacks by Island Caribs from St. Vincent the following year. They sailed to Trinidad, establishing themselves for some time in the Toco area (see Chapter 7). A new group was sent under Captain Marshall to Tobago in 1642. Probably settling at present Carapuse Bay on the windward coast, they planted tobacco and indigo, but were 'often disturbed by the Caribees and at length for want of Supplyes were forced to quitt' in 1643, leaving for Suriname where they were massacred by the Kali'na two years later. A final, similarly unsuccessful, attempt at colonizing Tobago was undertaken by a group of merchants under the Warwick patent in 1646. It probably did not last longer than a few months.

Simultaneously with the last two English efforts to settle in Tobago, a second Courlander colony was established in the southwestern part of the island. In 1642 Duke Jacob (Jekabs), who had just succeeded his father Friedrich, sent a few hundred people from Zeeland led by Captain Caron to Tobago who established themselves under Courlander flag in the present Buccoo/Mount Irvine area. Caron, who had been employed by the WIC in Brazil and was considered in Holland to be a somewhat untrustworthy character, was advised by his old masters in the Dutch Republic 'to carry a faire Correspondancy with the Arrawacoes', suggesting that he was urged to re-establish the trade contacts with the Nepoio and Arawak of Trinidad which the Dutch had in the 1630s. By apparently following this advice, he raised the 'Disgust of the Careebs of St. Vincents, who tooke their advantage, and distroyed a great part of that hopefull Colonie'. While Caron's settlers 'were in this distresse', the Arawak of Trinidad came to the relief of the survivors, taking them to the Pomeroon area of coastal Guiana 'where they became a Flourishing Colonie'. This apparently took place in 1650. Indeed, it has been reported that in this very year the Island Caribs of Dominica (not St. Vincent) were preparing a war expedition to Tobago. All in all, the picture of the period of European settlement in Tobago terminating in the mid-seventeenth century is one of fierce resistance against the subsequent invaders by both the local Amerindians of the island, and especially the Island Caribs of St. Vincent and Grenada: it was Amerindian hostility that ended most early attempts to establish European colonies on Tobago.

Further Dutch and Courlander ventures

By the early 1650s Tobago had become an island unoccupied by Europeans again. For a short period it was left once more to its autochthonous inhabitants and only frequented by ships for watering and refreshing, or seasonally by French fishers and turtlers from Guadeloupe and Martinique. Besides, according to a contemporary source, Island Caribs came to Tobago occasionally in order 'to take refreshments which they needed before going to war against the *Arovagues* [Arawaks], or after returning from such expeditions'. The island was apparently still inhabited primarily by Kali'na. In 1653 or 1654 Father Pelleprat, a French missionary, met a Kali'na (Galibi) chief from Tobago at a major Kali'na village on the Guarapiche River in east Venezuela who had travelled that far with 25 to 30 of his followers for trading purposes. He records a conversation with this Kali'na chief who, on hearing that Pelleprat had arrived from France for proselytizing purposes, wished him to confirm that the priest had not come for trading in cotton, birds or other things. By this time the established French and English colonies in the Lesser Antilles had gradually changed their core economic activity from the cultivation of tobacco to sugar cane. In the 1640s the sugar processing technology was introduced by the Dutch from Brazil simultaneously into the French West Indies, Barbados and St. Kitts. In addition, Dutch merchants supplied the local planters of these islands the necessary credit for investment in sugar machinery and black slaves. Indeed, in these years the importation of African slaves increased considerably while the previously dominating smallholdings of a few acres each, often worked by limited numbers of white indentured servants, were amalgamated to form capital-intensive, large-scale estates operated by the forced labour of a multitude of black slaves.

It was with the purpose of establishing colonies based on sugar that in 1654 both the Courlanders and the Dutch renewed their attempts to settle in Tobago. This time the Courlander enterprise was financed by the Duke himself. A multi-ethnic group of a few hundred people settled under a Dutch governor, Willem Mollens, at and around the old Dutch fortification of Plymouth on Great Courland Bay, baptizing it Fort Jacobus. Tobago was renamed *Neu Kurland* (German for 'New Courland'). A few months later a Dutch (Zeeland) group of colonists arrived at the windward side of the island who established themselves at present Rockly Bay, then called *Roodklip* ('Red Cliff') Bay. Afterwards, they claimed to have concluded a treaty of friendship with the local Amerindians. Indeed, the Courlanders only learned of the Dutch presence at the other side of the island when they came across three Dutchmen who had been left as hostages for the son of an Amerindian chief in a village in the mountainous central part of Tobago. The Courlanders lost no time and immediately overran the Dutch encampment. Although both parties agreed to leave each other undisturbed, the Dutch were forced to accept the nominal sovereignty of the Courlanders over the island. Undeterred, they started to build a town on the shore of Rockly Bay, actually at the site of present Lower Town Scarborough. It was called *Lampsinsstad* after the patrons and financial supporters of the colony, the Lampsins brothers, wealthy merchants from Zeeland. The town had a fortification with the governor's residence, a strong house and an arsenal, as well as warehouses, residences and a church, all constructed along present Milford Road. The entire expanse of the windward coast from Petit Trou and Little Rockly Bay in the southwest to present Hillsborough Bay in the northeast was cleared and gradually brought under cultivation.

The Dutch colony was rapidly strengthened by new immigrants, including groups of Jews and French Huguenots (Protestants), and Dutch planters who left Brazil after its surrender to the Portuguese (1654). The latter took their black slaves and many Amerindian allies with them. Some of these may have been employed as auxiliaries in the renewed Dutch Tobago colony of New Walcheren as they had been in Brazil. All together, in 1662 there were some 1250 white settlers and 400–500 African slaves in the Dutch-occupied part of the island. Four years later there were eighteen sugar mills on Tobago, the majority of which were operated by animal traction. By this time *Lampsinsstad* had become a major centre of regional trade and Tobago was becoming the store of European manufactures for the Lesser Antilles. Apart from sugar cane, the Dutch planted a variety of tropical crops for export to the mother country, such as cotton, cocoa, indigo, cassia fistula (golden shower tree), roucou, and tobacco while cattle and horses were imported for stock breeding. Apart from agriculture, hunting, turtling and fishing were practised. In addition, the Dutch cut dyewoods in the present Bloody Bay area. (The latter name is derived from this activity which coloured its water red.) Meanwhile, the Courlander colony on the leeward side of Tobago was faring less well. In spite of regular reinforcements and new settlers, sent by the Duke of Courland, the mixed population of New Courland dwindled due to illnesses and Amerindian attacks. All together, the colony never had more than some 500 inhabitants, mainly white farmers and soldiers.

From the outset the Courlanders wished to establish a trade relationship with the Tobago Kali'na. In 1654 Mollens reported that the latter had five villages on the island. Each of these settlements probably consisted of one extended family as he notes that each hamlet counted some 25 people under a captain, having one (war) canoe. According to a map, probably drawn by Mollens, one of these villages was situated close to the Courlander settlement, probably in present Plymouth. Hoping to conclude a treaty of friendship with the Amerindians, the Courlanders exchanged iron axes, knives and mirrors for hammocks with the Kali'na. Indeed, the Lutheran pastor, serving the Courlander community, had been instructed by Duke Jacob to study the indigenous language so as 'to look to it seriously that the minds of the savages could be directed to proper revelation of God'. He had to avoid any kind of religious dispute, but in every case 'to act with gentleness and tenderness'. Noting that the Kali'na ('Kriben') of Tobago went to war against the Arawak of Trinidad and the mainland, Mollens commented that the latter were accustomed to visit the island in 50–60 canoes, each containing some 25 warriors. The Kali'na would be 'very worried about these arawacoes for they are hellishly strong and begin large battles'. Apparently Arawaks from the mainland and Island Caribs from St. Vincent attacked the Courlander settlement several times, killing various of its inhabitants. Although in 1655 the Courlanders were still able to send a ship with tropical produce home, three years later their situation had worsened to such an extent that a Dutchman could report that only some fifty Courlanders remained of the original population who, besides, were unable to work on their farmlands for fear of leaving the fort 'on account of epidemics and the savages who are hunting them'. When due to war in Europe the Duke was unable to send supplies to Tobago, the Dutch incited a mutiny among the garrison of Fort Jacobus and in 1659 the Courlander colony was incorporated into that of the Lampsins.

Although documentary evidence that the Dutch colony on Tobago's windward coast was ever attacked by Amerindians is lacking, it is recorded that individual estate owners near present Hillsborough Bay fortified their houses 'against incursions of the Savages'. This suggests that these raids occasionally took place. One of the planters in this area reportedly had a small fortification around his house with two cannons. Obviously, *Lampsinsstad* was too populous and well defended to be attacked by the Amerindians. After the incorporation of the Courlander colony, the Dutch fortified the leeward coast against Island Carib attacks by refurbishing the Courlander fortification at Plymouth and by constructing a redoubt called *Belleviste* in the Buccoo/Mount Irvine area in order to 'prevent the Indians to disembark here'. The Dutch demanded that visiting Island Caribs obtained permission to land on Tobago from the governor of the island. Also, the inhabitants of the small, isolated community of Sandy Point at the southwestern tip of Tobago, where during the dry season potable water could be obtained only from wells, fortified one of these 'cisterns', undoubtedly in order to prevent interference with the water supply by the Amerindians. Nevertheless it is recorded that in 1660 the leeward part of Tobago suffered a major attack by Amerindians (Island Caribs?) during which the Dutch used the old Courlander supply of gunpowder.

The flourishing Lampsins colony came to an end due to the increased rivalry among the European powers. The Dutch trade monopoly annoyed both the French and English governments to such an extent that they initiated a series of attempts to shut out the Dutch from the West Indian market by proclaiming 'navigation laws' which (to the dismay of the planters) forbade foreigners to purchase the produce of their colonies. After the English Crown had vowed official support for the Courlander claim to Tobago, the patron of New Walcheren, Cornelis Lampsins, sought support from the French. By paying a considerable sum of money to the French monarch, he was raised to a peerage and made the Baron of Tobago. Actual support for the Dutch colony was not forthcoming, however, and during the Second Anglo–Dutch War *Lampsinsstad* was captured and plundered by a party of Jamaican buccaneers (1666). They just forstalled a force of a few hundred men from Barbados, assisted by Island Carib auxiliaries. The buccaneers 'destroyed all that they could not carry away'; only the fortress and the governor's house were spared. The English left a small garrison which after a few months in its turn was overrun by a small French force from Grenada. Finally, the Dutch led by the Zeeland admiral Crijnssen retook the island in 1667 after having conquered the English colony of Suriname. Some members of Crijnssen's crew accidentally met an Amerindian while walking along the beach, probably at Rockly Bay. Invited to pay a visit to the latter's village, they passed through a forest and arrived at another side of the island. Here they came across a large number of Amerindians, altogether more than a hundred men, armed with bows, arrows and war clubs. At last they arrived at a village consisting of some fifty houses where they shared a meal and some cassava beer with the Amerindians. They parted in friendship. Crijnssen now restored the fortification of *Lampsinsstad*, leaving a small garrison to protect the remnants of the town.

New settlers and soldiers were sent from Zeeland to Tobago by the Lampsins family in 1668. An attempt was made to rebuild *Lampsinsstad* and to resume the cultivation of cash crops. Settlement apparently took place in a more random manner than before and new areas on the windward coast were occupied. The colony was ill-fated, however. While the Dutch commander reported soon after disembarkation that a friendly relationship was kept up with the local Kali'na (Galibis), who counted sixty good archers, the settlement was attacked by twenty pirogues with 150 Nepoio ('Nipoirs') from Trinidad only a few months later. Assisted by the Kali'na, the Dutch were able to repulse this assault. The Kali'na were rewarded with iron axes, cutlasses and knives. Soon, however, an attack by Island Caribs from St. Vincent took place which cost the lives of 19 men, women and children. The planters and the governor of the island now petitioned the States of Zeeland to send more soldiers and some vessels in order 'to keep free the coast from the barbarians'. To no avail, and the outbreak of the Third Anglo–Dutch War, in which the French sided with the English, meant the end of the second Lampsins colony. The island was taken by a force from Barbados which looted and destroyed the fort and all buildings. After what was to become known as the 'Tobago Plunder', many planters, their African slaves and cattle were taken to Barbados. Numerous slaves escaped to the forest, however. Some 75 black slaves were captured and taken to the Windward Islands by a party of Island Caribs 'who came thither to glean up such remains of plunder as the English had left'.

By the Peace of Westminster, which ended the Third Anglo–Dutch War (1674), Tobago was awarded to the Dutch again. The heirs of the Lampsins now sold their colony to the States of Holland and West Frisia and with the Dutch still at war with France, the responsibility for the defence of Tobago was given to the Admiralty of Amsterdam. A squadron under Admiral Binckes with new colonists was sent from Holland in 1676. It was decided to construct a new fortification in former *Lampsinsstad*, the *Sterreschans* ('Star Fort'), close to the old one built in the 1650s, actually at present Dutch Fort. Binckes was unable to finish the work on the stronghold before Tobago was attacked by a French force under the Count d'Estrées in February/March 1677. A murderous encounter between the French and Dutch fleets took place in Rockly Bay.[42] Severe losses forced the French to withdraw, but d'Estrées returned with a new squadron in December 1677. Now he

42 An elaborately ornamented French cannon and two simple Dutch ones, recovered archaeologically from ships sunk during this battle in Rockly Bay, have been mounted at Scarborough's harbour.

was able to take the *Sterreschans* after an explosion in the Dutch powder magazine had killed Binckes and half the fort's garrison. D'Estrées took 600 prisoners whom he carried to Martinique. Some 70 to 80 black slaves, who had hidden in the woods during the Dutch–French hostilities, were captured by Island Caribs who, after the departure of the French, came to search for booty in five or six pirogues. They were seized by an English expedition sent from the Leeward Islands and after some years the slaves were returned to the Dutch. Peace was concluded between the Dutch and the French in 1678. Although throughout the 1680s and indeed as late as 1699 the States General of the Dutch Republic were petitioned for approval of schemes for settlement of Tobago, actual efforts to occupy the island were no longer made by the Dutch.

Following the demise of the Dutch colony, for a while Tobago was used only occasionally by Barbadians for hunting wild hogs and woodcutting. As the French neglected to establish themselves on the island, the Duke of Courland seized the opportunity to make a new series of attempts to found a colony on Tobago's leeward coast. In 1680 a new fortification was built at Stone Haven Bay by a small group of soldiers in Courlander service led by the English lieutenant Bennet, but lack of provisions and attacks from Island Caribs forced him to leave Tobago again the next year, just before the arrival of a multi-ethnic group of a few hundred Courlander settlers under a Scottish colonel, Monck. Finding the colony in a bad shape, the latter decided to construct a new fortification at Rocky Point. While being instructed by the Duke of Courland to conclude treaties of friendship with the Indians of the Windward Islands and Trinidad, Monck was soon assaulted by Island Caribs from St. Vincent and St. Lucia, aided by French interlopers, 'as wild and savage' as the Amerindians themselves, as the governor of Barbados noted. Illnesses decimated his people and as a relief party never reached Tobago, in 1683 Monck decided to abandon the colony. Again, Tobago was left for some years to the resident Amerindians (about whom nothing is reported in these years) and to be used only for turtling and hunting or woodcutting by visiting foreigners. Probably during a Barbadian woodcutting trip in 1684 an English longboat was taken by the 'natives' at Tobago and the crew killed.

Meanwhile, Duke Jacob, who died in 1682, and his successor Duke Friedrich Casimir, had entered negotiations with an English merchant-adventurer from Barbados, Captain John Poyntz, to have Tobago settled by Englishmen under Courlander flag. Poyntz reportedly visited Tobago several times and wrote a glowing prospectus on Tobago and its possibilities of colonization which would be published in London in 1683.[43] Calling Tobago 'the most Convenient, Commodious, and Salubrious Island in the Caribes', it extolled its virtues and opportunities. Besides, at the time Poyntz befriended the 'Indian Emperor of Trinidad', a Kali'na, whom he allowed to board his vessel together with his 'war captain', their wives and sons. This Amerindian, who would have been travelling to Tobago 'with thousands of his vassals', assured Poyntz of his peaceful intentions. The latter took the 'Emperor's' son to Barbados where he was presented to the governor. Afterwards

---

43 Reissued in 1695, this prospectus would become Daniel Defoe's main source for his description of the uninhabited island in the Caribbean where his immortal hero Robinson Crusoe was shipwrecked.

Poyntz exchanged names with him, the traditional Amerindian way of accepting individuals as linked by kinship. As late as 1704 one of Poyntz's associates referred to this Kali'na chief as the 'Emperor of the Carib nation', stating that he 'comes once a year, in his periagoes processioning round the Island of Tobago, claiming it as his own'. Nothing came of Poyntz's schemes, however, and in 1683 the English Crown ordered him to cease all preparations for Courlander settlement. Fears that Tobago, if properly cultivated, would be able to compete favourably in sugar production with Barbados and, moreover, would 'steal' the English trade to the latter island, were behind this decision.

The last Courlander attempts to colonize Tobago were made in the late 1680s. A new multi-ethnic group of settlers, led by a German commander, Captain Schmoll, arrived at the island in 1686. They built a new fortification at present Mount Irvine; reinforcements were sent by the Duke of Courland the following year. An effort to exchange timber for provisions and manufactures at Barbados failed as its governor forbade the trade, obeying London's policy which rejected Courlander rights to Tobago. Nevertheless, an English frigate assisted the settlers in fighting a party of Amerindians, probably Island Caribs, and a French barque from Martinique. A diary kept by a Dutch sailor in Courlander service, Jan Waebes, from 1686 to 1688 records the hostilities with these Island Caribs who apparently mingled with local Amerindians from the southwestern part of Tobago, near present Crown Point. Waebes' diary suggests that the local Amerindians 'wished to trade in all friendship' with the Courlanders and indeed did so, e.g., by supplying the settlers with fish. Some thirty of them visited the fortification with their wives and a few children. After a month the first 'foreign' Amerindians appeared, significantly showing French flags at their canoes, simultaneously with a French barque. An English frigate from Barbados, which subsequently arrived in Little Courland Bay, captured the French vessel and some pirogues 'full of Indians with some white men among them'. During the hostilities which followed several Courlanders were killed by the Amerindians. After a few months Schmoll surveyed the southwestern part of Tobago, but was unable to spot any pirogues here. Nevertheless the hostile encounters between the Courlanders and the Amerindians continued.

Meanwhile, the number of settlers steadily diminished due to sicknesses which reached epidemic proportions in the rainy months at the end of the year. By then already one-third of the colonists had died. As the Amerindians kept harassing the Courlanders, Schmoll attacked some of the Amerindian encampments near Crown Point. Several Courlander soldiers now deserted into the woods, but were killed by the 'savages'. In March 1687 Schmoll left Tobago with most remaining colonists and soldiers. Only two months later a ship with provisions and new settlers reached the island, discovering that, after having been abandoned, the Courlander fortification and buildings had been destroyed by a French party which accidentally visited the island. After the fort had been refurbished, the hostilities started again in 1688. In all 800 Amerindians reportedly now assaulted the colonists who were forced to use artillery and did not dare to leave the fort any longer. Finally, most settlers shipped on board an English vessel bound for Barbados with a cargo of wood chopped in Tobago. In 1693 a Danish captain called at Tobago and met a few Courlanders still living on the island. They said that they had not seen a Courlander ship for six years. Apparently, the colonists had been left in peace by the Amerindians for some time as they claimed to have piled up a large quantity of tropical produce for shipment. This represents the last report of Courlanders on Tobago as soon the last survivors left for Barbados. Although the Dukes of Courland held to their claims to Tobago throughout the eighteenth century, actual attempts at settling the island were no longer made by the Courlanders.

A peaceful interlude: Tobago as a 'neutral' island

Though claimed by France and Britain, Tobago now became a no man's land for more than half a century. It was only used occasionally for refreshing and refitting by warships of both countries in order to uphold their rights to the island. Meanwhile, the northern part of Tobago developed into a pirates' nest in spite of regular expeditions sent from Barbados to suppress buccaneer activities. In 1694 a Barbadian sloop, which had called at Tobago for trade with the local Amerindians, was captured by French privateers. It had the sons of some Amerindian 'kings' from Trinidad on board who wished to visit Barbados 'to make peace and settle trade' with the English. The sloop was taken to Martinique and a 'very considerable cargo' was lost. Also, in 1723 an English warship surprised a group of pirates who were using Man-of-War Bay, part of which is still known as Pirates' Bay, for refitting their vessels. The outlaws fled into the woods, but were reportedly taken by the British as the result of some treachery by Amerindians who had originally befriended them. Groups of Barbadians frequently visited Tobago in these years for periods of two or three months to cut timber, fire-wood and dyewoods. The ever 'wood-hungry' Barbadians even declared that 'Tobago is to Barbados as a piece of woodland to a private person'. Furthermore, the island was inhabited by a fluctuating group of Amerindians and some dozens of Barbadians, Spanish and French turtlers (*coureurs des* îles), the latter from Martinique and Guadeloupe, all of whom came to Tobago periodically during the turtling season.

By the early-eighteenth century Tobago became a refuge area for Amerindians of the mainland as well as the Lesser Antilles (Fig. 43). In the 1730s the island was invaded by groups of Chaima and Pariagoto Amerindians from Cumaná and the Paria peninsula who wished to escape from the attempts of Aragonese Capuchins to concentrate them in mission villages. According to Spanish records, many Chaima were induced by French itinerant traders to go with them to Tobago. Furthermore, in the early 1740s groups of Island Caribs from St. Vincent sought refuge in Tobago under pressure of their growing conflicts with the increasingly powerful Black Caribs, escaped African slaves mainly from Barbados who had mingled with the existing Amerindians on the island. Both the French and British attempted to influence the indigenous inhabitants of Tobago by gifts and signs of friendship. Accordingly, in 1714 the acting governor of Barbados informed London that he had encouraged the Tobago Amerindians to continue their alliance to the British Crown. An act of wishful thinking as the latter instead closely associated (and intermarried) with the French turtlers who formed the majority of the Europeans

Figure 43. Conventionalized picture of an Amerindian couple, shown in cartouche of an English manuscript map of Great Courland Bay, Tobago, by John Byrne, 1760. Coll. THM.

on the island. By this time the Amerindian population of the Lesser Antilles in general had started to decline steeply. Imported diseases such as smallpox, measles, chicken pox, influenza, and diphtheria, spreading through human contact, obviously formed the major factors in the diminution of the indigenous people of the archipelago. The Island Caribs probably were in relatively good health as late as the 1650s, due to their dispersed occupation pattern in the Lesser Antilles and the separation of their villages on the various islands, all of which contributed to isolation of potential focuses of infection. The steep decline in population seen towards the end of the seventeenth century may have been due to the importation of African diseases such as yellow fever and malaria, which probably spread due to the increased presence of escaped black slaves among the Island Caribs in these years.

A bold attempt to break the status quo between the French and the British was made by the governor of Martinique, the Marquess de Caylus, in 1749. Some 300 buccaneers from the French West Indies assisted by Island Carib auxiliaries were sent to Tobago, who started the construction of a fortification at Lambeau Hill on Rockly Bay. In order to establish friendly relations with the local Amerindians, the French took along a great quantity of glass beads and some 60 Flemish knives for gift giving. On learning of this expedition, the governor of Barbados sent some men-of-war to Tobago, ordering the French to leave. The incident ended peacefully with the French ships sailing back to Martinique, leaving some 150 French settlers and Island Caribs. Meanwhile the governments of France and Britain had followed up on an earlier French proposal and concluded the Treaty of Aix-la-Chapelle, assigning a neutral status to Tobago, Dominica, St. Vincent, and St. Lucia (1748). The French agreed to evacuate all four islands and their fortification at Lambeau was burned and the settlers removed. Not all of the Island Caribs returned, however. While in the 1740s there may have been a few dozen Chaima in the island, and less than a hundred local Kali'na and some 40 Island Caribs who had fled from St. Vincent, Caylus' expedition led to the settlement of a further group of 80 Island Caribs from Martinique. In 1757 an English sea captain notified the governor of Barbados that there were some 300 families of Amerindians on Tobago, of whom two-thirds belonged to 'the flat headed tribe', most likely Island Caribs, who inhabited the southern part of Tobago, while one-third were 'Red Indians', probably Kali'na (Galibis), occupying its northern portion. The two nations were 'at peace', and behaved 'in a friendly manner to each other'; both seemed 'to live in great union with the French'. Indeed, most of the Amerindians of the two groups spoke French. Besides, Tobago was visited seasonally for fishing purposes by Amerindians of the Guianas.

British maps drawn after surveys of the island in the 1760s indicate that at the time the principal Amerindian village was situated just west of the mouth of the Great River on present Goldsborough Bay. Other, smaller settlements were to be found on present King's Bay, at Belle Garden on Carapuse Bay and Richmond Bay. A British map published in 1765 shows the abode of a certain 'Indian King Cardinal with his Wives and about 80 People' on a hill at the back of present Prince's Bay, west of the Roxborough River. Besides, according to this map, a 'King Peter the Indian Chief with about 14 or 16 People' lived on the Caribbean coast, actually close to the inlet which at present is still known as King Peter's Bay. (The name of an estate just east of Moriah, Indian Walk, probably reminds of this same 'King Peter'.) Finally, this map shows the residence of the 'Indian King Rouselle with his Wives and People about 30 in Number' on present Signal Hill at the back of Lambeau. However, this was not a 'pure' Amerindian, but the son of a Frenchman from La Rochelle, André Jadouïn, who lived with his Island Carib wife at Great Courland Bay in 1748 and 1752. A bridle path connected Rouselle's abode with Petit Trou, while another one linked Buccoo Bay with La Guira, passing through present Canaan. La Guira was reportedly established as a mission post for the 'conversion of the Indians' by Spanish priests from Trinidad in the mid-eighteenth century. (The toponym is derived from *guairia* or *guaira*, the name of a specific type of Venezuelan vessel provided with a triangular sail.) By this time, due to their association with the French turtlers, the Amerindians of Tobago had become thoroughly gallicized, speaking French and influenced by French culture. In fact, only one present toponym in the island is of originally Amerindian (Island Carib) derivation, Man-of-War Bay, which represents a meaningful English corruption of *mánhore* (*manowa*, *man-o'-war*), the indigenous name of the magnificent frigatebird. This bird, which is reported by Poyntz with reference to Tobago as early as 1683, 'makes to the shipping some distance from the Coast, ere ever the Seaman can discover Land'.

From marginalization to extinction

Tobago's definite development as a plantation colony was initiated after the conclusion of the Seven Years' War in 1763 when France ceded its claims to the island to Britain. The following year the actual occupation of Tobago took place when the first lieutenant-governor, Alexander Brown, landed in present King's Bay. According to his private secretary, George Gibbs, the ship was welcomed by the 'Charaib chieftain' of Tobago's windward coast, Cardinal, who 'came off in his Canoe, to pay a visit of Respect'. His people are described by Gibbs as short in stature, but well proportioned, muscular and active, showing a copper-coloured skin and 'long and coarse black hair' flowing 'loosely on their shoulders'. Men and women went naked 'with the exception of a small clout [cloth] passing between the legs, attached by a girdle of twines of different colours, in which was held their knife'. In 1766 Gibbs visited Rouselle in the Signal Hill area. In spite of the latter's mixed parentage, Gibbs called him 'an Indian chief [...] settled in a vale, at a short distance from Rockly Bay'. He had noted already that the Carib women did all the house work and the labour of the garden, also making 'articles for domestic use'. Rouselle showed Gibbs a separate hut where his wives and daughters were at work, some making cassava bread and others spinning 'from the distaff'. One woman was weaving a cotton hammock, using a loom. On a plot of ground, close to the hut, the women cultivated Indian yams, sweet potatoes, cassava, plantains, and sugar cane. Rouselle offered Gibbs and his party huts to stay overnight and supplied the British with wild meats and fowl, as well as conchs, river mullets and oysters from Buccoo Reef.

Meanwhile, the British plans for the settlement and agricultural development of Tobago were in an advanced state of preparation. The island was surveyed and mapped, and divided into lots of 100 to 500 acres which were put up for sale to planters, while fortifications were established at strategic points along the shoreline. The forested area on the Main Ridge was reserved as Crown Lands for the supply of timber and to conserve water supplies. Besides, small lots of 10–30 acres were allocated to 'poor settlers'. These were situated on the edges of the swampy forelands of the larger river estuaries or on waterless tracts in the southwest of the island. Part or all of this land set aside for 'poor settlers' was apparently meant for resident Amerindians. Also, specific lots were assigned to them, for instance on the leeward coast to 'King Peter the Indian Chief' and his family, at Signal Hill to Rouselle, and at Studley Park on the windward coast to 'the Indian Francis and his family'. Land sales continued until 1771. By this year the entire island (except the Main Ridge Reserve) had been given out to private enterprise. Planters from Barbados, England, Ireland, and especially Scotland flocked in. Land clearing operations rapidly progressed. Most land was brought under sugar cane or cotton cultivation although pimento (allspice), cinnamon, ginger, nutmeg, and indigo were grown as well. Many sugar estates also had rum distilleries, and numerous cattle, horses and mules were imported. The projected towns developed less easily. Only Scarborough, the present capital, and to a lesser extent Plymouth materialized. Population grew exponentially: in 1780 the island had 474 white inhabitants and 10,613 African slaves. As late as 1777 there were still a few hundred Amerindians living on Tobago. The excessive labour involved in the land clearing operations and in general the harsh living conditions of the black population led to slave insurrections in 1769, 1771 and 1774. They were put down by the militia, possibly with the assistance of the local Amerindians. The runaway slaves either took refuge in the 'high woods' or fled to the Toco area of northeast Trinidad. They were joined by groups of Tobagonian Caribs. Due to the clearing of the forests the hunting grounds of the Amerindians became more and more limited 'and their dwellings were open to intrusion', as a result of which parties of them abandoned the island, settling in northeast Trinidad where there were still vast forests. (The Toco area has remained a favourite area for migrating Tobagonians until the present.)

Although after 1778 various efforts were taken to strengthen Tobago's defence, including the construction of Fort King George, they proved insufficient when a French force attacked and conquered the island in 1781. Officially ceded by Britain to France two years afterwards, the agricultural development of the island progressed uninterruptedly. Population increased moderately. In 1786 the island had 437 white inhabitants, 149 free coloureds, 11,638 African slaves, and as few as 24 Amerindians (Caribs), the latter residing at Man-of-War Bay. Four years later only five Amerindians were counted, living on the islet of Little Tobago. In 1793 Tobago changed hands again when the British retook the island. Sugar exports peaked in the 1790s while due to falling prices cotton cultivation declined drastically. The expression 'as wealthy as a Tobago planter', current in these years, is suggestive of the prosperity of the island's plantocracy. The few remaining Amerindians led a marginalized existence, far from the island's major centres of population. Three families of Red (Yellow) Caribs reportedly lived in a corner of Betsy's Hope (present Louis d'Or) estate, then owned by Sir William Young (Junior), opposite Queen's Island in the 1790s. (At present this part of Louis d'Or is still called Indian Point.) Recording his meeting with 'chief' Louis of the 'Charaibes' living on his estate in 1792, Young, a wealthy planter who was to be governor of Tobago between 1807 and 1815, noted that Louis was only five years old when his father and family fled from St. Vincent because of Black Carib pressure some fifty years previously, around 1740. The family was since divided into three distinct ones by increase in numbers. Louis is portrayed as 'a very sensible man' who 'in his traffick of fish and other articles, has obtained some knowledge of the French language'. Young was impressed by the appearance of two of the young women in Louis' family, calling them 'really handsome', but continued that the 'old Indian dress is lost' as they wore 'handkerchiefs, cotton petticoats, and jackets like the negroes'. In 1803 only three families of Island Caribs, in all 26 individuals, were still living on Tobago. (The island was ceded to France for a second time at the Treaty of Amiens in 1802, but was recaptured by the British as soon as the Napoleonic Wars reopened the year after.) Seven years later reportedly only one Island Carib family of some twenty people, that of Louis, was left in Tobago. Louis now resided on the north coast of the island 'amidst the woods and near the beach of a small unfrequented bay (for fishing)'. When inspecting the coastal batteries about 1810, Young was introduced to two European-dressed Caribs, probably members of Louis' family, who had been enrolled with the militia artillery. Louis visited Young three times during the latter's governorship of Tobago, each time accompanied by his two sons who were carrying a turtle. They were the last recorded Amerindian residents of the island.

9. Mission villages in Spanish Trinidad (1686–1797)

Initiated in 1686, the novel Spanish policy of establishing mission villages among the Amerindians of Trinidad, aimed at pacifying them, was quite successful in the long run: it ensured the gradual conversion and Hispanicizing of many of the island's indigenous inhabitants and hence their political submission. However, this process did not take place without major setbacks, first, the revolt which in 1699 destroyed one of the missions, Arenales in the centre of Trinidad, and led to the killing of the local missionaries, the island's governor and several colonial officials. Second, it proved impossible to found stable mission villages along Trinidad's south and east coasts as a result of violent attacks by Warao from the mainland, who themselves were under Spanish pressure in the Orinoco Valley and delta. Besides, the northeastern coastal zone remained an area of refuge for Amerindians of varying ethnicity from the mainland, the Windward Islands and Tobago as well as for runaway slaves from the latter island. During the eighteenth century it was the gradual decline in population due to imported sicknesses, against which the Trinidad Amerindians had no resistance, that reduced their power, and the French (and African) immigration of the 1780s that minimized their demographic relevance. By this time they had been fully reconciled with their subordinate position in the island, being largely assimilated to Spanish language, culture and society.

Establishment of Capuchin missions in Spanish Trinidad

Throughout the Spanish empire mission villages were typically frontier institutions, designed to convert, discipline, Hispanicize, and exploit the Amerindians who were compelled to live in them. They were subjected to religious instruction, rudimentary learning to read and write, and industrial training by being taught crafts, agriculture and stockbreeding. The mission was a village with the indigenous inhabitants performing both civil and religious duties. Generally speaking, the missionaries had absolute authority over the Amerindians during the mission's first twenty years of existence, known as a *pueblo de viva conversión* (or *reducción*). Afterwards the mission became a *pueblo de doctrina* over which civil authority was assumed by the Spanish government, while the missionary authority was limited to spiritual matters. Now a *corregidor* (chief magistrate) was appointed by the government as the mission's administrative and executive officer while the Church assigned a *cura doctrinero* as the priest in charge. The common attitude of the clergy was authoritarian paternalism and in varying degrees the regime they imposed was maintained by force. The Capuchins were experienced missionaries who had been active in Cumaná (Venezuela) for several decades when in 1686 the Spanish Crown ordered twelve Catalan Capuchins to travel to Trinidad in order to 'reduce' its Amerindians by founding mission villages. Arriving in August 1687, after some months most of them embarked on a voyage by pirogue along the west coast, ascending the Guaracara and Cipero rivers and walking along trails, guided by Amerindians, in order to select locations for the establishment of mission villages in west, central and south Trinidad. The mission sites were chosen taking into account the density of the indigenous population, the availability of a fresh water supply, access to the sea and/or the local agricultural potential. More priests arrived in 1691, deciding to establish additional missions, especially along Trinidad's south coast.

In all five missions were founded by the Capuchin priests among the Nepoio of west and central Trinidad, who from now on were called the 'Naparima Indians' in order to distinguish them from the Nepoio (and Arawaks) of the *encomiendas*, also referred to as the 'commands' (Fig. 39).[44] The first mission village, *La Purísima Concepción de María Santísima de Guayria*, was established at the foot of Naparima Hill on the Gulf of Paria in 1687. Its location, reportedly near the villages of three indigenous chiefs, is well known since the ruined church of the then abandoned mission was still standing, just north of present St. Vincent Street, when the Spanish planned the layout of the town of San Fernando in 1786. Clearly, the mission occupied the hill slopes north of Mariquire Valley with a landing place in the bay to the west. The oldest town of San Fernando had a central market square, the Plaza de San Carlos, between St. Vincent and Chacon Streets. It is now known as the 'Old Cemetery', a name which may reflect the mission. At the 'small port' of Guayria the island's Lieutenant-Governor was stationed in order to 'guard and protect' the converted Amerindians. Almost 10 km to the east, as the crow flies, another Capuchin mission settlement, *La Anunciata de Nazaret de Savana Grande*, was founded in the vicinity of nine indigenous villages (perhaps exaggeratingly estimated to be occupied by a thousand Amerindians), north of the present centre of Princes Town. The Roman Catholic church of this town, which Spanish-speaking Trinidadians called *La Misión* until recently, still stands at the site of the former mission, founded in 1687, relatively far from the current town which developed in the nineteenth century. A third mission, *Santa Ana de Savaneta* (*Sabaneta*), was established in 1687 near two indigenous villages on the left bank of the Savonetta River, a tributary of the Rivulet River. It was situated on top of a ridge in a former sugar cane area some 250 m west of the Sir Solomon Hochoy Highway, close to the Couva crossover.[45] Between 1700 and 1705 a fourth mission village, *Nuestra Señora de Montserrate*, was founded west of the Mayo River, a right tributary of the Guaracara River, in the Montserrat Hills of west Trinidad. Its location is exactly known, too. As at Savana Grande, the Montserrate mission occupied the area around the present Roman Catholic church in the centre of the village of Mayo, which originated in the mid-nineteenth century at the location

44 In 1680 it was reported that Trinidad was inhabited by Naparima Indians and Arawaks of whom the latter were 'unconverted albeit very docile'.

45 The indigenous name is derived from that of a small tree (*savonette*), the roots of which were traditionally used as a means of stupifying fish.

of the former mission settlement. (In the 1850s there still existed 'a few vestiges' of the then deserted mission.) Finally, a fifth mission village, *San Francisco de los Arenales*, was founded early in 1688 on the bank of the Arena River, southeast of present San Rafael (Tumpuna) in central Trinidad. Its original site is not precisely known, although it is claimed to have been located by a French Dominican priest in 1885, using local Spanish/Amerindian oral traditions.

Attempts to establish stable missions along the south and southeast coasts of the island proved abortive as none of these survived for more than a decade and often less. On the east coast a Capuchin mission, *San Francisco de los Cocos*, was settled on Cocos Bay, perhaps near the Nariva River, in 1689. It was abandoned for unknown reasons this same year. In the southeast the mission of *San Joseph de Mayaro* was founded in 1691 on the shore of Mayaro Bay, possibly at present St. Joseph, north of Pierreville. Some of its inhabitants fled from the mission the following year while others revolted in 1697. Those captured were taken to Guayria. The Mayaro mission existed perhaps until 1698. On the south coast the easternmost Capuchin mission, *San Francisco de Careiro* (*Cariero*), was founded probably at Guayaguayare in 1691. It was attacked by Warao from the mainland in 1693 and 1697, on the latter occasion the two resident priests barely escaping assassination. The mission was abandoned the following year. Its exact location is not known, although an archaeological site yielding Mayoid ceramics associated with historic glass beads is known from the western end of Guayaguayare Bay.[46] Further west along the south coast another abortive mission was founded, probably among Arawaks, in 1691 near the Moruga River at a location where reportedly the English had a small fort (half a century previously). It was abandoned before 1706. Finally, another Capuchin mission village was founded on the Cedros Peninsula near the Serpent's Mouth, a reportedly 'well populated' area. It probably lasted less than a year.

The missions were supposed to resemble miniature versions of Spanish towns. Ideally a square formed the centre of the mission settlement. Its eastern side was occupied by the church, the presbytery and store houses with food stocks and agricultural instruments. The other communal buildings, such as the *casa de cabildo* for village meetings and craft shops, were often to be found on the north side of the plaza. The church, which was invariably east–west oriented, dominated the village. In Trinidad it had walls of *tapia* and a thatched roof, with statues of coloured wood inside. (The original church of the Savaneta mission measured 8.4×4.3 m.) The Amerindian houses were laid out in orderly pattern within the mission confines. They were rectangular and provided with some form of attic. On average one house would have sheltered some 9.5 people. It is not known whether all Capuchin missions in Trinidad resembled this ideal layout. In several cases perhaps a church was built close to an existing Amerindian settlement without forcing its inhabitants to move into a newly designed mission village, which they had to build themselves. At any rate, the missions in west Trinidad were connected with each other by old indigenous footpaths, some of which would

---

46 These beads include seventeenth to eighteenth-century Spanish beads, including two cornaline d'Aleppo seed beads (1575-1820) and numerous embroidery beads.

develop into 'Royal Roads'. For instance, an Amerindian dirt track went from the Guayria mission to the east, passing south of the Mariquire Valley through present High Street and Coffee Street to the Naparima–Mayaro Road, which leads to the former Savana Grande mission and still traverses Princes Town. Montserrate was connected with Savaneta by the present Mayo Road, which beyond Tortuga is still known as the Indian Trail Road and passes through a hamlet called Indian Chain.

From the outset the tasks of the missionaries were clear to Trinidad's governor: to begin with baptizing the Amerindians, then teaching them to work for wages, in order first to buy clothes so as to abandon their habit of going to church naked, and then to pay a small tribute to the Crown. The missions were self-supporting agricultural colonies; the resident Amerindians cultivated cassava, maize, bananas and cocoa on the village's common grounds. The profits were used for decorating the church, the furniture of the presbytery and the rations of the missionaries. Two days a week were entirely devoted to cocoa production (which demanded limited labour), four days to work on the Amerindians' own plots, cultivating food crops for themselves or for sale. The Sundays were for religious instruction. The latter was facilitated by the availability of Chaima grammars in Savana Grande and Montserrate, while in 1714 the Savaneta mission had two (now lost) manuscripts, apparently put together by the local priests, on the Naparima language.[47] The missionaries could call on the Amerindians for work on the church, presbytery or cemetery. They were obliged as well under the *mita* to work outside the missions for the Spanish landowners during a limited time period. The Capuchin priests had full judicial powers and could inflict corporal punishment by whipping or have unruly Amerindians put into the local prison. Although each mission was supposed to have its own *cacique* or *capitán* (chief) and *cabildo* (council), as well as *regidores* (councillors), *alcaldes* (magistrates), and *alguaciles* (policemen), the paternalistic authority of the priests was unlimited. Until 1696, the latter received an annual allowance from the colonial treasury; the Amerindians did not pay any tithes or fees to the priests and were exempted from paying tribute for twenty years. Chiefs were given the title '*don*' and had special uniforms and insignia. The Naparima missions as a whole had one 'General', trained by the Spanish, who commanded the male warriors acting as 'ethnic soldiers'. Festivals were held on the name days of the patron saints of the missions. From now on, the Nepoio and Arawak of Trinidad are referred to by Spanish rather than indigenous personal names in the historic documents, suggesting their relative acculturation to Spanish society.

Escaping remained the major problem of the Trinidad missions. As the governor of Trinidad wrote to the Crown in 1694, the Amerindians preferred to live in their own way in the forests and did not wish to settle in missions. Their mutinous behaviour was encouraged by attacks on the missions carried out by Warao (Guarano, Guarauno, Guaraoon) from the mainland who saw the Amerindians living in them as allies of the Spanish. By this time the Warao, mainly occupying the delta of the Orinoco, were under pressure from the Spanish who attempted to enslave them. In 1694 a priest from Guayria complained that this mission had been

47 In 1732 it was noted that Nepoio and Naparima represented 'the common language' of the Amerindians in Trinidad's missions.

attacked the previous year by Warao, aiding local Amerindians who were hiding in the forests and mountains and inciting the inhabitants of the mission to revolt. Indeed, all attempts to found missions along Trinidad's south and east coasts turned out to be unsuccessful due to revolt and desertion, partially resulting from Warao attacks. This failure of the mission system in the island's southern portion formed an area of major concern to the Spanish. Besides, during a visit of 1688 to the *encomiendas* or 'commands' in north Trinidad, the governor found that spiritual condition of these villages was poor: twelve years had passed since they were visited by a priest. Only Aricagua had a chaplain. Following an official decree to forbid personal service by the Amerindians, this same governor, Don Sebastian de Roteta, freed 302 Amerindians kept effectively as slaves by the Spanish colonists. (Practically all of them had been captured on the mainland, most of them in the Orinoco Valley and a few in Cumaná.) These Amerindians were granted land near St. Joseph where they established a village, *Santa Cruz de Buenavista*, in 1689 (Fig. 39). In all 37 houses were built here, mainly occupied by women and children. A large wooden cross took the place of a church. Another village was founded near Port-of-Spain. Consisting of only six houses, it had twenty Amerindians who were employed as security forces assisting with ship inspections. Here a church existed already.

A series of events, which for the Spanish inhabitants of Trinidad were most shocking, took place during and following a major uprising of the Nepoio at the Arenales mission in central Trinidad in December 1699. Unrest started when they learned from others about the atrocities committed by the Spanish during a visit by the governor of Trinidad and his officials to the mission villages of Guayria, Savana Grande and Savaneta. It appears that the inhabitants of these Naparima missions had not abandoned all their indigenous beliefs in spite of their conversion and, in the words of the Spanish, were 'living like barbarians using their false idolatries', indulging in 'sorceries, abuses and superstitions' by following their shamans (*peai-men*) who were 'speaking with the devils'. The Spanish punished these 'Indian sorcerers and those who contradicted the instruction of the holy doctrine' severely, apparently by hanging them. Fearing this same fate, the captain of the Arenales mission planned the rising together with a few accomplices. Indeed, when the next day during work on a new church the Amerindians refused to place a beam in position, they were warned that the governor was due to arrive in the mission and would take stern measures if they persisted in their refusal to work. This incensed the Amerindians so much that they murdered the resident priests and a carpenter attached to the mission. With the assistance of other members of the mission, subsequently the governor and his retinue were ambushed; they had just crossed the Aripo (Caroni) River on their way to Arenales. Almost all the Spanish priests and government officials in his party and some African slaves were killed, using poisoned arrows. Returning to the mission, the Amerindians destroyed the homes of the clerics and ransacked the church with everything in it. Saints' figures and ornaments were desecrated, the sacred vestments torn into strips (and converted into loincloths), while the altar wine was drunk and the holy oils spilled. Afterwards all the Amerindians left the mission, fleeing into the forests.

Warned by a seriously wounded survivor of the assault, immediate action was taken by the *cabildo* of St. Joseph. Fearing the possibility of a general indigenous revolt in the island, its *alcaldes* (magistrates) first made sure that the Amerindians of the *encomiendas* still remained loyal to the Spanish. Indeed, the assistance of those living in Tacarigua and Arauca could be ascertained easily. (The *cabildo* rewarded their captains (chiefs) by freeing them from forced labour for several years.) Several search expeditions were organized in order to find the rebels. A first patrol of thirty Spanish and a hundred Amerindians from Tacarigua and Arauca went as far as the Aripo River and encountered the bodies of the governor and his party, realizing that the mutineers had fled to the east and southeast. Another Spanish–Nepoio detachment found that some of the fugitives had gone to Mount Tamana and afterwards moved to an 'island' in the Nariva Swamp, close to the beach of Cocos Bay.[48] Here the pursuing squad encountered a fully Amerindian army of eighty Nepoio from Savana Grande and some from Moruga, led by Don Antonio de la Cruz, the indigenous 'General' of all the Naparima Amerindians, assisted by a Spanish lieutenant. After some skirmishes with the rebels and provisioned by a few Spanish and twenty Amerindians from Arauca, the detachment with Nepoio from Tacarigua and Arauca returned to St. Joseph. Having dislodged the rebels from their hiding in the Nariva Swamp, the Naparima general now pursued them as far as present Point Radix where several of them jumped off the rocks and were drowned in the sea. All the original instigators of the mutiny were killed, including their leader who had put on the governor's uniform and was carrying his staff and sword. Only a few rebels escaped by fleeing to the Caribs of Arrecifes (present Salybia) on the northeast coast. All 84 captives were taken to Savana Grande and then to St. Joseph. Also, Captain Calixto of Savaneta delivered to the Spanish two Amerindians from Arenales, who had come to his mission with the news of the uprising. In all 61 male rebels were put to death while the women and children below 12 years of age were enslaved. Don Antonio de la Cruz was congratulated by the newly arrived governor and given four of the captured women as slaves. All in all, the Arenales rising represented the last notable eruption of indigenous power in the island. It is quite ironic that this final attack on Spanish control was put down by other Amerindians, acting as auxiliaries for the Spanish. Apparently by now their allegiance to the Spanish had begun to supersede the indigenous tribal loyalties, as both the Arenales insurgents and their pursuers were principally affiliated to the Nepoio people.

Abolition and reinstatement of the missions

The early years of the eighteenth century saw a growing conflict between the missionaries and the colony's landowners, who resented their limited access to the Amerindian labour force in the island. By this time the economy was gradually improving due to the wide cultivation of cocoa (of the '*criollo*' variety), especially since trees deriving from seeds imported from Caracas and Cumaná had been

48 Later it appeared that some of the rebels wished to hide on Mount Tamana, awaiting the opportunity to join a party of Warao from the mainland on one of their raids on the island.

planted. Because of the lack of coinage, cocoa now became the local currency, as on the mainland coast. Trinidad's cocoa was of excellent quality and, bought and paid for in advance, it fetched high prices. The main foreign traders were Dutch privateers and slavers. Otherwise, the cocoa was exported to Caracas where it could be loaded on registered vessels from Spain. French and English pirates occasionally interfered with the trade by seizing ships loaded with cocoa. In 1701 an English frigate from Barbados threatened to attack the island; it was chased away by sixty Amerindians under a Spanish captain. (Eventually the cocoa industry was so successful that in 1719 Trinidad could afford to equip and arm a ship-of-war to protect its trade.) Due to the growing prosperity in the island, the demand for labour increased correspondingly. The Spanish settlers, some 120 now, complained that the Amerindians in the missions were pampered and kept in idleness while they were denied the use of Amerindian labour. (Black slaves were difficult to get.) Indeed, the Church controlled all this labour and the missions were leading in the production of cocoa for export. As an experiment, the Spanish landowners were granted permission to employ Amerindians from the missions as labourers in the cocoa fields in return for pay, food and religious instruction. However, the planters reportedly disregarded these obligations and after a period of 6–8 months the Amerindians returned to the missions, exhausted, sick with hunger and unclad. Understandably, the missionaries refused to continue the arrangement.

In 1708 the Spanish Crown decided to act on the requests of Trinidad's governor, who supported the planters, and demanded the withdrawal of the missionaries. Due to appeals by the Capuchins, it was not until 1713 that the royal order was put into effect. By this time the four Naparima mission villages of west Trinidad had in all 1171 inhabitants. With 401 people, Savana Grande was the largest. The missions were now transformed into *pueblos de doctrina* in which the authority of the priest (*cura*) was reduced to religious indoctrination, while *corregidores*, appointed by the governor, dealt with aministrative and judicial matters. The latter now had direct access to the Amerindian labour in the missions as well as the *encomiendas* and disposed of it as they wished. As the Capuchins left Trinidad in 1714, the secular clergy had to take over. This posed a major problem and in 1719 some of the previous missionaries were allowed to fill posts temporarily in their former missions as they were the only priests who knew the 'Indian languages'. By this time obviously only members of the local Nepoio elite were able to speak Spanish, as during the 1700 trial of the Arenales insurgents, none of the accused was able to understand the proceedings without the assistance of an indigenous interpreter, Captain Martin de Mendoza of the Arauca *encomienda*. Following the dismissal of the Capuchins, the mission villages began to disintegrate and many Amerindians left them in order to live in the interior 'with the savages of the other nations reverting to idolatry', as a Spanish document of 1721 expressed it. Besides, attacks by the Warao from the mainland still took place, reportedly inciting the mission Amerindians to rebellion and carrying out enslaving raids. The four Naparima villages had only 623 Amerindians in 1722, just over half the number ten years previously.

Probably forced, Chaima and Warao from the mainland took up residence in the *encomienda* villages in 1712.[49] The latter were abolished throughout the entire Spanish empire and transformed into *pueblos de doctrina* in 1716. By this time there were some 650 Amerindians living in them. Their inhabitants had been under such pressure to pay tribute in the form of personal service or by producing crops, that the governor complained in 1711 that they had too little time to cultivate their own lands. Things were not improving after the abolition of the *encomienda* system as the *corregidores*, who were often related to their owners, kept misusing the Amerindians at times. Also, religious instruction was neglected: priests were not paid and the *encomenderos* refused to provide them with wine, bread, oil, and ornaments. Nevertheless, in 1717 the Amerindians of Arauca built an entirely new church since the old one was completely ruined. Throughout these years, the Spanish settlers remained almost wholly dependent on the Amerindians of the former *encomiendas* for food supplies. In spite of this, the Spanish kept complaining that they were rather lazy, and heathens 'with as many women as each wishes'. Besides, they enjoyed much more freedom than the Amerindians of the missions whom they reportedly tried to lure away, as apparently happened with forty families in 1716. Converted Amerindians were rewarded with freedom from tribute for twenty years. This had to be paid in goods, for lack of currency: maize, cassava, black wax, tobacco, hardwood, and rope of the mahoe tree. However, in 1705 the Amerindians were working one third of the year on the estates of the *encomenderos* instead of paying their prescribed tribute in money or agricultural produce. By the 1720s, apart from ground provisions and maize, fruits such as plantains, pawpaws, pineapples, oranges, lemons, and watermelons were cultivated in the former *encomienda* villages, now *pueblos de doctrina*, while pigs, goats, mares, horses and chicken were raised. Besides, their male inhabitants remained enlisted in the militia while they kept guard at the mouth of the Caroni River as well. In 1705 St. Joseph had in all 80 men who could bear arms, among whom there were very few Spanish; most of them were *mestizos*, *mulatos* and free blacks, 'all poor people'. In 1722 it had in addition 181 Nepoio auxiliaries from the four 'commands' and the village of Buenavista near St. Joseph.

The production of cocoa rose rapidly after the landowners were allowed to employ the Amerindians from the former missions and *encomiendas* on their estates. Being of superior quality, it fetched high prices. However, the island's prosperity did not last long, as in 1725 a disastrous fungus disease ruined the entire stock of cocoa trees, as a result of which poverty struck all the planters. Many settlers (and slaves) now emigrated to the mainland and Trinidad's non-Amerindian male population declined to a mere 162 adults, while St. Joseph gradually lapsed into oblivion. In desperation, in 1728 the governor even sent an expedition to the mainland in order to search for El Dorado. Indeed, the colony was nearly bankrupt. The Spanish settlers reportedly 'fed themselves with what little they could personally get in the woods and in the sea'. Besides, being in a 'miserable state' and suffering 'much sickness and distress from the want of food, medicines

49 Of these, Aricagua had been administered by the Crown since 1689.

and attendance', many Amerindians now left the former *encomienda* and mission settlements in order to live 'in the hills as if they were heathen', as a Spaniard noted disapprovingly in 1732. As the Nepoio of the three 'commands' had assisted the Spanish as boat hands, armed with bows and arrows, during an expedition against Caribs in the Orinoco Valley in 1733, which did not yield them any booty, and in order to ease the burden on the loyal Amerindians in general, all were relieved of tribute for six years. Nevertheless, the movement to the interior continued. (In this respect it should be kept in mind that in this period a few thousand Amerindians, about which the Spanish historic documents are virtually silent, were permanently inhabiting the parts of the island which were beyond Spanish control.) To add to the misery, virulent smallpox epidemics hit the island in 1739 and 1741.

For a long time requests to the Crown to send more clerics to the island were unsuccessful: in 1739 there was only one priest (without any knowledge of the Nepoio language) for all four Naparima mission villages. He received goods in payment for his duties which 'were not of much value'. Finally, by royal decree Aragonese Capuchins, who had been active in Cumaná on the mainland for many years, were given charge of the Trinidad Amerindians, thereby reinstating the mission system, in 1744. It was not until 1749 that action was taken and two new mission settlements (*pueblos de doctrina*) were founded in the island. The first of these, *Los Santos Reyes de Mucurapo*, was apparently situated not far from the original site of sixteenth-century Cumucurapo village (Fig. 39). It was established probably among Amerindians of Arawak ethnicity originating from the mainland, but could not retain them for very long, because of their 'natural inconsistency' as the Spanish explained. Abandoned in 1751, the mission was re-established three years afterwards and closed again soon after. This was mainly because the governor refused to contribute to its upkeep. A second mission, *Santa Rosa de Arima*, was founded in the existing Nepoio settlement of Arima, just south of the Northern Range. It was located in the neighbourhood of the present Roman Catholic church of this village, which is situated on the bank of the Arauca River. Here land to construct the mission was donated to the Church by a Spanish settler. However, this mission, too, was abandoned in 1754. (The layout of the present town of Arima developed out of that of the mission which was revived in 1786.)

In these years the population of the four Naparima settlements was enlarged by groups of Chaima and Pariagoto Amerindians from the mainland. Partly, this may have been induced by a smallpox epidemic which ravaged the Paria Peninsula in 1736, while reportedly French itinerant traders incited these Amerindians to join them and go to Tobago (see Chapter 8). In 1739 150 'pagan' Chaima were living in the Naparima villages. Also, in the 1740s large numbers of 'Yellow' (Island) Caribs moved from St. Vincent to northeast Trinidad and the mainland, fleeing from the pressure of the Black Caribs. These Island Caribs settled, with the Chaima and Pariagoto, on the north coast at Arrecifes (Salybia Bay), just east of present Toco, and the latter also on the eastern shore at Cumana Bay.[50] As we have seen, Caribs

50 The name *Salybia* is of Island Carib (Kali'nago) derivation and occurs as a toponym in the Carib Territory of Dominica as well. It is related to the Island Carib name for Trinidad, *chaléibe* (pronounced as šaléybe) and perhaps the Island Carib term *chalíbaboüe*, meaning 'separate'.

(Kali'na) were settled here in 1699 when they were joined by Nepoio fugitives from Arenales. Being beyond direct Spanish control, northeast Trinidad clearly became a refuge area for various Amerindian groups, and after the British settlement of Tobago also for runaway slaves from this island.

In the 1750s the cocoa industry recovered somewhat due to the introduction of the Brazilian '*forastero*' variety which proved to be hardier than the one grown previously. Some colonists returned to the island, but cocoa production never again assumed the importance it had in the early 1700s. People remained miserably poor and were struck by perpetual outbreaks of smallpox, malaria and yellow fever. In 1757 St. Joseph was such a derelict place that a newly arrived governor could not find a proper house for himself and went to live in Port-of-Spain. It led to lingering conflicts with the *cabildo* which held to St. Joseph as the island's capital. These years also saw the establishment of new mission villages (*pueblos de doctrina*) by the Aragonese Capuchins who wished to continue their efforts at evangelization of the Trinidad Amerindians following the failure of Mucurapo and Arima. Accordingly, in 1758–1759 in all five new missions were founded, while the Capuchins nominally took charge of the four Naparima villages and the former *encomienda* settlements as well. Most of the new missions were established in northeast Trinidad. The first of these, *Nuestra Señora de la Asunción*, was founded among Chaima and Caribs in the neighbourhood of the present Roman Catholic church of Toco, which is situated in an isolated hamlet still called The Mission, some 2.5 km west of the centre of this north coast village. The present church is located on a small promontory opposite two hills, from west to east, the Mission Hill and the Kalifonia Hill. Until the early 1900s the church stood on top of the Mission Hill. The name Kalifonia is a corruption of the name the female Island Caribs gave to their people, Kali'puna. (A track going up this hill was called the Kalifonia Road until recently.) Another mission, Arrecifes, was established at Salybia Bay, less than 2 km east of Toco, among Caribs, Chaima and Pariagoto, of which the two latter groups were recent arrivals. Its exact location is not known. This applies also to a third mission, Cumana, which was created among Caribs, Chaima and Pariagoto at Cumana Point on the east coast. Obviously, the name is a commemorative toponym, reminding of the area of origin of the two latter ethnic groups. A fourth, similarly unlocated, mission was founded among Chaima somewhat inland from the east coast at Matura, about 20 km, as the crow flies, south of Cumana.[51] Finally, a fifth mission, *La Divina Pastora*, was established among Arawaks and Warao from the mainland at Siparia in southwest Trinidad. It was located in the vicinity of the present Roman Catholic church in this village.

All these missions were shortlived as the Capuchins left the island again after a few years since the local government was unwilling to support them financially. They continued to exist as Amerindian villages, since all of them except Matura are shown as such on the first detailed map of Trinidad, drawn by Agustín Crame in 1777. Little is known about daily life in the various Amerindian villages in this period, although clearly Hispanicization was developed furthest in the former

51 Somewhat later, in the 1770s small groups of French turtlers and coconut planters settled illegally among the Amerindians of Trinidad's north and east coasts at Toco, Cumana and Manzanilla.

encomiendas, which in 1765 encompassed in all 703 Amerindians, including Nepoio joined by some newly arrived Chaima. Their inhabitants still supported the Spanish as military auxiliaries in addition to provisioning St. Joseph and ships calling at Port-of-Spain. In 1763 the Amerindians of Tacarigua assisted in building a fortification at Port-of-Spain, as a reward for which their annual tribute was acquitted. Highlight of the year was the celebration of the local patronal feast which included offerings of game and produce, dancing and merry-making, with the male Amerindians displaying their military skills. Only one priest (*cura doctrinero*) was available for all three 'commands'. (In 1764 the former missions had been without one for nine years.) Apart from agriculture, hunting and fishing formed the mainstay of the local subsistence economy. Fish was dried and in this way could be kept for a long time. By the 1770s primarily maize and cassava were grown.

Archaeological research has given some further insight into the Amerindians' daily life in the Naparima villages, especially Savaneta, Montserrate (Mayo) and Savana Grande (Princes Town). Midden deposits at these mission sites have yielded Spanish and, predominantly, Amerindian (Mayoid) pottery, including cassava griddles, food remains such as shells and animal and fish bones, stone tools, and metal artifacts, glass, gunflints, and pipes. European metal objects comprise iron nails, horseshoes, musket balls, knives, and door hinges. Fine, colourfully glazed Spanish tableware (*majolica*) is extremely rare; all that has been recovered was made in Mexico and can be dated between 1650 and 1745. Clearly, only the church possessed this kind of expensive earthenware. In addition, fragments of olive jars (*botijas*) and other storage vessels have been found, as well as eighteenth-century Dutch polychrome delftware and brown French 'faience' from Rouen. The recovery of pieces of hematite (red ochre) suggests that body painting had not been entirely abandoned. Besides, the presence of tools such as hammerstones, polishing stones for pottery, stone anvils, and grinding stones is indicative of the at least partial continuation of an originally 'pre-Columbian' pattern of subsistence technology. Fishing (of catfish) and shell collecting apparently took place predominantly at the shore of the Gulf of Paria. The shells include mainly tiger lucinas, Caribbean oysters and West Indian crown conchs. In addition, a few freshwater species have been found such as ramshorn snails and river conchs. The animal bone fragments point to hunting armadillos, ant eaters, howler monkeys, porcupines, pacas, agoutis, collared peccaries, black-eared opossums, brocket deer, and turtles, and keeping hunting dogs, pigs and sheep.

By the 1760s the island's economy was slowly improving. In addition to cocoa, small quantities of tobacco, coffee, indigo, vanilla, and cinnamon were grown for commercial exploitation. Sugar cane was cultivated only for local consumption. Domestic livestock remained scarce. Also, sea turtles and timber were traded with the mainland. In 1765 the island had in all 2503 inhabitants among whom were 1277 (nominally) converted Amerindians. (In addition, there were perhaps a thousand or so Amerindians living beyond Spanish control in Trinidad's interior.) Natural disasters hit the island at irregular intervals. Smallpox epidemics raged in 1764 and 1770–1771, killing Spanish and Amerindians alike. In 1766 a major earthquake destroyed many houses and both churches of St. Joseph, the fortification and governor's residence in Port-of-Spain, and the mission churches of Savana Grande, Guayria, and Montserrate, as well as those of the 'commands' of Arauca and Tacarigua. The entire village of Savaneta had burned down two years previously due to a fire caused by clearing the mission's common grounds. Only some religious objects such as a silver chalice, some sacred vestments and a holy figure could be saved from the church. The Amerindians were moved to Montserrate. Money for rebuilding the village was donated by the Crown in 1769. Three years later a disastrous drought caused the complete failure of the cocoa crop. Again, the island's population experienced a complete relapse into poverty. Many settlers as well as Amerindians emigrated to the mainland. By the 1770s the Spanish government finally realized that, lacking manpower and capital, Trinidad whose strategic importance was recognized at last, would remain undeveloped unless its policy regarding the island drastically changed. Following its acceptance that foreign immigration would be essential to develop the island into a profitable plantation economy based on slave labour, far-reaching reforms were implemented. Ultimately the success of these economic and socio-political changes would lead to the marginalization of Trinidad's Amerindian population.

Foreign immigration and the development of a plantation economy

In 1776 the newly arrived governor, Don Manuel Fálquez, reported to the Crown that conditions in Trinidad were deplorable: it had become a semi-deserted island whose remaining settlers were highly uncivilised. Besides, the available government buildings were not more than straw shacks. This same year Madrid allowed the immigration of foreign planters under certain conditions (notably their being Roman Catholic), granting them land on easy terms coupled with tax incentives. From 1777 onwards especially French people from Grenada, which, like Tobago, was one of the islands ceded to Britain in 1763, and some Irish settlers moved in. The stream swelled when in 1783 even more generous terms were offered to immigrants in the famous *Cédula* of Population, specifically designed to attract wealthy French planters, both white and coloured. (France was closely allied with Spain since 1761.) Other reforms were made as well: trade between Spain and its colonies was liberalized while in 1777 Trinidad was brought under the Captaincy-General of Venezuela and the Intendant at Caracas.[52] From 1784 onwards, the island's socio-political and economic reconstitution was energetically and skilfully guided by a new governor, Don José Maria Chacón. Bringing with them their slaves, capital and know-how, the French newcomers set up plantations of cotton, cocoa, coffee and sugar. Tools and equipment, horses, mules and oxen for transport and work on the estates were imported. Soon the immigrants by far outnumbered the Spanish in the island. With the French, their food, dances, music, and social customs, including carnival, were introduced. Indeed, Trinidad had become a

52 The island had been officially separated from (Venezuelan) Guayana as early as 1762. It was made a separate intendancy in 1791.

French colony ruled by Spain. While in 1780 commercial agriculture was confined to the growing and export of cocoa, vanilla, indigo, annatto, cotton, and maize, by the 1790s sugar had become the most important crop. By this time some 150 sugar plantations, most of them French owned, had been established in the valleys of the Northern Range, along the west coast and near the new town San Fernando. Many forested areas were brought under cultivation now. Trade increased tremendously and Port-of-Spain became a bustling port where the *cabildo* finally moved in 1784. Mainly British shipping profited, however.

While prior to 1780 the number of African slaves was insignificant and the available labour force was dependent on the Amerindian presence in the island, French immigration completely reversed this picture. Indeed, within a decade Trinidad's demographic structure changed completely from Spanish-Amerindian to French-African. In 1789 the slave trade was declared open and the number of African slaves grew exponentially. The island's total population increased from 3432 in 1778 to 5899 in 1784 and not less than 17,718 in 1797. While the percentage of whites and free coloureds remained practically the same, moving from 40.3% to 35.9% and 37.4%, that of African slaves grew from 6.6% to 38.8% and 56.5%, and that of the Amerindians declined from 53.1% to 25.3% and finally 6.1%. However, it should be kept in mind that an uncounted number of Amerindians were still living beyond Spanish control. Besides, the actual decrease in the number of converted Amerindians in the island was relatively limited, from 1824 to 1495 and 1082. It had various causes, including primarily miscegenation, disease and emigration to the mainland. The growth of the numbers of free coloureds was due partially to the fact that a royal decree of 1789 instructed the Spanish colonies to welcome escaped French and British slaves, as a result of which throughout the 1790s Trinidad received numerous seaborne runaways including many from Tobago. Moreover, in 1783 groups of Island Caribs from Dominica migrated to northeast Trinidad, three years later followed by Black Caribs from St. Vincent. In spite of objections by Chacón, the *cabildo* granted land on the east coast to the latter of these fugitives, at least some of whom returned to St. Vincent in order to continue their war against the British in 1795. Many fled to Trinidad again after its conclusion in 1797. Their settlement may have been at Salybia (the second toponym of this name in northeast Trinidad) on the shore of Saline Bay and immediately south of Balandra Bay. Like Salybia, the latter name is a corruption of an Island Carib term, *balánna*, meaning 'sea'.

The foreign immigration and the concomitant pressure on the available land induced Chacón to reduce the number of indigenous mission villages, so as to be able to distribute the communal lands of these settlements to new French arrivals. The Amerindians did not have any claims to private property in the missions and, besides, by now they had apparently become so subservient to the Spanish that they lacked any ability or desire to resist Chacón's measures. About 1780 a visitor to the missions remarked that the 'temperament and docility' of Trinidad's Amerindians made them 'very likeable', adding that their dogs 'and drunkenness constitute all their delights'. Similarly, in 1788 an English captain reported that the Nepoio of the missions were 'an inoffensive and indolent race of people' who were highly 'tractable and obedient' to the Spanish. Indeed, the Amerindians, who remained available for hire by the planters, were highly desired for labour on the estates, particularly for clearance work in which they were considered to be adept, since they were felt to be more sober and peaceable than the black slaves. In 1782 there were complaints that the *corregidores*, who dispensed the Amerindian labour as they wished, were bribed to supply the indigenous labour. In 1787 the daily life of the inhabitants of the three remaining 'commands', Tacarigua, Cuara and Arauca, was reportedly 'more miserable' than that of 'slaves being forced to work the greater part of the year in the service of the same subjects entrusted with their protection and help'. Generally speaking, the Amerindian villages were in a poor state: about 1780 a visitor called Arauca a 'wretched settlement' and noted that the Nepoio of Cuara lived 'in total neglect'. Only one priest took care of the three remaining 'commands'. The situation in the Naparima missions, which had two *curas doctrineras*, was slightly better. By 1785 the churches of Savaneta and Montserrate, both structures of wattle-and-daub covered with palm leaves, had been completely renovated. The latter was reported as 'quite neat' in 1774.[53] However, in 1785 Savana Grande's church was called 'totally ruined' by Chacón. Besides, about 1780 its Amerindians were reportedly living in 'poor, badly constructed huts'. All in all, the annual tribute collected from the Amerindians was abolished by Chacón due to their poverty. Finally, throughout these years (actually until 1810) none of the villages of the northeast had a resident missionary, although they may have been visited occasionally by a priest. (Matura had disappeared as a settlement by 1784.)

In order to take over the extensive and largely uncultivated lands in Tacarigua Valley belonging to the former *encomiendas* and grant them to new settlers, Chacón decided to abolish the three remaining 'commands', Tacarigua, Arauca and Cuara, and move their 662 largely Nepoio inhabitants to Arima, thus reinstating the mission of *Santa Rosa de Arima* in 1786. Don Pedro Reyes Bravo, the *cura* of the three villages, went with them to Arima and supervised here the building of its church and houses for the Amerindians. Chacón had the 16 last indigenous inhabitants of the village of Santa Cruz de Buenavista near St. Joseph move to Arima as well. In order to compensate the Amerindians, they were granted 320 *fanegas* (2368 acres) on the banks of the Arauca River, but since this appeared to be less fertile than the land they had occupied previously, in addition they received a sum of money which was put in the community chest. Six Spanish settlers were placed in the village as well to afford 'a good example' to the Amerindians. Cocoa was the primary commodity grown by the mission Amerindians. Arima is the only mission village in Trinidad which has preserved its original layout. (It would exist as such until the mid-nineteenth century.) The village was arranged in traditional manner around a large rectangular plaza (present Lord Harris Square) with the church and presbytery on the eastern side and the Amerindian houses on the other three. The *casa real* (government house) was probably on the west side of the plaza. Part of the area between present De Gannes and Church Streets, north of

53 In 1785 the altar of Montserrate's church had an image of the Virgin Mary wearing a golden necklace with greenstone beads and a crown of silver.

Harris Square, is still Church property. The main concentration of the Amerindian population was to the northwest of the centre of the mission, on Calvary Hill and between a small tributary of the Mausica River and King Street. At present the Roman Catholic cemetery covers most of the latter area. The original footpath which connected Arauca (Arouca) with Arima is still recognizable in the Eastern Main Road, the Arima Old Road and Sorzano Street. (The latter street is called after the Spanish family which supplied the first *corregidores* of the Arima mission.) Amerindian (Mayoid) pottery as well as some Spanish ceramics have been found in the area at the back of the church and its vicinity.

Chacón further decided to amalgamate the four Naparima missions at Montserrate, but in 1794 only the Amerindians of Savaneta had moved there. Guayria ceased to exist after 1784 when its inhabitants numbered only 18. Two years later Chacón established San Fernando at the site of the old mission. It was declared a town in 1792. Subsequently, Montserrate was abandoned and by 1797 the 463 Amerindians of the Naparima missions had been gathered in Savana Grande. It would exist as an Amerindian mission settlement until the mid-nineteenth century. At Siparia in south Trinidad a previously abandoned mission, *La Divina Pastora*, was revived with Arawaks and Warao in 1784. In 1795 it still had a resident Capuchin as the *cura doctrinero* of the village who was its founder. In 1797 it counted 139 indigenous inhabitants. From its inception the Siparia mission was often visited by Warao from the mainland. Shell refuse, European ceramics (including late eighteenth-century pearlware and earthenware), stone fragments, metal objects, and pipestems have been found in the neighbourhood of Siparia's present Roman Catholic church which stands at the site of its predecessor of mission times. Spiritual guidance was lacking in the remaining Amerindian villages of northeast Trinidad, Toco, Cumana and Salybia, although they had *capitánes pobladores*, instituted as government officials to take care of their administrative and judicial matters, like the *corregidores* of the Naparima missions. In 1797 155 Amerindians were counted in these villages. Finally, in these years there still remained an unknown number of Amerindians in the interior of the island, part of whom formerly lived in the mission settlements. About 1780 a foreign visitor noted that there were 'many families who have been living a nomadic life in these woods', who, when 'they happen in their wanderings to arrive near these [mission] villages, they enter them confidently and present their children to the priests for baptism. This they perform apparently with great devotion and sincere faith, presenting the priest with games and cassava cakes'. This suggests that these Amerindians had become as Hispanicized and at least nominally converted as those living in the mission villages. It was not long before they and the other Trinidad Amerindians witnessed the humiliating defeat which Spain, the colonial power which ruled the island for two hundred years and had reduced them to submission, suffered during the French-inspired and self-declared Anglo–Spanish War, as a result of which Trinidad became part of the British empire (1797).

10. British colonization and Amerindian persistence in Trinidad (1797–present)

The system of Amerindian mission villages was finally abandoned after half a century of British rule. By the 1850s only the former missions of Arima and Siparia remained as towns inhabited by relatively many people of 'pure' and mixed Carib and Warao ancestry, respectively. In these years increasing numbers of small subsistence farmers of mixed Spanish–Amerindian–African descent, so-called peons, immigrated into Trinidad from the mainland, thereby reinforcing the Hispanized indigenous population element in the island. The peons also revitalized the annual celebrations of the Santa Rosa Festival in Arima which have attracted people from all over Trinidad until the present. The ongoing pilgrimages and trade expeditions of the mainland Warao to San Fernando and Siparia, and their involvement in the annual feasts of La Divina Pastora in the latter town, have similarly kept alive the remembrance of the indigenous population element in the multi-ethnic configuration of Trinidad society. By supporting financially and morally a series of local initiatives seeking for recognition of Arima's indigenous roots, the recent governments of Trinidad and Tobago have shown to be quite sensitive to the desire of the Caribs of this town to be recognized as a distinct ethnic group proud of its ancestry and cultural heritage.

The end of mission times in British Trinidad

In February 1797 it took the British only a few days to conquer Trinidad. Sailing into the Gulf of Paria with a major fleet, they induced the Spanish to set fire to their own small squadron moored at Chaguaramas while the latter put up merely token resistance on land.[54] According to the rather generous terms of capitulation, Spanish civil and criminal law would be maintained and this was confirmed at the official cession of the island by the Spanish by the Treaty of Amiens (1802). Since it was not allowed an Assembly elected by the local white planters (as Tobago in 1763), Trinidad became a British 'Crown Colony', a situation which, with occasional constitutional changes, would last until Trinidad and Tobago became an independent country in 1962. Under British rule the island's economic circumstances developed without major setbacks. In 1797 Trinidad had primarily sugar, coffee, cotton, and some cocoa plantations. Now a major influx of money took place and many prospective planters (with their slaves) flocked in. Especially

54 Lacking military supplies and troops, Chacón had organized the land defence to the best of his abilities: one of his few fortifications was armed with the militia and even 'a few Indians [...] with bows and arrows'.

the sugar industry flourished: while Trinidad produced 14.2 million pounds weight of sugar in 1802, this amount had risen to 37.7 million in 1838. In 1809 sugar was grown on almost 70% of the total acreage of cultivated land in the island. By the 1830s large tracts of land, especially in the Caroni Basin and along the west coast as far south as San Fernando, had been reclaimed especially for sugar cultivation. Besides, in these years the world prices for cocoa plummeted, which, added to several years of crop failures, led to a sharp reduction in its production. Although as early as 1806–07 the slave trade had been forbidden in the British empire, it was not until 1838 that slavery was abolished and full 'Emancipation' was granted to the enslaved black population of the island, following four years of 'apprenticeship'. Free coloureds had already been placed by law equal to whites in 1829. While Spanish was still spoken in parts of the island and in the Amerindian enclaves, most people spoke a French *patois*, while English represented the language of government and business.

Meanwhile, the Amerindian segment of Trinidad's population gradually declined and became increasingly marginalized. In 1810 the official census of the island counted in all 1659 indigenous people, falling to 710 in 1820 and 520 in 1838. This would mean that in the latter year not more than 1.3% of the total population (39,328 people) could be called of Amerindian descent. Although no doubt miscegenation, disease and emigration to the mainland affected the number of Trinidadian Amerindians in these years negatively, it is likely that the situation was less bleak than painted by these official counts, as they would have taken into account only the Amerindians living in the remaining mission villages, notably Arima, Savana Grande, Siparia, and Toco. European visitors to these missions generally expressed unflattering stereotyped opinions of their inhabitants. The Amerindians were seen as 'harmless and inactive children' of whom the 'total want of mental and [...] bodily energy is beyond credibility'. In 1825 an Englishman emphasized the perceived lifeless character of the mission Indians of Arima and Savana Grande, noting about the latter that 'nothing seems to affect them like other men; neither joy nor sorrow, anger, or curiosity, take any hold of them. Both mind and body are drenched in the deepest apathy; [...] silence is in their dwellings and idleness in all their ways'. He remarked that during his visit to Arima the Amerindians of this mission were sitting for hours in motionless silence. Similarly, in 1803 an English sea captain commented on the Caribs of Trinidad's northeast coast that their indolence was extreme, the 'greatest part of the time is spent in swinging in their hammocks'. He added that most work was done by the women while the men only went fishing. In fact, the European visitors seemed surprised that the Amerindians were quite satisfied when their basic subsistence needs were fulfilled, devoting the rest of their time, as a contemporary wrote, to 'smoking, dancing, and all kinds of amusements'. Besides, a visitor to the Siparia mission noted in 1847 that he 'saw none of the apathy so often mentioned'.

In 1819 Toco, Cumana and possibly Salibia were still separate villages, although only Toco had a resident priest. The mission's baptismal registers, which started in 1837, refer to all Amerindian mothers as 'Caraibesse'. The Carib ethnicity of the early nineteenth-century Amerindian inhabitants of Trinidad's northeast

Figure 44. Church of the Arima mission, Trinidad. Drawing by Captain Wilson, 1837. Courtesy Gérard A. Besson.

coast is confirmed by their contemporary *corregidor*, who noted that they called themselves *Califournans*, which clearly represents a corruption of Kali'puna, i.e., the name the female Island Caribs gave to themselves. Besides, in these years groups of Chaima still lived in the mountainous area north of Arima. Occasionally they came down to the mission village in order to exchange wild meats for small household goods. After 1854 these Chaima were seen no more as a major cholera epidemic which struck the Amerindians of the north coast and the Northern Range extinguished them. The indigenous population of the north coast also diminished due to emigration. In the early 1800s reportedly Amerindians from this region fled into the woods and to the mainland in order to withdraw themselves and their families from the dictatorial behaviour of Toco's commandant, a 'contemptible little tyrant', who, together with another plantation owner, forced them to work as slaves on their estates. Not all Amerindians of the north coast were as submissive to the Europeans. A blind shaman called Sylvester, who was 60 years of age in 1806, is recorded to have exercised an almost absolute authority over the Caribs of the north coast. Apparently he poisoned another shaman who caused his blindness. Besides, he reportedly obstructed the conversion of the Caribs and tore down the cross in some village because, he said, priests 'are more expert magicians than myself'.

In the early nineteenth century Arima became Trinidad's most important mission village. Its church was rebuilt and a bell-tower added following a hurricane which blew down the church in 1810 (Fig. 44). Two years later an influx of Island Caribs from St. Vincent took place after a series of eruptions of this island's Soufrière volcano.

The British Secretary of State ordered the governor of Trinidad to grant land to these 'Charaibs', who subsequently were allowed to settle around the mission. It was now that the name 'Carib' was adopted by the Amerindians of Arima since reportedly, following these years, although originally of Nepoio ethnic affiliation, they called themselves *Califournans*, just as the Caribs of Trinidad's north coast.[55] In 1818 Governor Sir Ralph Woodford, taking a special interest in the mission, decided to 're-establish' it. First he removed its curate on the grounds of neglect of duty, noting that after Sunday mass a cockfight was allowed to be held in front of the presbytery next to the church. Secondly, Woodford appointed a new Protector (*corregidor*) to the Arima mission and added 320 acres to the 1000 acres granted to the village since Spanish times. Supporting the *cabildo* of Arima, Woodford tried to consolidate and enforce the mission, taking a leading role in preserving Amerindian rights over its territorial integrity. He also assumed the right to appoint or dismiss the indigenous chief at the head of the *cabildo*. With respect to corporal punishment, Woodford advised the mission's priest that 'the rule should be severe in appearance but mild in reality'. In 1825 Arima, then counting 278 people, was described as consisting of one large square and a street or two, having a large church, presbytery, government house, prison, and two schools. The most densely populated portion of the mission faced King Street and was called the 'Carib Village'. A visitor noted that 'in the middle of the town and quite irregularly, the plantains, the tamarinds, the breadfruit are planted, under which the Indians were sitting in groups, smoking, the children playing about, the women with the older girls preparing the cassava bread. Everyone seemed happy, and all was harmony...' A few Spanish were living in the mission and also some coloured men married to Amerindian women. Accordingly, in 1837 the militia was reportedly composed of Caribs, Spanish and *sambos* (people of mixed African–Amerindian extraction). They appeared 'barefoot, in short pantaloons and lasso in hand', armed with rifles.

Although celebrated from the beginning of the Arima mission in the late eighteenth century, in Woodford's time the festivities on the name-day of its patron saint, the Santa Rosa Festival, developed into a public feast which was celebrated with pomp and splendour, long processions during which the statue of Santa Rosa was paraded through the streets, and a gaily decorated church. On this day the Amerindians elected a king and a queen, usually a young man and a young woman, and all appeared in their best apparel. The king and queen presided over the festivities and acted as their principals on solemn occasions. The church was especially decorated for the festival with palm leaves, local produce and fruits. After mass, ceremonial dances were performed in the church and afterwards the Amerindians went to the government house in order to pay compliments to the *corregidor*, who gave the signal for dancing, drinking palm beer, and games and various sports, especially archery competitions. Woodford regularly patronized the Santa Rosa Festival, awarding prizes to schoolchildren who had earned them by good behaviour or by progress at school. In these years the festival lasted for one week; on the last Sunday of August its most grandiose procession took place during

55 The Spanish consistently used the term *indios* for the inhabitants of the mission, thereby emphasizing their subordinate and Hispanized character.

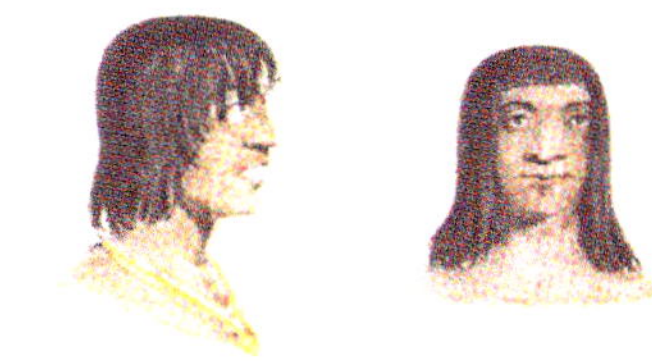

Figure 45. Portraits of two Amerindians of the Savana Grande mission, Trinidad. Coloured lithographs by Richard Bridgens (1820), published in his *West India Scenery* [...], London 1836.

which the statue of Santa Rosa was carried through the mission by four Caribs. Clearly, the festival, which attracted people from all over the island, formed a major event and an enduring vehicle for ensuring community cohesion, reinforcing it as a unit whilst making it publicly visible. Indeed, it would remain the prime institution and cultural symbol of the Caribs of Arima throughout the nineteenth and twentieth centuries until the present.

The Amerindians of the mission village of Savana Grande (present Princes Town) were less fortunate than those of Arima in terms of support by the early nineteenth-century Trinidad government (Fig. 45). In 1825 Savana Grande, then counting 229 people, was described as consisting of chiefly two parallel rows of 'large and lofty' houses with a spacious grass-covered street or promenade between them. The houses, which stood at intervals of 3–4.5 metres, were 'beautifully constructed' of spars of bamboo, thatched with palm branches, and 'ventilated in the most agreeable manner'. A projection of the roof at their front, supported by posts, formed a shady gallery 'under which the Indians will sit for hours together in motionless silence'. Traditionally, the mission was taken to extend to a radius of 600 *varas* (some 500 m) diverging from its church, beyond which the Amerindians had their farming plots. In these years the church was in a bad state: in 1824 it was described as 'a very miserable barn'. Besides, the situation of the Amerindians was quite gloomy. In 1806 a Venezuelan visitor, the revolutionary general Francisco de Miranda, noted that they were exploited by the resident priest who had settled a Spaniard in a rum shop in the mission, with whom he shared the profits, 'for the love of spirits is the chief vice of the Indians'. Miranda was 'disgusted with the manner in which the Indians were treated'. Things were not improving when Woodford appointed Robert Mitchell, the manager or owner of several estates, as the commandant of North Naparima. The Amerindians had to work for the commandant when ordered and, according to a contemporary, they were 'put into a gang like a set of slaves'. In this way Mitchell had the 'Royal Road' between San Fernando and Savana Grande graveled in 1818, but the Savana Grande Amerindians had to work on his own estates as well. In order to keep them obedient, they were 'whipped, positively whipped, almost daily'. The mission priest was as tyrannical as the commandant. Called 'a scandal to his order, and a curse to his flock', he 'went from the altar to the tap, where he sold rum by drams or gills'. Besides, he forced the Amerindians to work in his gardens and collected all the young girls under his roof. The situation improved under his successors in the later 1820s and 1830s, but after 1835 the mission did not have a resident priest any longer.

The Amerindians of the southernmost mission, Siparia, fared better than those of Savana Grande. Established among Warao and Arawak, it lost a number of its inhabitants when at the cession to Britain in 1802 the resident priest predicted that they would be mistreated by the new rulers of the island. Many took to the woods south of the mission or migrated to the mainland. Woodford attempted to reorganize the mission by locating therein royalist emigrants from Venezuela, as a result of which after this country's War of Independence (1811–1823) Siparia's population rose to almost 500 people. In 1847 the mission is described as consisting of about 25 houses built of arrow reed (*roseau*) wattled with incombustible 'tinmeet', plastered with yellow mud. They were provided with bamboo ladders. Furniture consisted only of hammocks; tables and chairs were rare. Live wild hogs were kept inside in bamboo cages; domestic utensils consisted of calabashes and baskets. Besides, houses of hunters had many dogs. The mission had a resident priest, a schoolmaster and a *corregidor*. Siparia was a centre of trade which was visited often by mainland Warao (Waraoons), exchanging baskets and hammocks for yellow and red *roucou*, rum and tobacco. Landing at Quinam or Moruga, they walked up to Siparia or Savana Grande, respectively. Part of the track to the latter mission has become known as 'Indian Walk'.[56] As in Arima, the celebration of the name-day of the mission patroness, La Divina Pastora, was an annual festival which was highlighted by a solemn procession of the statue of the Holy Shepherdess through the streets of the village. This statue is described as carved from red cedar and wearing a straw hat and silk gown. Rumour has it that the statue was carried from the mainland by a priest who had to flee from persecution. This may have happened during the Venezuelan War of Independence when many priests, most of whom were royalists, left the mainland for Trinidad.

In these years the political unrest on the mainland also led to an increasing number of other immigrants who wished to escape the turmoil at home. In fact, refugees from both sides, republicans and royalists, fled to Trinidad. The British first encouraged the Venezuelan rebels to use Trinidad as a base for planning their uprising, but became more sympathetic to the royalist camp afterwards. The majority of immigrants were small subsistence farmers (*conuqueros*), in Trinidad commonly known as peons (*peones*), who came as early as Spanish times as seasonal labourers to the sugar and cocoa estates of the island or as woodcutters and petty traders. In spite of Woodford's utterance that 'nothing can exceed the laziness of the Spanish peons but the Indians', in the 1820s they were generally judged as 'tractable and laborious'. In these years the peons were encouraged by the (Spanish) mission priests to settle in Arima, not because of their abilities as estate workers and subsistence farmers, but to maintain the dominance of Spanish customs, language and traditions, thus reinforcing the dwindling numbers of Hispanized Amerindians. Indeed, the peons were typically of mixed Amerindian–Spanish–African descent and culturally as well as physically peons and Amerindians formed overlapping categories. Both were Spanish-speaking subsistence farmers or peasants, accustomed to live in Spanish-style wattle-and-daub houses (*ajoupas*), sleep in hammocks, weave baskets and eat cassava bread and maize pies. Besides, they were identified with the Spanish cultural heritage, and with time the peons, Amerindians and Spanish of Trinidad were conflated into one broad population

56 In 1817 Erin (San Francique) formed a rendezvous for Warao from the mainland as well. Still further west, there is a Quarahoon River on the Cedros Peninsula.

group by the other segments of society. The increase of the Spanish-speaking population due to this peon immigration led to the strengthening and revival of the Spanish language in the island, which had been under pressure from French *patois* and English since the British takeover.

Woodford's successors, being busy with the preparations for Emancipation, did not care about the preservation of the Spanish-founded missions. In 1834 the office of *corregidor* was abolished and subsequently stipendiary magistrates were appointed to deal with non-spiritual matters in the still surviving missions, bringing the Amerindians under common law. The missions were never officially terminated, but the reorganization of Trinidad's internal administrative boundaries under Governor Lord Harris in 1849, creating the system of wards, brought about their dissolution anyway. From now onward people had to demonstrate formal titles to land and have the land deeds registered. This worked against the Amerindians as none of them possessed such deeds and many could not read or write. All lots of land in the mission villages were put up for sale at an upset price and the mission Amerindians, who by law were not permitted to own property, lost their land. (Of course, all of this was in flagrant contravention to the conditions under which the Spanish ceded the island to the British in 1802.) No information is available on Toco, but in Arima this happened to more than 200 Caribs who found themselves without land or work and in depressed economic circumstances. After the dissolution of the Arima mission, its inhabitants retreated to Calvary Hill and further into the Northern Range. Squatters, especially former slaves, all engaged in cocoa cultivation, moved into the mission lands and surrounding areas. In 1843 only seven Amerindian families were still living in Savana Grande, all the others had retreated into the forest. By this time most of the latter were intermarried with peons and came to the mission only for selling game or 'grass' hammocks. Others had gone to the mainland, in the 1850s reportedly visiting the former mission once a year to pay respect to the graves of their ancestors, taking with them some baskets and mats for sale. By the 1840s Siparia was inhabited by a mixed population of Spanish-speaking Arawaks, peons, and former African slaves engaged in tobacco, cocoa and coffee cultivation.[57] At the time it still formed a lively centre of trade for the mainland Warao. During their visits, the latter, including their shaman, often stayed in the house of the (former) mission *corregidor*. In spite of the disappearance of the Toco and Savana Grande mission villages, in Arima and Siparia a distinctive spirit of communality was kept alive among their largely Hispanized population of 'pure' or mixed Amerindian descent, even after the dissolution of the mission system.

Becoming a small segment of a plural society

Following the abolition of slavery, most of the former slaves moved off the plantations, settling in villages which sprang up around the island's major towns. Some became urban labourers, porters and domestics or settled as skilled workers,

57 In 1847 a visitor saw in one house of the village two men rolling cigars, claiming that they made 900 of them per day.

while others kept working seasonally at the estates, simultaneously cultivating small plots of farm land. By growing fruits, ground provisions, peas, beans, some cocoa or coffee, and keeping a few cows, pigs, goats, and chickens, these peasants, often squatting on Crown lands, adopted a way of life which closely resembled that of the peons and mixed Spanish–Amerindians throughout the island. The labour problem, faced by the French Creole and British estate owners, was solved by the immigration of groups of workers from various places. First of all, the relatively high wages paid on the Trinidad plantations attracted people from the small islands of the West Indies. From the 1840s onwards they were followed by 'indentured' labourers from Portuguese Madeira, China, and (then) British India. Only the East Indian immigrants remained agricultural workers, many of whom became peasant farmers from the 1870s onwards. (Their immigration was halted in 1917.) Small tradesmen from Syria and Lebanon came a few decades afterwards. Sugar, grown by increasingly larger companies, remained the island's major income earner until 1898. As a result of the increasing demand for chocolate on the British market the cultivation of cocoa boomed on Trinidad after the 1870s. This was mainly the achievement of the peons, who, like the black peasants, were helped by the opening up of the Crown lands to smallholders during the late 1860s and 1870s.[58] Indeed, by the 1870s there were as many as 2000 Venezuelans arriving each year. Settling close to the Spanish-speaking population in the island, they occupied parts of the Northern Range, the Central Range and the south coast, preserving their own traditions of language, food, music, dancing, and religion. It was in 1865 that the first oil well was drilled in Trinidad. This meant the start of the petrochemical industry which would become the island's prime economic activity in the next century. All in all, by the early 1900s the complicated fabric of Trinidad's plural society, a true '*callaloo*' of population groups, had been formed. It was further enriched due to the unification of the island with Tobago in 1889.

What was the place of the Hispanized 'pure' or mixed Amerindians in this multi-ethnic social and cultural conglomerate during the late nineteenth century and thereafter? By this time only a few families of indigenous descent, all peasant farmers, were still living an isolated life in the forests of the Northern Range. Reduced in 1870 by an outbreak of smallpox, the Caribs of the north coast were limited to a dozen 'pure' families at the end of the century. Nevertheless, at present there are still people of mixed indigenous descent living in the Toco/Cumana area of the northeast. The smallpox epidemic of 1870 also affected the population of Arima, although it is claimed that in 1888 there were still some 70–80 'pure' and some 200 mixed Amerindians living near the former mission, notably on Calvary Hill. All had adopted Spanish names or intermarried with Spanish families, carrying surnames such as Hernandez, Lopez, Calderon, and Campo. Besides, mixture with peons and coloured immigrants from the small islands of the West Indies took place as well. The cocoa boom of the 1870s led to a major influx of peons and renewed the fortunes of the Spanish and French Creole families, the so-called *gens d'Arime*, who had been able to acquire much land in and around the former

58 The central position of the peons in the expansion of cocoa in Trinidad earned them the nickname *cocoa panyols* (a corruption of *español*).

mission. It led to a revival of interest in the local church, which was rebuilt in 1869 and enlarged in 1888, reportedly from stone hewn at Calvary Hill and carried by the Caribs on their shoulders to the town. Moreover, the local 'cocoa elite' moved to achieve municipal self-government for Arima. They were successful and in 1888 the town was granted a royal charter bestowing it the status of borough, which allowed Arima to have its own borough council, budget and tax base. Most inhabitants of indigenous or mixed Spanish–Venezuelan–Amerindian descent in the town's region lived like peasants elsewhere in Trinidad: in 1931 out of the 1909 dwellings in Arima, 1528 (80%) were typically Spanish-style wattle-and-daub houses thatched with palm leaves (Fig. 46a-b). They stuck to traditionally Amerindian household items such as hammocks, cassava graters and squeezers (*sebucán*), log mortars and wooden pestles for pounding maize, cocoa or coffee, river stones for crushing spices, so-called Carib baskets, and bamboo fish pots.

The ongoing peon immigration reinforced and revitalized Trinidad's Spanish–Amerindian culture. In Arima this was most obvious from the annual celebrations of the Santa Rosa Festival in which typically peon dances and music, so-called parang (from *parranda*, 'going out and singing'), now had a central position. Parang is grounded primarily in an old peon tradition of house-to-house caroling in rural towns and villages especially around Christmas, involving string bands playing *cuatros*, guitars, mandolins, violins, and Amerindian *shac-shacs*. Also, the peons introduced the *sebucán* dance, a variety of the European maypole dance, in which the dancers were dressed like Amerindians, and other dances in which the participants depicted animal figures. Finally, it may have been due to peon influence that in these years the roles of the festival kings and queens, who originally were elected for a week, were essentially reformulated. Now an elderly lady became instituted for life as the 'Carib Queen' in charge of coordinating the overall efforts for the Santa Rosa Festival. This elevation of the position of the festival queen reflected the changing character of the Santa Rosa Festival in these years, which in various respects became a public rendition of a household religious ritual particular to the peons known as the 'cross wake' (*velorio de la cruz*). The chief organizer of this ceremony was always the female head of the household, the so-called 'keeper of the cross' (*ama de la cruz*). Indeed, the symbol of authority of the Carib Queen was a flat silver cross. While being elected for her traditional knowledge regarding the processing of cassava and maize, basket weaving, the preparation of herbal remedies, and *oraciónes* (prayers used in healing), successive Carib Queens were often related. Her office has remained until the present. As late as the 1880s there was a 'King' as well, who was elected for life for overseeing the men's work for the celebrations, such as the cleaning of the cemetery and the cutting of *tirite* palms for decorating the church and the bamboo poles used to secure the colourful flags which were placed around Harris Square.

In the second half of the nineteenth century gradual changes took place as well in the secular amusements which had always been secondary to the spiritual aspects of the festival. In 1857 only seven 'pure' Amerindians could be found to present the governor with a flag at the beginning of the celebrations. Now the traditional dances and sports such as archery disappeared with the actors therein,

Figure 46. Carib houses, Arima, Trinidad, 1904. Photos by Jesse Walter Fewkes, published in his *The Aborigines of Porto Rico and Neighboring Islands*, Washington, DC, 1907.

being replaced by quadrilles, waltzes, horse races, and card games such as blind hookey. The annual races at Arima during the Santa Rosa Festival became famous island-wide. A cannon installed at Calvary Hill was used to signal the start of the celebrations. It was placed here in 1931 through Governor Sir Claude Hollis. The cannon blast replaced the firing of a rocket which, according to the local tradition, itself substituted for the blowing of a conch shell in order to announce the beginnings of the festivities. Of course, the solemn processions remained the central element of the Santa Rosa Festival. The statue of the saint, which was normally kept inside the church, was and is taken to the Carib Queen for the week of the celebrations. Here it is placed on a throne and decorated in garlands of pink, red, yellow, and white paper roses, made by the females of the community. Beautified in this way, it was carried through the streets of the town in order to be finally placed again in the church of the former mission. In these years several oral traditions sprang up on the appearance of Santa Rosa de Lima in Arima. One legend has it that the statue of the saint was found by three male Carib hunters at the entrance of a cave (or a natural spring) in the forests of the Guanapo Heights north of the town. According to others, they encountered a seemingly lost, young, dumb Spanish girl, whom they took to the mission. However, the next morning she had disappeared, but the hunters found her back at the place where they had come across her the first time. Again she disappeared and a third time as well. Now the Caribs found only a corona of roses at the cave (or spring) and a necklace, after which they went to the mission priest who identified the girl as the spirit of Santa Rosa herself and ordered the hunters to carve her statue, honor her and keep her feast day.

Interestingly, comparable traditions are told on the (black) Virgin of Montserrat, worshipped at Tortuga in the Central Range, and La Divina Pastora, celebrated in the former mission of Siparia in south Trinidad. Although basically of Spanish origin, some indigenous elements are obvious, notably the finding of the girl (or statue) at the cave entrance or the spring, both typically entries to the 'Other World' in Amerindian belief (see Chapter 5).[59] Besides, the legends associated with the devotions to the Holy Shepherdess, which attract pilgrims from all over the island up to the present, incorporate elements clearly of Warao derivation. With Arima, Siparia represents the modern town in Trinidad with the most distinct indigenous remembrances. The feast of La Divina Pastora has been celebrated a few weeks after Easter since the origin of the mission in the late eighteenth century. On this day a solemn procession of the statue of the Holy Shepherdess is held through the streets of Siparia. Numerous claims are made of miracles performed and favours granted through the divine intercession of the Holy Shepherdess especially during the celebrations. Over the years the statue of La Divina Pastora has become the object of veneration by non-Roman Catholics, notably Protestants of various denominations, Warao Amerindians, East Indian Hindus and Muslims, and formerly also Chinese. Hindus call the statue *Suparee Ke Mai* ('Mother of Siparia') and identify her with their goddess Kali. They have worshipped the saint

59 The Siparia legend says that hunters heard the crying of a child on Siparia Hill and on investigating found the statue of La Divina Pastora which they took to the priest of Oropuche. After the statue had disappeared three times, the priest decided to build a shrine at the place where it had been found.

from the time of indentureship on Holy Thursday and Good Friday, making offerings to the statue of jewelry, oil, rice, candles, and money. La Divina Pastora is claimed to heal the sick, grant wealth to the needy and allow barren women to give birth, demanding gifts of love and sincere thanks in exchange. Similarly, the Warao have paid homage to the Holy Shepherdess, who is considered to be their 'special protector' since time immemorial. The statue is seen as embodying *Dauarani* ('Mother of the Forest'), a goddess who, manifesting herself as a (red) tree serpent, originated as the transformation of the canoe made by Haburi, the Warao culture hero who after his flight from the mainland found his final home at Naparima Hill (see Chapter 5). Indeed, there are oral traditions in and around Siparia that the statue is originally Warao and was usurped by the Spanish.

The close relationship between the Warao and Trinidad, especially Siparia and Naparima Hill, no doubt originated in pre-Columbian times. In fact, at present there are still people of 'pure' or mixed Warao (and Arawak) ancestry living in south Trinidad. Besides, until the 1940s groups of mainland Warao regularly visited their sacred site of Naparima Hill for collecting quartz crystals and pieces of quartzite to be put inside shaman's rattles, also exchanging trade items for household goods and tobacco on the market of San Fernando (see Chapter 5). Some of them may have descended from Warao who formerly lived in south Trinidad. Although these journeys were forbidden by the Venezuelan government in the 1940s, Warao canoes, laden with for instance bows and arrows, hammocks, and birds, reportedly have been seen as far north as Port-of-Spain until recently.[60] Similarly, the presence of mainland Warao in the neighbourhood of Siparia was common until well into the twentieth century. About 1850 an English traveler reported he saw temporary huts made by visiting Warao, of a few poles with some branches of *carat* palms along the bridle path from Moruga to Savana Grande. By these years the Warao began to be seen as untameable, independent and elusive characters. Indeed, to this day individuals perceived as wild or gypsy-like in their behaviour are referred to as Warahoons. In south Trinidad horror stories are told of the Warao entering yards at night and stealing clothes off the drying lines or even snatching babies. In addition, according to folk tradition throughout the island, the Warao acquired supernatural powers. In the 1940s as far north as Toco they were seen as powerful shamans. By the 1890s the Warao became enshrined in the figure of the Wild Indian at Trinidad's carnival, although almost half a century earlier the first portrayals of 'Indians from South America' were performed during the carnival parade in Port-of-Spain by peon masqueraders daubed with red ochre and carrying Amerindian bows and arrows, quivers and baskets.[61]

60 In the folk tradition of south Trinidad the Warao were sometimes referred to as 'Caribs' and this may have been the origin of topographical names such as Carib Valley in Pointe-à-Pierre and Carib Street (with its Carib House) in San Fernando. The latter road initially was a foot path going up Naparima Hill, typically a track taken by the Warao during their pilgrimage to the sacred home of their culture hero Haburi.

61 In the 1930s Afro–Trinidadians took up Amerindian masking at carnival with its connotation of savagery and wildness. However, they dressed as 'Red Indians' from the North American plains, carrying bows and arrows. While this Amerindian masking was quite popular for some time, it lost its central place in carnival after the 1950s, although it remained important in San Fernando.

The present Amerindian community of Trinidad

According to the national population census of 2011, 1461 people in Trinidad and Tobago, or 0.11% of the twin islands' total population of 1.328 million people, consider themselves of 'indigenous' ancestry. However, it is quite obvious that (notably in Trinidad) there are people who, though subsumed in the census under the categories of 'African' or 'mixed ethnicity', in fact are of (partly) Amerindian descent. As noted already, most Trinidadians of full or partial indigenous extraction are to be found in the Toco/Cumana area and in and around the towns of Arima and Siparia. It is especially in Arima that the (Hispanized) Amerindian roots of its inhabitants have been emphasized by a dedicated couple of them during the past forty years or so. In 1976 Ricardo Bharath Hernandez founded the Santa Rosa Carib Community, which has recently renamed itself as the Santa Rosa First Peoples Community (SRFPC) in order to show that its membership is open to Amerindians of all ethnic affiliations. The SRFPC gradually has received recognition and support from successive governments of Trinidad and Tobago and the attention of the national media. Still at present Hernandez is the president of the SRFPC; he also held the office of deputy mayor of Arima. Thanks to him and the other SRFPC members, including the Carib Queen, in 1990 the organization was officially recognized by the government as the 'sole legitimate representative of Trinidad's retained community of Amerindians'. Besides, ten years later the government proclaimed October 14 (the anniversary of Hierreyma's destruction of St. Joseph in 1637) as the annual 'National Day of Recognition of Trinidad's Indigenous Peoples'. Recently, the SRFPC adopted a 'smoke ceremony', involving tobacco smoking by a New Age shaman accompanied by offerings of cassava bread and corn, and the burning of incense with the shaking of *shac-shacs*, as a means of reviving what are assumed to be original Amerindian beliefs and ritual.

The SRFPC has built a Carib Resource Center at Paul Mitchell Street on land donated by the Roman Catholic Church of Arima, where it attempts to revive the preparation of cassava bread and traditional indigenous handicrafts such as the weaving of baskets, mats, fans, and cassava sifters and strainers, using tirite bush ropes, and heavy baskets made of mamuri (*mamoo*) vines. Also, educational activities are being pursued in order to promote awareness and appreciation for the culture, history and traditions of the Caribs in Trinidad and Tobago. From 1990 onwards the SRFPC has received an annual subvention from the government as well as one from the Arima Borough Council for the Caribs' maintenance of the Santa Rosa Festival. Two years later, when Trinidad and Tobago played host to the Caribbean Festival of the Arts (CARIFESTA), Arima was allocated a generous grant by the government to act as the centre for Amerindian delegations from across the West Indies, what has since been referred to as 'The First Gathering' of Caribbean Amerindians in Trinidad. The following year the government in cooperation with the SRFPC hosted 'The Second Gathering' in Arima, and the SRFPC was formally applauded for its 'support of Indigenous causes worldwide'. Still in 1993 the organization received a National Award, the Chaconia Medal (Silver), for Culture and Community Service from the then President of the Republic of Trinidad and Tobago, Noor Hassanali. Finally, the government has leased five acres of land in

order for the SRFPC to establish a 'Model Amerindian Village', serving as an educational and cultural tourism facility. The Trinidad Regiment has offered the SRFPC assistance with the structural work, engineering and manpower needed in clearing the lands and constructing this village. This major project, which has been pursued by the SRFPC for years, still has to take shape.

The SRFPC activities intended to revive the Amerindian identity and to retrieve the old-time indigenous traditions of Arima has served as an example for other people of Amerindian descent in Trinidad, who wish to seek for their indigenous roots. Indeed, people of 'pure' and mixed Warao ancestry in the Siparia region, led by 'Elder' Rabina Shar, have recently organised a group, the Warao Nation, representing this ethnic community. The struggle for recognition as a distinct ethnic unit in the plural society of Trinidad and Tobago, as shown by the members of the Santa Rosa First Peoples Community and the Warao Nation, certainly contributes to the growth of local pride in being descended from the earliest peoples who occupied the twin islands, indeed the first inhabitants of the West Indian archipelago (Fig. 47).

Figure 47. The Carib Queen of Arima, accompanied by other Carib ladies, in traditional dress at the First Peoples' Heritage Day in October 2014. On the first row, from left to right: present Santa Rosa Carib Queen Jennifer Cassar, Catherine Hummingbird Ramirez and Joycelyn Coa.

Epilogue. The Amerindian heritage of Trinidad and Tobago

Although, as we have seen, the Amerindians disappeared from Tobago about two hundred years ago while at present only a small segment of Trinidad's population considers itself to be of 'pure' or mixed indigenous ancestry, the Amerindian influence on the material, linguistic and cultural characteristics of the twin islands' complicated modern society remains considerable. First of all, the some 300 registered archaeological sites in Trinidad and Tobago testify to the former occupation by successive Amerindian peoples of both islands well into the historic period, indeed until today. The lack of adequate legal protection of these places of former settlement and other activities by the first inhabitants of the two islands continues to be a sore point, which should be a matter of urgent interest to all those striving for the conservation of our cultural heritage. Sites such as Banwari Trace, Cedros, Palo Seco, Erin, St. Bernard, Savaneta, Golden Grove, Sandy Point, and St. Catherine's, to mention only a few which are still (partly) existing, are of more than local interest: they are of Caribbean-wide importance and should be treated as such.

A second category of hallmarks of the rich cultural heritage of indigenous origin in Trinidad is formed by the numerous toponyms (place names) of Amerindian derivation (Fig. 48). They are to be found all over Trinidad. (Indigenous place names are rare in Tobago.) In all 200 of Trinidad's toponyms are of Amerindian derivation, but since a single name may refer to five or six different topographical features, occurring in geographical clusters, actually not less than 450 of these carry Amerindian toponyms.[62] Moreover, the most important geographical elements of Trinidad have typically Amerindian names. While several of these toponyms may originally date from pre-Columbian times, others are more likely of more recent date, for instance coined by Amerindian-influenced Spanish or peons. The large number of Amerindian toponyms in Trinidad is unique for the Caribbean and reflects the limited Spanish occupation of the island until the 1780s and the long history of uninterrupted European–Amerindian interaction on the island. Besides, many of these names are derived from the indigenous names of trees, plants and animals which had no counterparts in Europe and, as a result, were adopted by the Spanish. Icacos (from *hicáco*, 'coco plum or fat pork' tree), Chaguaramas (from *chaguaramo*, 'palmiste' palm), Cunupia (from *cunupia*, 'mardi-gras' plant), and Carapal (from *carapa*, *crappo*, 'crabwood' tree) are examples. Various Amerindian names show Spanish influence, creating hybrid forms, for instance by the addition of terminals such as *-al* (meaning: 'a place of abundance of') and *-ito* or *-ita*

62 These topographical features include towns, villages, rivers, bays, springs, points (promontories), hills, mountains, estates, roads, forests, and reefs.

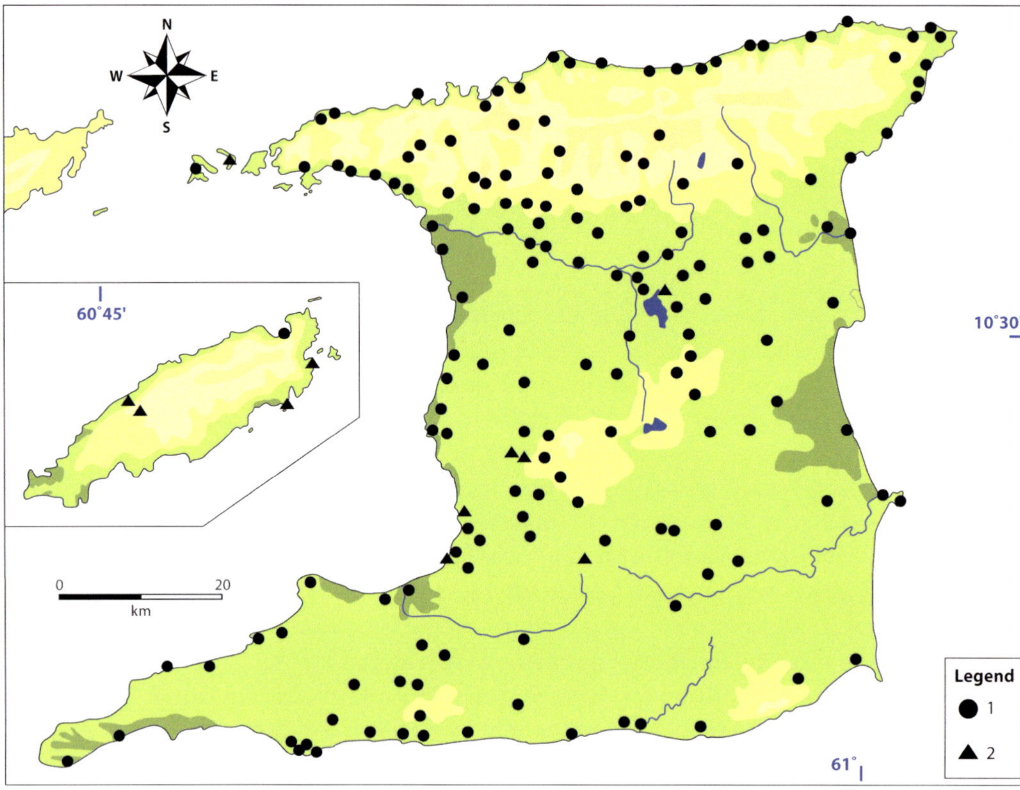

(meaning: 'a place of few'). Atagual, Morichal, Timital, Ariapita, Caurita, and Moriquito are examples. Also, spelling variations occur which are due to Spanish influence: Cuba/Couva, Marabal/Maraval, and Nariba/Nariva.

Figure 48. Map of Trinidad and Tobago (inset), showing: (1) Amerindian toponyms; (2) English and Spanish place names pointing to past Amerindian occupation or activity.

Interestingly, most indigenous toponyms of Cariban derivation are to be found in the northern part of Trinidad while those of Arawakan origin are restricted to the south and southwest coasts of the island. This reflects the settlement areas of the Amerindian peoples living in Trinidad at the time of Columbus. Besides, a few Warao names are to be found in the southwest. Many toponyms similar to those of Trinidad appear on the mainland as well, especially in eastern Venezuela, pointing to the close relationship between the Cariban and Arawakan dialects of Trinidad and those of the continent. Typically Cariban place names include El Cerro de Aripo (from *aripo*, 'cassava griddle'), El Tucuche (from *tukusi*, 'humming bird'), Tunapuna (from *tona*, 'water, river', and *-pona*, 'up, upon', thus: 'on the river'), Corozal (from *corozo*, 'grugru' palm), and Toco (from *toco*, 'wild sapodilla' tree). Arawakan place names are for instance Ceyba Point (from *ceiba*, 'silk cotton tree'), Siparia (from *tcipir*, 'hardwood', and *-ari*, 'rough, coarse'), Guarapiche (from *-piche*, 'stream, flow'), and Moruga (from *morekuie*, 'wood stork'). In addition to indigenous place names, there are English and Spanish toponyms in Trinidad which remind of Amerindian occupation, such as Indian Walk, Carib Valley, Carib Street, Indian Trail Road, and Raya del Caribe. Only one toponym in Tobago is probably of indigenous (Island Carib) origin, Man-of-War Bay (from *mánhore*, 'magnificent frigatebird'), although there are three English toponyms reminding of the Amerindian presence in the island, including King Peter's Bay, Indian Walk, and Indian Point, of which the latter name occurs at two locations.

There are various terms in the present English creole of Trinidad and Tobago which have been adopted directly from one of the Amerindian languages that were spoken on the two islands or from a European language, notably Spanish or French, which had incorporated particular Amerindian expressions. Many of these words are names of plants, trees and animals, some of which are found also in the Trinidadian toponyms. Such names are quenk (from *cuenco*, 'peccary'), iguana ('lizard'), lappe (from *lapa*, 'large rodent'), manicou ('opossum'), colibri ('humming bird'), genip (from *genipa*, 'genip fruit'), pachro (from *pakro*, 'chiton'), and chipchip (from *chipichipe*, 'donax clam'), to mention only a few. In addition, there are names of objects of Amerindian material culture which have passed over into the modern English of Trinidad and Tobago. Examples are pirogue (from *piragua*), barbecue (from *barbacoa*), boutou (from *aputu*, 'weapon stick'), sebucan (from *cibucan*, 'cassava squeezer, coulev'), and canoe (from *canoa*). The same can be said of names of food or dishes such as arep (from *arepa*, 'fried cornmeal pie with meat filling'), maize (from *maisi*), and cassava (from *cazabi*). Finally, a quite interesting group of nouns, current in the present creole of the twin islands, made a long journey to arrive here. They originate from the Tupian language of the Amerindians of the Brazilian coast where these words were adopted by French traders in the early sixteenth century. Incorporated in French, these names of plants, animals and items of indigenous material culture were introduced to the Caribbean, notably the French West Indies. (Here several of them were adopted by the local Island Caribs.) Finally, they landed in Trinidad with the French immigration of the 1780s and spread to Tobago afterwards. These words include agouti (from *acuti*), tapir (from *tapira*), ajoupa (from *aiupaue*), boucan (from *mocaem*, 'barbecue'), roucou (from *urucu*, 'red colouring'), and callaloo (from *caaruru*).

Apart from names of places, animals, plants, and things, the present people of Trinidad and Tobago owe much in terms of ecological knowledge, subsistence practices, ways of food preparation, material culture, traditional medicines, and folk beliefs to the indigenous inhabitants of the two islands. This is especially due to the transmission of lifeways between the Amerindians (with the peons) and the African slave population of colonial times and their descendants, the island peasantry which developed after Emancipation. Besides, there are nowadays still very viable social phenomena which belong to the Amerindian (and peon) legacy of Trinidad and Tobago. *Gayap* (or *lend-hand*) forms an example. Important cultural transfers from the Amerindians (and peons) to the island peasantry also took place with respect to the technology of subsistence agriculture and the food crops and fruits cultivated (see Chapter 5). Actually, small farming in the twin islands today can be seen to form a syncretic fusion of African and European elements with already existing systems of indigenous cultivation and food preparation. The same applies to the fishing and hunting techniques which are or were being applied by local people. Besides, among the small farmers of Trinidad and Tobago the traditional division of labour between men and women regarding the various subsistence activities closely resembles that of Amerindian (and peon) society. Similarly, the knowledge of medicinal plants and their use for the treatment of injuries and in the preparation of 'bush teas', taken for curing illnesses, which exists among many local people, most likely owes much to old Amerindian and peon curative practices which were handed down from generation to generation, and shared with the small farmers of African ancestry in colonial times. Of course, this applies also to the use of baths as protection against perceived evil spells and mischievous forces, and for ritual cleansing. Finally, the Spanish *mestizos* and African slaves and their descendants were profoundly influenced by Amerindian religious convictions and cosmological views, leading to various forms of amalgamation between Amerindian, African and European beliefs (see Chapter 5). All of this suggests that although people of 'pure' or mixed Amerindian descent form only a small segment of the population of Trinidad and Tobago, nowadays many originally Amerindian linguistic, social and cultural traditions are generally shared by people of all kinds of ethnic derivation throughout the twin islands.

Glossary

Acarewana **:** (C) Indigenous term used for Amerindian chiefs or 'great men' in Trinidad and the Orinoco Valley.

Adornos **:** (S) Human- and animal-like or geometric head lugs shown on the pre-Columbian pottery of the Caribbean.

Ajoupa **:** (T) Small wattle-and-daub cottage in traditional Spanish style, thatched with palm leaves, of which the loam used for plastering the walls was applied to a stick framework (see also: '*tapia*').

Alcalde **:** (S) Magistrate in Spanish town.

Alguacil **:** (S) Constable or police officer in Spanish town.

Anglophone : English-speaking.

Anthropophagus : man-eater, cannibal.

Anthropozoomorphic head lugs : Modeled faces on pottery vessels showing both human-like and animal-like features (see also '*adornos*').

Appliqué fillets : Narrow strips of clay applied as a form of decoration to the wall of pottery vessels.

Aragon : Formerly independent kingdom in northeast Spain.

Arauquinoid : Amerindian cultural tradition (called after the Arauquín site in the Middle Orinoco Valley on the mainland), distributed in the Guianas, Venezuela and Trinidad, marking the last part of the Ceramic Age, in Trinidad from ca. AD 650/800 until 1450.

Arawak (Aruac) : (A) Arawakan-speaking Amerindian people originally living in the Guianas, the Orinoco Valley and south Trinidad (see also: 'Lokóno', 'True Arawak').

Arawakan : Family of related Amerindian languages distributed in Amazonia, the Guianas and the Caribbean.

Archaeology : systematic study of past human culture and society through the recovery and excavation of material remains.

Archaic Age : Stage in the development of Amerindian culture and society, characterized by a subsistence economy based on hunting, fishing, collecting, and incipient horticulture, and a technology typified by stone, bone, and shell artifacts, generally lacking pottery.

Arquebus : Fifteenth-century matchlock gun, usually fired from a support.

Artifact : Man-made, used or modified object.

Autodenomination : Common name given by the members of an ethnic group to themselves.

Barrancoid : Amerindian cultural tradition (called after the Barrancas site in the Lower Orinoco Valley on the mainland), distributed in the Guianas, Venezuela and Trinidad, marking the middle part of the Ceramic Age, in Trinidad from ca. AD 300 until 650/800

Bergantine **:** (S) Two-masted Spanish sailing vessel.

Biotic community : All living organisms living in a particular environment.

Black Carib : Offspring of the Island Carib and African slaves escaped especially from Barbados who organized themselves as an Amerindian people on St. Vincent, adopting language, culture and society from the Island Carib (see also: 'Red (Yellow) Carib').

Boutou **:** (C) Wooden war club, used by the Amerindians in the contact period.

Cabildo **:** (S) Spanish town council.

Cacique **:** (A) Indigenous term for an Amerindian chief.

Camp or bivouac sites : Locations utilized shortly by the Amerindians for dwelling during hunting, fishing or collecting expeditions.

Capitán **:** (S) Term adopted by the Amerindians for 'chief' under European influence.

Capitán poblador **:** (S) Officer in charge of the Spanish missions in northeast Trinidad with similar functions as the *corregidor*.

Capuchins : Roman Catholic Order of friars, which has undertaken missionary activities in many parts of the world.

Caraculí **:** (C) Decorative ornaments made of an alloy (mixture) of gold, copper and silver, originating from the South American mainland and distributed into the West Indies (see also: '*guanín*').

Carib : (C) Cariban- and Arawakan-speaking Amerindian people originally living in the Guianas, the Orinoco Valley, north Trinidad, Tobago, and the Lesser Antilles (see also: 'Island Carib', 'Kali'na', 'Kali'nago', 'Mainland Carib', 'Red (Yellow) Carib').

Cariban : Family of related Amerindian languages distributed in Amazonia, the Guianas and the Caribbean.

Carinepagoto : (C) Cariban-speaking Carib people living in northwest Trinidad throughout the contact period.

Casa de cabildo **:** (S) Spanish town hall.

Casa real **:** (S) Governor's residence in Spanish town.

Catalonia : Region of northeast Spain, formerly part of the independent kingdom of Aragon.

Cayo complex : Amerindian cultural tradition (called after the Cayo site on St. Vincent), identical to that of the Island Carib, distributed in the Lesser Antilles and Trinidad and Tobago, marking the end of pre-Columbian times and the contact period until well into the eighteenth century.

Cedrosan : Amerindian cultural subtradition of the Saladoid series (called after the Cedros site in Trinidad), distributed in the Guianas, the Venezuelan coast and the West Indies, marking the early and middle parts of the Ceramic Age, in Trinidad and Tobago from ca. 200 BC until AD 650/800.

Ceramic Age : Stage in the development of Amerindian culture and society, characterized by a subsistence economy based on hunting, fishing, collecting, and developed horticulture, and a technology typified by pottery (ceramics), and stone, bone and shell artifacts.

Chaguanes (Siawani) : (W) Waraoan-speaking subgroup of the Warao, originally living in west Trinidad and the Orinoco delta.

Chert : hard and dense rock type used by the Caribbean Amerindians for making small tools employed for various purposes.

Clan : Kin group, not necessarily living together ('non-residential'), tracing descent from a common (often mythical) ancestor.

Cocoa panyols **:** (S) Nickname (derived from *español*) for the 'peons' who migrated to Trinidad from the mainland in the late eighteenth through early twentieth centuries, referring to their strong involvement in the cocoa industry (see also: 'peons').

Complex (style) : The characteristic material culture traits of a group of people, retrieved through archaeological means.

Conquistador **:** (S) Spanish conquerer.

Contact period : Episode of the first Amerindian–European contacts, generally taken to last into the sixteenth and seventeenth centuries.

Contrabandistas **:** (S) Term ('smugglers') used by the Spanish to refer to the English, French and Dutch who came as traders to the Spanish Caribbean in the sixteenth through seventeenth centuries.

Conuco (swidden) **:** (A) Small plot of agricultural land, often cleared by slash-and-burn methods and cultivated with simple means for only a few years (see also: '*conuquero*').

Conuquero **:** (S) Peasant or small farmer (see also: '*conuco*').

Corregidor **:** (S) Spanish official appointed by the government and charged with the protection of the mission Amerindians, the collecting of tribute and the regulation of the *mita*.

Coulevre **:** (F) Cassava press made of twilled basketry used to expel the poisonous hydrocyanic acid from the grated pulp (see also: '*matapee*', '*sebucán*').

Coureurs des îles **:** (F) Traders, woodcutters and turtlers from the French West Indies who moved around the Lesser Antilles during the seventeenth and eighteenth centuries.

Cuatro **:** (S) Small Latin American stringed instrument, usually with four strings, especially popular in Venezuela and introduced to Trinidad by the peons.

Cultigen : Domesticated plant.

Cura doctrinero **:** (S) Spanish priest charged with the conversion and instruction of the mission Amerindians.

Diorite : Rock type with a black-and-white mottled appearance, typically found in central Tobago.

Distaff : Small staff for holding the wool or cotton in spinning.

Ducat **:** (S) Spanish monetary unit and gold coin.

Encomendero/a **:** (S) Recipient of an *encomienda*.

Encomienda ('command') **:** (S) Grant of Amerindian village given to Spanish colonists as a personal reward for services or merits, including the benefit of the natives' labour.

Entrada **:** (S) Spanish exploration journey, searching for treasure.

Estuarine environment : Brackish transition zone between a river mouth and the sea.

Ethnic group : Group of people ('nation'), historically established on a given territory, possessing relatively stable linguistic and cultural characteristics and recognizing their unity and difference as expressed in a self-appointed name.

Ethnocentrism : judging another culture solely by the values and standards of one's own culture.

Exogamy : Requirement for marriage outside a particular social group or range of kinship.

Factor : Head of a Dutch trading post in the interior of the Guianas in colonial times.

Frontier : Transition zone or shifting borderland between areas inhabited by different peoples, in the Americas that between the Amerindians and Europeans.

Galeones **('galleons') :** (S) Spanish colonial fleet of merchant vessels with accompanying warships (galleons), destined for the *Tierra Firme* ('mainland') and occasionally sailing through the Galleons' Passage between Trinidad and Tobago.

Gayap (gaiappe) **:** (C) Communal work of a group of male in-laws, neighbours and friends, being rewarded with food and drinks after completion of the task, for instance the clearing of a garden and the construction of a house or a boat.

Greater Antilles : The group of large islands in the northwest of the Caribbean, including Cuba, Jamaica, Hispaniola (Haiti and Dominican Republic), and Puerto Rico.

Guanín **:** (A) Alloy (mixture) of gold, copper and silver, used for making ornaments on the South American mainland (see also: '*caraculí*').

Guatiao **:** (A) Amerindians who were considered to be friends and allies of the Spanish in the contact period.

Guayabitan : Amerindian cultural subtradition of the Arauquinoid series (called after the Guayabita site in Northeast Venezuela), distributed in east Venezuela and Trinidad, marking the last part of the Ceramic Age, from ca. AD 650/800 until 1450.

Guayaco **:** (C) Small loin cloth tied on both sides by a string encircling the waist, worn by male Amerindians in the contact period.

Haburi : (W) Warao culture hero, legendary inventor of the canoe and the paddle, who fled from the mainland with his mother and her sister to south Trinidad and found a refuge on Naparima Hill.

Hallucinogenic drugs : Psychoactive substances that induce hallucinations.

Hematite : Red iron stone, used by the Amerindians for obtaining red colouring used for decorating pottery and other material items.

Humus : Brown to black soil, originating from the decomposition of plant or animal matter.

Indios **:** (S) Term applied by Columbus to the inhabitants of the Americas as he mistakenly assumed that he had discovered a western route to Asia ('India').

Inhumation (burial) : Ritual deposition of a dead person's body into a grave, subsequently to be covered with earth.

Invertebrates : animals without a vertebral column, such as insects, crabs, lobsters, snails, clams, octopuses, starfish, sea-urchins, and worms.

Island Arawak : Term applied by nineteenth-century linguists to the Amerindians of the Greater Antilles, as in the contact period most of the latter spoke a language belonging to the Arawakan language family.

Island Carib : Term given by anthropologists to the Kali'nago/Kali'puna of the Lesser Antilles.

Isotope analysis : See 'strontium isotope analysis'.

Jumbie **:** (Afr) Spirit character of often malevolent character, the ghost of a dead person.

Kali'na (Kari'na) : (C) Name which the Mainland Carib gave to themselves, meaning 'the people'.

Kali'nago : (C) Name, derived from Kali'na, which the male Island Carib gave to their people.

Kali'puna : (A) Name which the female Island Carib gave to their people.

Language (linguistic) family : Group of related languages (see also: 'Arawakan', 'Cariban', 'Tupian').

Legua **('league') :** Spanish unit of distance, about 5.5 km.

Lesser Antilles : Archipelago of small islands stretching from Trinidad and Tobago to Puerto Rico and the Virgin Islands, including Barbados, the Windward Islands and Leeward Islands.

Lignite : Brownish-black coal, in Trinidad naturally occurring in the Central Range.

Lithic : First stage in the development of Amerindian culture and society, characterized by a subsistence economy primarily based on hunting and collecting, and a technology typified by chipped stone and bone artifacts.

Loam : Soil consisting of a friable mixture of clay, silt and sand.

Lokóno : (A) Name the Arawak gave to themselves, meaning 'the people' (see: 'Arawak').

Mainland Carib : Term given by anthropologists to the Cariban-speaking Kali'na of the Guianas and the Orinoco Valley.

Mait-source **:** (F) Mythical folk creature acting as the protector of the fishes which developed out of the Amerindian spirit character known as the Master of Fish.

Majolica **:** (S) Tin-enamel glazed, colourful Italian and Spanish tableware (dishes and plates), first made in the Middle Ages.

Maloca **:** (T) Amerindian multi-family house, formerly to be found in large parts of the South American mainland (and Trinidad).

Maman-Dlo **:** (F) Mythical folk creature, believed to live in pools and rivers, which developed out of a female Amerindian spirit character acting as a protectress of women in childbirth.

Maraca, marac **:** (A/C/T) Calabash rattle, used by Amerindian shamans during nocturnal healing séances (see also: '*peai*-man', '*shac-shac*', 'shaman').

Matapee **:** (C) Cassava press made of twilled basketry used to expel the poisonous hydrocyanic acid from the grated pulp (see also: '*sebucán*', '*coulevre*').

Mayoid : Amerindian cultural tradition in Trinidad (called after the Mayo site in the Central Range), marking the end of pre-Columbian times and the contact period until well into the eighteenth century.

Mean sea level (MSL) : Average level of the ocean's surface.

***Mestizo* :** (S) Spanish term for the offspring of a white and an Amerindian.

Micaceous schist : Rock type, containing large quantities of (shiny) mica particles, with a tendency to split in layers. It is typical of Trinidad's Northern Range.

Midden deposit : Refuse heap, often consisting of large accumulations of shells and other food remains, fragments of pottery and/or artifacts of stone, bone, shell, and coral, forming part of a former settlement site.

***Misiónes* ('missions') :** (S) Villages established on the mainland and Trinidad by the Spanish in order to convert, discipline and exploit the Amerindians who were compelled to live in them.

***Mita* :** (S) Draft labour system for public works, compulsory for each Amerindian village under Spanish control.

Morisco : Spanish Moor, descendant of the Arabs who inhabited Spain before the fall of Granada (1492).

Mortuary (burial) gift : Object(s) put into a grave in order to accompany a dead person's body.

***Mulato* :** (S) Spanish term for the offspring of a white and an African.

Nepoio : (C?) Probably Cariban-speaking Amerindian people living in central and east Trinidad and the Orinoco Valley during the contact period.

New Age : Spiritual movement drawing on ancient concepts from various Amerindian and Eastern traditions.

***Oraciónes* :** (S) Prayers and prayer songs used in curing by peon healers.

Ortoiroid : Amerindian cultural tradition (called after the Ortoire site in southeast Trinidad), distributed in the Guianas, Venezuela and the West Indies, marking the Archaic Age, in Trinidad and Tobago from ca. 6000 to 500 BC.

***Papa-Bois* :** (F) Mythical folk creature acting as the protector of the forest animals, which developed out of the Amerindian spirit character known as the Master of Animals.

***Parang* :** (S) Hispanic American music and songs introduced to Trinidad by the peons of Amerindian–Spanish–African descent and usually played during the Christmas season.

***Patois* :** (F) Creole French spoken in the Lesser Antilles and Trinidad and Tobago.

***Peai*-man *(piaye)* :** (C) Amerindian shaman (medicine man), employing hallucinogenic drugs in order to contact the spirit world for healing, predicting the future and to cast evil spells (see also: 'hallucinogenic drugs').

Pearl islands : Cubagua, Margarita and Coche offshore east Venezuela, where the Spanish had Amerindians dive for pearl oysters during the sixteenth century.

Pelagic fishes : Fish species living in the open sea.

***Peones* ('peons') :** (S) Small farmers of Amerindian–Spanish–African descent who migrated to Trinidad from the mainland especially from the late eighteenth to early twentieth century (see also: '*cocoa panyols*').

Petroglyph : Amerindian rock drawing made by pecking, grinding and abrading.

Plural society : Society composed of a medley of peoples, each holding its own religion, language and culture to a certain extent.

Pottery repertoire : Complete variety of different vessel forms characterizing a site or cultural tradition.

Pre-Columbian period : episode in the Amerindian past before the arrival of Columbus (1492) in the West Indies (see also: 'prehistory').

Prehistory : era in the human past before the first written documents (in Trinidad before the arrival of Columbus in 1498).

***Pueblo de doctrina* :** (S) Spanish mission village in which a *corregidor* acted as its administrative and executive officer while the authority of the resident priest was limited to spiritual matters (see also: '*pueblo de viva conversión* (*reducción*)').

***Pueblo de viva conversión (reducción)* :** (S) Spanish mission village during its first twenty years of existence when the missionary had absolute authority over the Amerindians in civil as well as spiritual matters (see also: '*pueblo de doctrina*').

Radiocarbon dating (14C dating) : A scientific dating method, used for archaeological finds, based on measuring the decay of the radioactive isotope of carbon in organic materials, notably charcoal, wood, shells, and bone.

***Real* :** Spanish monetary unit and coin.

Red (Yellow) Carib : Term used in the eighteenth century to refer to the Island Carib of the Lesser Antilles in order to distinguish them from the Black Carib (see also: 'Island Carib', 'Kali'nago', 'Kali'puna').

***Regidor* :** (S) Councillor attached to the *cabildo* of a Spanish town.

***Repartimiento* :** (S) System of land partition among the first Spanish invaders of the Caribbean islands.

***Rescate* :** (S) Spanish slave raiding and trade expeditions in the contact period.

***Roucou* :** (T) Red pigment and food colouring/flavouring obtained from the seeds of a cultivated shrub or small tree.

Saladoid : Amerindian cultural tradition (called after the Saladero site in the Lower Orinoco Valley on the mainland), distributed in the Guianas, Venezuela and the West Indies, marking the early and middle parts of the Ceramic Age, in Trinidad and Tobago from ca. 200 BC until AD 650/800.

***Sambo* :** (S) Spanish term for the offspring of an Amerindian and an African.

Santa Rosa First Peoples Community : Amerindian organisation originally founded at Arima as the 'Santa Rosa Carib Community' (1976), intended to revive the Amerindian identity and retrieve the old-time indigenous traditions of the town.

***Sebucán* :** (A) Cassava press made of twilled basketry used to expel the poisonous hydrocyanic acid from the grated pulp (see also: '*coulevre*', '*matapee*').

Series : Cultural tradition reconstructed from archaeological finds.

Serpentinite : Greenish rock type, in prehistory often used for carving ornaments or tools.

***Shac-shac* :** Calabash rattle, at present used by *parang* and calypso musicians, developed out of the Amerindian shaman's rattle (see also: '*maraca*').

Shaman : Medicine man (see also: '*peai*-man').

Shebaio : (A) Arawakan-speaking Amerindian people living on the south coast of Trinidad and the coastal zone of the Guianas during the contact period.

Spindle whorl : Small flywheel that regulates the speed of a hand-operated spindle.

***Staten* ('States') :** (D) Local government of the seven provinces that made up the Dutch Republic, also represented in the joint *Staten Generaal* ('States General').

Strontium isotope analysis : Scientific method of determining the relative ratio of the radioactive isotope of strontium in human bones, used in archaeology to provide information on the diet and geographical origin of the individuals sampled.

Swidden : garden plot, cleared by slash-and-burn techniques and planted with a few crops, often cultivated for only a few years.

***Taíno* :** (A) Term applied by anthropologists collectively to most of the Amerindian peoples of the Greater Antilles (see also: 'Island Arawak').

Tapia **:** (S) Loam mixed with straw and occasionally animal dung, used for plastering the wattle-work walls of cottages built in the Spanish fashion (see: '*ajoupa*').

Tierra Firme **('mainland') fleet :** (S) See: *galeones* ('galleons').

Troumassoid : Amerindian cultural tradition (called after the Troumassée site on St. Lucia), distributed in Tobago and the Lesser Antilles, marking the last part of the Ceramic Age, in Tobago from ca. AD 650/800 until 1450.

True Arawak : Term applied by anthropologists to the Arawak (or Lokóno) in order to distinguish them from the Arawakan-speaking peoples (or '*Taíno*') of the Greater Antilles (see: 'Island Arawak').

Tupian : Family of related Amerindian languages distributed on the Brazilian coast.

Vecino **:** (S) Householder in a Spanish town.

Virilocality : Residence of a married couple with the husband's kin.

Vocabulary : List or collection of words or words and phrases, alphabetically organized, defined and explained.

Warao : (W) Waraoan-speaking Amerindian people originally living in southwest Trinidad, the Orinoco delta and northwest Guyana.

Waraoan : Language spoken by the Warao.

Yaio : (C) Cariban-speaking Amerindian people living in southwest Trinidad and on the coast of the Guianas in the contact period.

Yopa **:** (A) Hallucinogenic sniffing powder made from the crushed seeds of the *Anadenanthera* tree, used by Amerindian shamans in order to induce an ecstatic trance during which they are able to contact the spirit world (see 'hallucinogenic drugs', '*peai*-man').

Abbreviations: A, Arawakan; Afr, African language; C, Cariban; D, Dutch; F, French; S, Spanish; T, Tupian (Brazil); W, Waraoan.

Bibliography

Pre-Columbian and historic Amerindian archaeology

Boomert, Arie, 1982 – Our Amerindian heritage. *Naturalist Magazine* 4 (4): 26–61.

Boomert, Arie, 1982 – The rock drawings of Caurita. *Naturalist Magazine* 4 (6): 38–44.

Boomert, Arie, 1985 – The Guayabitoid and Mayoid series: Amerindian culture history in Trinidad during late prehistoric and protohistoric times. *Proceedings Tenth International Congress for the Study of the Pre-Columbian Cultures of the Lesser Antilles, Martinique 1983*: 93–148.

Boomert, Arie, 1986 – The Cayo complex of St. Vincent: Ethnohistorical and archaeological aspects of the Island Carib problem. *Antropológica* 66: 3–68.

Boomert, Arie, 1996 – *The Prehistoric Sites of Tobago: A Catalogue and Evaluation*. Alkmaar: The author.

Boomert, Arie, 2000 – *Trinidad, Tobago and the Lower Orinoco Interaction Sphere: An Archaeological/Ethnohistorical Study*. Alkmaar: Cairi Publications.

Boomert, Arie, 2001 – Saladoid sociopolitical organization. *Proceedings Eighteenth International Congress for Caribbean Archaeology, Grenada 1999*, II: 55–77.

Boomert, Arie, 2001 – Raptorial birds as icons of shamanism in the prehistoric Caribbean and Amazonia. *Proceedings Nineteenth International Congress for Caribbean Archaeology, Aruba 2001*, II: 121–157.

Boomert, Arie, 2002 – Agricultural societies in the continental Caribbean. In: Jalil Sued Badillo, ed., *General History of the Caribbean*, I: *Autochthonous Societies*: 134–194. Paris/London: UNESCO Publishing/Macmillan Caribbean.

Boomert, Arie, 2005 – Golden Grove: A late-prehistoric ceramic complex of Tobago. *Leiden Journal of Pottery Studies* 21: 27–60.

Boomert, Arie, 2007 – Plymouth: A late-prehistoric ceramic complex of Tobago. *Leiden Journal of Pottery Studies* 23: 121–158.

Boomert, Arie, 2009 – Between the mainland and the islands: The Amerindian cultural geography of Trinidad. *Bulletin of the Peabody Museum of Natural History* 50 (1): 63–73.

Boomert, Arie, 2010 – Crossing the Galleons' Passage: Amerindian interaction and cultural (dis)unity between Trinidad and Tobago. In: Corinne L. Hofman and Alistair J. Bright, eds., 'Mobility and Exchange from a Pan-Caribbean Perspective', *Journal of Caribbean Archaeology*, Special Publication 3: 106–121.

Boomert, Arie, 2012 – Gateway to the mainland: Trinidad and Tobago. In: William F. Keegan, Corinne L. Hofman and Reniel Rodríguez Ramos, eds., *The Oxford Handbook of Caribbean Archaeology*: 141–154. Oxford University Press.

Boomert, Arie, 2014 – The Caribbean Islands. In: Colin Renfrew and Paul Bahn, eds., *The Cambridge World Prehistory*, vol. 2: *East Asia and the Americas*: 1217–1234. Cambridge: Cambridge University Press.

Boomert, Arie, 2015 – Prehistoric Tobago: An outline. *Archaeology and Anthropology: Journal of the Walter Roth Museum of Anthropology* 19 (2): 35–50.

Boomert, Arie, Birgit Faber-Morse and B. Irving Rouse, 2013 – *The Yale University Excavations in Trinidad of 1946 and 1953*. Yale University Publications in Anthropology 92. New Haven: Yale University Press.

Boomert, Arie, and Peter O'Brien Harris, 1984 – The Pitch Lake in archaeology. *Naturalist Magazine* 5 (11): 34–47.

Boomert, Arie, and Peter O'Brien Harris, 1988 – *An Inventory of the Archaeological Sites in Trinidad and Tobago*. St. Augustine, Trinidad: The University of the West Indies.

Boomert, Arie, and Léonid Kameneff, 2003 – Preliminary report on archaeological investigations at Great Courland Bay, Tobago. *Proceedings Twentieth International Congress for Caribbean Archaeology, Santo Domingo 2003*, II: 457–468.

Boomert, Arie, Omar R. Ortiz-Troncoso and H.H. van Regteren Altena, 1987 – Archaeological-Historical survey of Tobago, West Indies. *Journal de la Société des Américanistes* 73: 246–258.

Boomert, Arie, and Cassandra T. Rogers, 2007 – Troumassoid stone artifacts in Tobago: Rock types and source areas. *Proceedings Twenty-first International Congress for Caribbean Archaeology, Trinidad 2005*, I: 282–294.

Chauharjasingh, Archibald S. 1994 – Sixteenth century chevron beads found in Trinidad. *Gayap: Review of the Arts 1984–1994*: 26. San Fernando Arts Council, Trinidad.

Clement, Christopher O., 2000 – Remnant Amerindian groups on eighteenth century Tobago, West Indies?: A comparison of coarse earthenwares from four sites. *The Florida Anthropologist* 53 (1): 12–25.

Dorst, Marc C., 2000 – *Manzanilla 1: An Archaeological Survey of a Pre-Columbian Site on Trinidad: Spatial Patterning, Ceramics, Lithics and Faunal Remains*. MA Thesis, Leiden University.

Dorst, Marc C., 2004 – Manzanilla 1: Creating a site-scale pottery classification at a multi-component Ceramic age site on Trinidad. *Leiden Journal of Pottery Studies* 20: 53–74.

Dorst, Marc C., 2008 – *The Pre-Columbian SAN-1 Site, Manzanilla, Trinidad: Preliminary Research Report Fieldwork October 2007*. Port-of-Spain: National Archaeological Committee of Trinidad and Tobago.

Fewkes, Jesse W., 1907 – *The Aborigines of Porto Rico and Neighboring Islands*. Washington, DC: Twenty-fifth Annual Report of the Bureau of American Ethnology (1903–1904).

Harris, Peter O'Brien, 1973 – Preliminary report on Banwari Trace, a preceramic site in Trinidad. *Proceedings Fourth International Congress for the Study of the Pre-Columbian Cultures of the Lesser Antilles, St. Lucia 1971*: 115–125.

Harris, Peter O'Brien, 1976 – The Preceramic period in Trinidad. In: Linda Sickler Robinson, ed., *Proceedings of the First Puerto Rican Symposium on Archaeology*: 33–64. San Juan de Puerto Rico: Fundación Arqueológica, Antropológica e Historica de Puerto Rico Report 1.

Harris, Peter O'Brien, 1978 – A revised chronological framework for Ceramic Trinidad and Tobago. *Proceedings Seventh International Congress for the Study of the Pre-Columbian Cultures of the Lesser Antilles, Caracas 1977*: 47–63.

Harris, Peter O'Brien, 1991 – Amerindian Trinidad and Tobago. *Proceedings Twelfth International Congress for Caribbean Archaeology, Cayenne 1987*: 259–269.

Harris, Peter O'Brien, 1991 – A Paleo-Indian stemmed point from Trinidad, West Indies. *Proceedings Fourteenth International Congress for Caribbean Archaeology, Barbados 1991*: 73–93.

Healy, Paul F., Anne Keenleyside and Marc C. Dorst, 2013 – Isotope analysis and radiocarbon dating of prehistoric human bone from the Manzanilla (SAN 1) site, Trinidad. *Caribbean Connections* 3 (1): 30–45.

Jansen, Richard, and Marc C. Dorst, 2007 – Spatial patterning and structures of the multi-component Ceramic age site SAN 1, Manzanilla, Trinidad. *Proceedings Twenty-first International Congress for Caribbean Archaeology, Trinidad 2005*, I: 315–327.

Laffoon, Jason E., 2012 – *Patterns of Paleomobility in the Ancient Antilles*. PhD dissertation, Leiden University.

Lopinot, Neil H., 2012 – *The La Reconnaissance Site, a Prehistoric Village in the Trinidad Interior*. Springfield, MO: Missouri State University.

Lopinot, Neil H., 2013 – *Summary of Archaeological Research by the Center for Archaeological Research, Missouri State University – March 21–April 13, 2013*. Springfield, MO: Missouri State University.

Mickleburgh, Hayley L., 2012 – Unusual patterns of dental calculus deposits in skeletal material from the site of Manzanilla, Trinidad: Bioarchaeological evidence for habitual coca leaf chewing? *Caribbean Connections* 2/1.

Mickleburgh, Hayley L., and Jaime R. Pagán-Jiménez, 2012 – New insights into the consumption of maize and other food plants in the pre-Columbian Caribbean from starch grains trapped in human dental calculus. *Journal of Archaeological Science* 39: 2468–2478.

Mones, Micah, 2007 – Amerindian lithics of Tobago: A preliminary report. *Proceedings Twenty-first International Congress for Caribbean Archaeology, Trinidad 2005*, II: 757–766.

Nieweg, Dennis C., 2000 – *Shells in Archaeology: Archaeological Shell on Trinidad and Guadeloupe: Two Case Studies*, 2 vols. MA Thesis, Leiden University.

Nieweg, Dennis C., and Marc C. Dorst, 2001 – The Manzanilla 1 (SAN-1) site, Trinidad. *Proceedings Nineteenth International Congress for Caribbean Archaeology, Aruba 2001*, I: 173–185.

Ostapkowicz, Joanna, Christopher Bronk Ramsey, Alex C. Wiedenhoeft, Fiona Brock, Tom Higham, and Samuel M. Wilson, 2011 – 'This relic of antiquity': Fifth to fifteenth century wood carvings from the southern Lesser Antilles. In: Corinne L. Hofman and Anne van Duijvenbode, eds., *Communities in Contact: Essays on Archaeology, Ethnohistory and Ethnography of the Amerindian Circum-Caribbean*: 137–170. Leiden: Sidestone Press.

Pagán-Jiménez, Jaime, Reniel Rodríguez-Ramos, Basil A. Reid, Martijn van den Bel, and Corinne L. Hofman, 2015 – Early dispersals of maize and other food plants into the Southern Caribbean and Northeastern South America. *Quaternary Science Reviews* 123: 231–246.

Ray, Jack H., 2015 – Procurement and use of chert from localized sources in Trinidad. *Journal of Caribbean Archaeology* 15: 1-28.

Reid, Basil A., 2003 – *Archaeological Surveys and Excavation of Lot 13 of Marianne Estate, Blanchisseuse, Trinidad (July–August 2003)*. St. Augustine, Trinidad: The University of the West Indies.

Reid, Basil A., 2011 – Interim report on the St. John Archaeology Project. *Archaeology and Anthropology: Journal of the Walter Roth Museum of Anthropology* 17 (1): 39–54.

Steadman, David W., and Sharyn Jones, 2006 – Long-term trends in prehistoric fishing and hunting on Tobago, West Indies. *Latin American Antiquity* 17 (3): 316–334.

Steadman, David W., and Anne V. Stokes, 2002 – Changing exploitation of terrestrial vertebrates during the past 3000 years on Tobago, West Indies. *Human Ecology* 30 (3): 339–367.

Steadman, David W., and Anne V. Stokes, 2003 – An archaeological survey and test excavation at the Saladoid Blanchisseuse site, Trinidad. *Proceedings Twentieth International Congress for Caribbean Archaeology, Santo Domingo 2003*, I: 399–406.

Primary historic sources and maps

Aguado, Pedro de, 1963 [1581] – *Recopilación Historial de Venezuela*, 2 vols. Ed. Guillermo Morón. Caracas: Academia Nacional de Historia.

Andrews, Kenneth R., ed., 1959 – *English Privateering Voyages to the West Indies 1588–1595*. London: Hakluyt Society.

Anonymous, ca. 1780 – *Concerning the Island of Trinidad which bears North-South in relation to the Dragon's Mouth*. Transl. from the Spanish by Kemlin M. Laurence. St. Augustine, Trinidad: University of the West Indies (typescript).

Basanta, Joseph, 1853 – *The Island of Trinidad, From the Latest Surveys*. London: John Arrowsmith.

Breton, Adele C., 1921 – The Aruac Indians of Venezuela. *Man* 21: 9–12.

Buissink, Father P.J., ed., 1938 [1699/1700] – *The Arena Massacre Trinidad: 1st December, 1699*. Port-of-Spain: Historical Society of Trinidad and Tobago.

Byrne, John, 1760 – *A Plan of great Courland Bay, surveyd in August 1760*. Manuscript map, Tobago Museum, Scarborough.

Carmichael, Gertrud, and Kendryk S. Wise, eds., *Trinidad (and Tobago) Historical Society Publications*, 1–999. Port-of-Spain: Historical Society of Trinidad and Tobago.

Caulín, Father Antonio, 1966 [1779] – *Historia de la Nueva Andalucía*, 2 vols. Ed. Father Pablo Ojer. Caracas: Academia Nacional de la Historia.

Colección de Documentos Ineditos Relativos al Descubrimiento, Conquista y Organización de las Antiguas Posesiones Españolas de Ultramar, 42 vols. (CDIU), 1885/1932. Madrid: Real Academia de la Historia.

Columbus, Christopher, 1994 – *Accounts and Letters of the Second, Third, and Fourth Voyages*, 2 vols. Ed. Paolo E. Taviani, Consuelo Varela, Juan Gil, and Marina Conti; transl. from the Spanish by Luciano F. Farina and Marc A. Beckwith. Nuova Raccolta Colombiana, English Edition. Roma: Ministry of Cultural and Environmental Assets.

Columbus, Ferdinand, 1992 [1571] – *The Life of the Admiral Christopher Columbus By His Son Ferdinand*. Transl. from the Spanish and ed. by Benjamin Keen. New Brunswick, NJ: Rutgers University Press.

Crame, Agustín, 1777 – *Mapa de la Ysla de Trinidad*. Manuscript map, Archivo General de Indias, Sevilla.

de Anguiano, Father Matheo, 1928 [1702] – Missión Apostólica en la Isla de la Trinidad de Barlovento, y en Santo Thomé de Guayana, Provincia de El Dorado [...]. In: Manuel Serrano y Sanz, ed., *Relaciones Históricas de las Misiones de Padres Capuchinos de Venezuela Siglos XVII y XVIII*: 95–143. Madrid: Suárez.

de Armellada, Father Cesáreo, ed., 1960 – *Por la Venezuela Indigena de Ayer y de Hoy*, 2 vols. Caracas: Sociedad de Ciencias Naturales La Salle.

de Carrocera, Father Buenaventura, 1968 – *Misión de los Capuchinos en Guayana*, 3 vols. Caracas: Academia Nacional de la Historia.

de Carvajal, Father Jacinto, 1985 [1648] – *Descubrimiento del río Apure*. Ed. José Alcina Franch. Madrid: Historia 16.

de Castellanos, Juan, 1962 [1589] – *Elegías de Varones Ilustres de Indias*. Ed. Isaac J. Pardo. Caracas: Academia Nacional de la Historia.

de Laet, Johannes (Jean), 1640 – *L'Histoire du Nouveau Monde ou Description des Indes Occidentales*, 2nd ed. Leyde: Elsevier.

de Laet, Johannes, 1931/1937 – *Iaerlyck Verhael van de Verrichtinghen der Geoctroyeerde West-Indische Compagnie*, 4 vols. Ed. S.P.L. l'Honoré Naber. 's-Gravenhage: Linschoten-Vereeniging.

de Las Casas, Father Bartolomé, 1957/1961 [1520/1561] – *Historia de las Indias*, 2 vols. Ed. Juan Perez de Tudela Bueso. Madrid: Biblioteca de Autores Españoles.

de Las Casas, Father Bartolomé, 1965 [1552] – Brevísima Relación de la Destruición de las Indias. In: Lewis Hanke and M. Giménez Fernández, eds., *Tratados de Fray Bartolomé de Las Casas*, vol. 1: 3–199. México: Fondo de Cultura Económica.

de Pamplona, Father Miguel, 1928 [1780] – Relación de las conversiones de Capuchinos aragoneses, de la Provincia de Cumaná; [...]. In: Manuel Serrano y Sanz, ed., *Relaciones históricas de las Misiones de Padres Capuchinos de Venezuela Siglos XVII y XVIII*: 145–256. Madrid: Suárez.

de Rionegro, Father Froilán, ed., 1918 – *Relaciones de las misiones de los PP Capuchinos en las antiguas provincias españolas – hoy República de Venezuela 1650–1817*, 2 vols. Sevilla: Zarzuela/La Exposición.

de Veracoecha, E. Troconis, ed., 1969 – *Documentos para el Estudio de los Esclavos Negros en Venezuela*. Caracas: Academia Nacional de la Historia.

Dorta, Enrique M., ed., 1967 – *Materiales para la Historia de la Cultura en Venezuela (1523–1828): Documentos del Archivo General de Indias de Sevilla*. Madrid: Gráficas Cóndor.

Dudley, Sir Robert, 1646 – [Map of Guiana], *Arcano del Mare*, America XIII. Firenze.

Dudley, Sir Robert, 1899 – *The Voyage of Robert Dudley* [...] *to the West Indies, 1594–1595*. Ed. G.F. Warner. London: Hakluyt Society.

Formisano, Luciano, ed., 1992 – *Letters from a New World: Amerigo Vespucci's Discovery of America*. Transl. from the Italian by David Jacobson. New York: Marsilio.

Gumilla, Father José, 1963 [1741] – *El Orinoco Ilustrado y Defendido*, 2 vols. Ed. José Nucete-Sardi. Caracas: Academia Nacional de Historia.

Hakluyt, Richard, 1903/1905 [1589] – *The Principal Navigations, Voyages, Traffiques and Discoveries of the English Nation* [...], 12 vols. Glasgow: MacLehose.

Harcourt, Robert, 1928 [1613] – *A Relation of a Voyage to Guiana* [...] *1613*. Ed. C.A. Harris. London: Hakluyt Society.

Harlow, Vincent T., ed., 1925 – *Colonising Expeditions to the West Indies and Guiana, 1623–1667*. London: The Hakluyt Society.

Hulme, Peter, and Neil L. Whitehead, eds., 1992 – *Wild Majesty Encounters With Caribs From Columbus To the Present Day: An Anthology*. Oxford: Clarendon Press.

Jane, Cecil, ed., 1988 – *The Four Voyages of Columbus*. Transl. from the Spanish by Cecil Jane. New York: Dover Publications.

Karijosemito, Rasijem, and Philip Dikland, eds., 2004 – *Zeeuwse archivalia uit Suriname en omliggende kwartieren 1667–1683*. Paramaribo: Surinaams Museum/KDV Architects.

Konetzke, Richard, ed., 1953/1962 – *Colección de Documentos para la Historia de la Formación Social de Hispanoamérica 1493–1810*, 3 vols. Madrid: Consejo Superior de Investigaciones Científicas.

Leal, Indefonso, ed., 1978 – *Libros y bibliotecas en Venezuela Colonial (1633–1767)*, 2 vols. Caracas: Academia Nacional de la Historia.

Lorimer, Joyce, ed., 2006 [1596] – *Sir Walter Ralegh's* Discoverie of Guiana. London: Hakluyt Society.

Mallet, Capt. F., 1802 – *Descriptive Account of the Island of Trinidad:* [...]. London: W. Faden.

Martire d'Anghiera, Pietro, 1912 [1493/1525] – *De Orbe Novo: The Eight Decades of Peter Martyr D'Anghera*, 2 vols. Transl. from the Spanish by Francis A. MacNutt. New York: Burt Franklin.

Millares Carlo, A., ed., 1966 – *Archivos de los Registros Principales de Merida y Caracas: Protocolos del Siglo XVI*. Caracas: Academia Nacional de la Historia.

Moreno, Antonio A., ed., 1964 – *Relaciones Geográficas de Venezuela*. Caracas: Academia Nacional de la Historia.

Morison, Samuel E., ed., 1963 – *Journals and Other Documents on the Life and Voyages of Christopher Columbus*. Transl. from the Spanish by Samuel E. Morison. New York: Heritage Press.

O'Brian, Patrick, and Verlyn Klinkenborg, eds., 1996 [ca. 1590] – *Histoire Naturelle des Indes: The Drake Manuscript in The Pierpont Morgan Library*. Transl. from the French by Ruth S. Kraemer. New York: W.W. Norton.

Oviedo y Valdés, Gonzalo Fernández de, 1959 [1535/1547] – *Historia General y Natural de las Indias, Islas y Tierra Firme del Mar Océano*, 5 vols. Ed. Juan Pérez de Tudela Bueso. Madrid: Biblioteca de Autores Españoles.

Pelleprat, Father Pierre, 2009 [1655] – *Relation des Missions des Pères de la Compagnie de Jésus dans les* Îles *et dans la Terre Ferne de l'Amérique méridionale*. Ed. Réal Ouellet. Québec: Presses de l'Université Laval.

Phillips, Jr., Williams D., and Mark D. Johnston, eds., 2000 – *Testimonies From the Columbian Lawsuits*. Transl. from the Spanish by Anne Marie Wolf. Repertorium Colombianum 8. Turnhout: Brepols.

Poyntz, Capt. John, 1901 [1683] – *The Present Prospect of the Famous Island of Tobago* [...]. Port-of-Spain: Yuille.

Ralegh, Sir Walter, 1848 [1596] – *The Discovery of the Large, Rich, and Beautiful Empire of Guiana*. Ed. Sir Robert H. Schomburgk. London: Hakluyt Society.

Ralegh, Sir Walter, 1928 [1596] – *The Discoverie of the large and bewtiful Empire of Guiana*. Ed. Vincent T. Harlow. London: Argonaut Press.

Ralegh, Sir Walter, 1997 [1596] – *The Discoverie of the Large, Rich and Bewtiful Empyre of Guiana*. Ed. Neil L. Whitehead. Norman, OK: University of Oklahoma Press.

Rochefort, Charles de, 1665 – *Le Tableau de l'Isle de Tabago, ou de la Nouvelle Oüalchre, L'une des Isles Antilles de l'Amérique*. Leyde: Carpantier.

Rochefort, Charles de, 1666 – *The History of Barbados, St Christophers, Mevis, St Vincents, Antego, Martinico, Monserrat, And the rest of the Caribby-Islands, In all XXVIII*, 2 vols. Transl. from the French by John Davies. London: Starkey & Dring, Jr.

Sainsbury, W.N., ed., 1860 – *Calendar of State Papers, Colonial Series, America and West Indies, 1574–1660*. London: Public Record Office.

Simón, Father Pedro, 1963 [1627] – *Noticias Historiales de Venezuela*, 2 vols. Ed. Demetrio Ramos Pérez. Caracas: Academia Nacional de la Historia.

Symcox, Geoffrey, and Jesús Carrillo, eds., 2001 – *Las Casas on Columbus: The Third Voyage*. Transl. from the Spanish by Michae Hammer and Blair Sullivan. Repertorium Colombianum 11. Turnhout: Brepols.

Thevet, Andrewe, 1971 [1568] – *The New Found Worlde Or Antarctike*. Transl. from the French. Amsterdam: Da Capo Press.

Vázquez de Espinosa, Antonio, 1942 [ca. 1628/1629] – *Compendium and Description of the West Indies*. Transl. from the Spanish and ed. by C. Upton Clark. Washington, DC: Smithsonian Institution.

Whitehead, Neil L., ed., 2011 – *Of Cannibals and Kings: Primal Anthropology in the Americas*. University Park, PA: Pennsylvania State University Press.

Young, Sir William, 1807/1812 – *An Historical, Statistical, and Descriptive Account of the Island of Tobago*. St. Augustine, Trinidad: University of the West Indies (manuscript).

Various historical and anthropological accounts

Anderson, Edgar, 1970 – *Senie kurzemnieki Amerikā un Tobāgo kolonizācija*. Stockholm: Daugava.

Alegría, Ricardo E., 1981 – *Las Primeras Noticias Sobre los Indios Caribes*. San Juan: Editorial Universidad de Puerto Rico/Centro de Estudios Avanzados de Puerto Rico y El Caribe.

Andrews, Kenneth R., 1966 – *Elizabethan Privateering: English Privateering during the Spanish War 1585–1603*. Cambridge: Cambridge University Press.

Andrews, Kenneth R., 1978 – *The Spanish Caribbean: Trade and Plunder 1530–1630*. New Haven: Yale University Press.

Andrews, Kenneth R., 1984 – *Trade, Plunder and Settlement: Maritime Enterprise and the Genesis of the British Empire, 1480–1630*. Cambridge: Cambridge University Press.

Anthony, Michael, 2001 – *Anaparima: The History of San Fernando and Its Environs (The Naparimas)*, 2 vols. San Fernando: City Council of San Fernando.

Bellour, Helene, and Samuel Kinser, 1998 – Amerindian masking in Trinidad carnival. *The Drama Review* 42 (3): 147–169.

Bolton, Herbert E., 1917 – The mission as a frontier institution in the Spanish-American colonies. *American Historical Review* 23: 42–61.

Boomert, Arie, 1984 – The Arawak Indians of Trinidad and Coastal Guiana, ca 1500–1650. *The Journal of Caribbean History* 19 (2): 123–188.

Boomert, Arie, 2002 – Amerindian–European encounters on and around Tobago (1498–ca. 1810). *Antropológica* 97/98: 71–207.

Boomert, Arie, 2009 – The earliest Dutch fortifications of Tobago. *Archaeology and Anthropology: Journal of the Walter Roth Museum of Anthropology* 16 (1): 31–42.

Borde, Pierre-Gustave-Louis, 1982 [1876/1883] – *The History of Trinidad Under the Spanish Government*, 2 vols. Transl. from the French by James A. Bain and Brigadier-General A.S. Mavrogordato. Port-of-Spain: Paria Publishing Co.

Boucher, Philip P., 1992 – *Cannibal Encounters: Europeans and Island Caribs, 1492–1763*. Baltimore/London: Johns Hopkins University Press.

Brereton, Bridget, 1979 – *Race Relations in Colonial Trinidad 1870–1900*. Cambridge: Cambridge University Press.

Brereton, Bridget, 1981 – *A History of Modern Trinidad 1783–1962*. Kingston: Heinemann.

Burns, Sir Alan C., 1965 – *History of the British West Indies*. London: Allen & Unwin.

Carmichael, Gertrud, 1961 – *The History of the West Indian Islands of Trinidad and Tobago 1498–1900*. London: Alvin Redman.

Coleridge, Henry N., 1826 – *Six Months in the West Indies, in 1825*. New York: Carvill, Bliss & White.

Cothonay, Father R.P.M. Bertrand, 1893 – *Trinidad: Journal d'un missionaire Dominicain des Antilles anglaises*. Paris: Rétaux et Fils.

Dauxion-Lavaysse, Jean François, 1820 – *A Statistical, Commercial, and Political Description of Venezuela, Trinidad, Margarita, and Tobago*. Transl. from the French. London: Whittaker.

Day, Charles W., 1852 – *Five Years' Residence in the West Indies*. London: Colburn.

de Carrocera, Father Buenaventura, 1968 – *Misión de los Capuchinos en Cumaná*, 3 vols. Caracas: Academia Nacional de la Historia.

de Verteuil, Father Anthony, 1973 – *Sir Louis de Verteuil: His Life and Times*. Port-of-Spain: Columbus Publishers.

de Verteuil, Father Anthony, 1995 – *Martyrs and Murderers: Trinidad 1699*. Port-of-Spain: Litho Press.

de Verteuil, Father Anthony, and Chris-Arthur de Wilde, 2009 – *The Black Earth of South Naparima*. Port-of-Spain: Litho Press.

de Verteuil, Louis A.A. Gaston, 1884 – *Trinidad: Its Geography, Natural Resources, Administration, Present Condition, and Prospects*, 2nd ed. London: Cassell.

Encinas, E.M., 1927 – Arima at the Time of Sir Ralph Woodford. In: Alfred Richards, ed., *Discovery Day Celebration 1927 Souvenir*: 73–74. Port-of-Spain: Franklin's.

Fernández-Armesto, Felipe, 2006 – *Amerigo: The Man Who Gave his Name to America*. London: Weidenfeld & Nicolson.

Forte, Maximilian C., 2003 – *How The Amerindians of Arima Lost Their Lands: Notes from Primary and Other Historical Sources, 1802–1880*. Arima, Trinidad: Santa Rosa Carib Community.

Forte, Maximilian C., 2005 – *Ruins of Absence, Presence of Caribs: (Post)Colonial Representations of Aboriginality in Trinidad and Tobago*. Gainesville: University Press of Florida.

Fraser, Lionel M. 1971 [1891/1896] – *History of Trinidad*, 2 vols. London: Frank Cass.

Gamble, W.H., 1866 – *Trinidad: Historical and Descriptive: Being a Narrative of Nine Years' Residence in the Island*. London: Yates & Alexander.

Gibson, Charles, 1966 – *Spain in America*. New York: Harper & Row.

Goldwasser, Michele, 1994/1996 – Remembrances of the Warao: The Miraculous Statue of Siparia, Trinidad. *Antropológica* 84: 3–42.

Goldwasser, Michele, 1998/1999 – Seeking the Ancestors. *Antropológica* 89: 3–24.

Goslinga, Cornelis Ch., 1971 – *The Dutch in the Caribbean and on the Wild Coast 1580–1680*. Assen: Van Gorcum.

Gullick, Charles J.M.R., 1985 – *Myths of a Minority: The Changing Traditions of the Vincentian Caribs*. Assen: Van Gorcum.

Harlow, Vincent T., 1932 – *Ralegh's Last Voyage*. London: Argonaut Press.

Harricharan, Father John T., 1975 – *The Catholic Church in Trinidad 1498–1852*. Port-of-Spain: Inprint Caribbean.

Heinen, H. Dieter, 1992 – The early colonization of the Lower Orinoco and its impact on present day indigenous peoples. *Antropológica* 78: 51–86.

Hemming, John, 1978 – *The Search for El Dorado*. London: Book Club Associates.

Hernandez, Ricardo Bharath, and Maximilian C. Forte, 2006 – "In this place where I was chief": History and ritual in the maintenance and retrieval of traditions in the Carib community of Arima, Trinidad. In: Maximilian C. Forte, ed., *Indigenous Resurgence in the Contemporary Caribbean: Amerindian Survival and Revival*: 107–131. New York: Peter Lang.

Herskovits, Melville J., and Frances S. Herskovits, 1947 – *Trinidad Village*. New York: Knopf.

Higman, Barry W., 2011 – *A Concise History of the Caribbean*. Cambridge: Cambridge University Press.

Hollis, Sir Alfred Claud, 1941 – *A Brief History of Trinidad Under the Spanish Crown*. Port-of-Spain: Government Printer.

Ingram, Amelia K., 2008 – Reading history, performing Carib: The Santa Rosa Festival and Amerindian identity in Trinidad. *Caribbean Studies* 36 (2): 65–94.

Jimenez G., Morella A., 1986 – *La Esclavitud Indigena en Venezuela (Siglo XVI)*. Caracas: Academia Nacional de la Historia.

Joseph, Edward L., 1838 – *History of Trinidad*. Port-of-Spain: H.J. Mills.

Kingsley, Charles, 1877 – *At Last: A Christmas in the West Indies*, 2nd ed. London: Macmillan.

Klooster, Wim, 1998 – *Illicit Riches: Dutch Trade in the Caribbean, 1648–1795*. Leiden: KITLV Press.

Knapp, Jeffrey, 1993 – Elizabethan Tobacco. In: Stephen Greenblatt, ed., *New World Encounters*: 273–312. Berkeley: University of California Press.

Leahy, Father Vincent, 1980 – *Catholic Church in Trinidad 1797–1820*. Arima, Trinidad: St. Dominic Press.

Leahy, Father Vincent, 1980 – *Bishop James Buckley 1820–1828*. Arima, Trinidad: St. Dominic Press.

Lorimer, Joyce, 1977 – Ralegh's first reconnaissance of Guiana? An English survey of the Orinoco in 1587. *Terrae Incognitae* 9: 7–21.

Lorimer, Joyce, 1978 – The English contraband tobacco trade in Trinidad and Guiana 1590–1617. In: Kenneth R. Andrews, N.P. Canny and P.E.H. Hair, eds., *The Westward Enterprise: English Activities in Ireland, the Atlantic and America 1480–1650*: 124–150.

Luke, Sir Harry, 1950 – *Caribbean Circuit*. London: Nicholson & Watson.

Martin, R. Montgomery, 1836 – *History of the West Indies: Comprising Jamaica, Honduras, Trinidad, Tobago, Grenada, the Bahamas, and the Virgin Islands*, 4 vols. London: Whittaker.

Massé, Armand, 1988 – *The Diaries of Abbé Massé 1878–1883*, 4 vols. Transl. from the French by M.L. de Verteuil. Port-of-Spain: De Verteuil.

Mattiesen, Otto H., 1940 – *Die Kolonial- und* Überseepolitik *der kurländischen Herzöge im 17. und 18. Jahrhundert*. Stuttgart: Kohlhammer.

M'Callum, Pierre F., 1805 – *Travels in Trinidad during the Months of February, March, and April, 1803*, [...]. Liverpool: The author.

Mohammed, Patricia, 2009 – *Imaging The Caribbean: Culture and Visual Translation*. Oxford: Macmillan.

Moodie-Kublalsingh, Sylvia, 1994 – *The Cocoa Panyols of Trinidad: An Oral Record*. London: British Academic Press.

Morales Padrón, Francisco, 2012 – *Spanish Trinidad*. Transl. from the Spanish and ed. by Armando García de la Torre. Kingston: Ian Randle.

Moreau, Jean-Pierre, 1992 – *Les Petites Antilles de Christophe Colomb à Richelieu (1493–1635)*. Paris: Karthala.

Morison, Samuel E., 1942 – *Admiral of the Ocean Sea: A Life of Christopher Columbus*. Boston: Little, Brown & Co.

Morison, Samuel E., and Mauricio Obregón, 1964 – *The Caribbean As Columbus Saw It*. Boston: Little, Brown & Co.

Naipaul, Sir Vidiadhar S., 1969 – *The Loss of El Dorado: A History*. Harmondsworth: Penguin Books.

Newson, Linda A., 1976 – *Aboriginal and Spanish Colonial Trinidad: A Study in Culture Contact*. London: Academic Press.

Newton, Arthur P., 1966 – *The European Nations in the West Indies 1493–1688*. London: Black.

Noel, Jesse A., 1966 – *Spanish Colonial Administration and the Socio-Economic Foundations of Trinidad, 1777-1797*. Unpubl. PhD Thesis, Cambridge University, Cambridge.

Ojer, Father Pablo, 1966 – La politica Indiana de Rodrigo de Navarrete, escribano de Margarita e informador de La Casas. *Anuario de Estudios Americanos* 23: 305–327.

Ojer, Father Pablo, 1966 – *La Formación del Oriente Venezolano*, vol 1: *Creación de las Gobernaciones*. Caracas: Universidad Católica "Andres Bello".

Otte, Enrique, 1977 – *Las Perlas del Caribe: Nueva Cadiz de Cubagua*. Caracas: Fundación John Boulton.

Ottley, Carlton R., 1971 – *The Story of San Fernando*. Port-of-Spain: The author.

Perera, Miguel Ángel, 2000 – *Oro y Hambre Guayana Siglo XVI: Antropología histórica y ecología cultural de un malentendido 1498–1597*. Caracas: Universidad Central de Venezuela.

Phillip, Jean-Baptiste, 1824 – *An Address to the Right Honourable Earl Bathurst relative to the Claims which the Coloured Population of Trinidad have to the same Civil and Political Privileges with their White Fellow Subjects, by a Free Mulatto of the Island*. London.

Pohl, Frederick J., 1944 – *Amerigo Vespucci Pilot Major*. New York: Columbia University Press.

Reyes, Elma, ed. 1978 – *The Carib Community*. Arima, Trinidad: Santa Rosa Carib Community.

Roos, Doeke, 1992 – *Zeeuwen en de Westindische Compagnie (1621–1674)*. Hulst: Van Geyt.

Rowan, J.C., 1934 – Queen of the Caribs. *The Trinidadian* 2 (1): 24–25.

Scott, Julius S., 1996 – Crisscrossing Empires: Ships, Sailors, and Resistance in the Lesser Antilles in the Eighteenth Century. In: Robert L. Paquette and Stanley L. Engerman, eds., *The Lesser Antilles in the Age of European Expansion*: 128–143. Gainesville: University Press of Florida.

Silva Montañes, Ismael, 1983 – *Hombres y Mujeres del Siglo XVI Venezolano*, 4 vols. Caracas: Academia Nacional de la Historia.

Sued Badillo, Jalil, 1978 – *Los Caribes: Realidad o Fabula: Ensayo de Rectificación Histórica*. Río Piedras, Puerto Rico: Editorial Antillana.

Underhill, Edward B., 1862 – *The West Indies: Their Social and Religious Condition*. London: Jackson, Walford & Hodder.

Vaughan, Alden T., 2002 – Sir Walter Ralegh's Indian interpreters, 1584–1618. *The William and Mary Quarterly* 59 (2): 341–376.

Vigneras, Louis-André, 1976 – *The Discovery of South America and the Andalusian Voyages*. Chicago/London: The University of Chicago Press.

Whitehead, Neil L., 1988 – *Lords of the Tiger Spirit: A History of the Caribs in Colonial Venezuela and Guyana 1498–1820*. Dordrecht: Foris Publications.

Whitehead, Neil L., 1990 – The Snake Warriors – Sons of the Tiger's Teeth: A descriptive analysis of Carib warfare, ca. 1500–1820. In: Jonathan Haas, ed., *The Anthropology of War*: 146–170. Cambridge: Cambridge University Press.

Whitehead, Neil L., 1990 – Carib Ethnic Soldiering in Venezuela, the Guianas, and the Antilles, 1492–1820. *Ethnohistory* 37 (4): 357–385.

Whitehead, Neil L., 1993 – Native American Cultures along the Atlantic Littoral of South America, 1499–1650. *Proceedings of the British Academy* 81: 197–231.

Whitehead, Neil L., 1993 – Ethnic Transformation and Historical Discontinuity in Native Amazonia and Guayana, 1500–1900. *L'Homme* 33 (2-4): 285–305.

Whitehead, Neil L., 1994 – The Ancient Amerindian Polities of the Amazon, the Orinoco, and the Atlantic Coast: A Preliminary Analysis of Their Passage from Antiquity to Extinction. In: Anna C. Roosevelt, ed., *Amazonian Indians from Prehistory to the |Present*: 33–53. Tucson: The University of Arizona Press.

Whitehead, Neil L., ed., 1995 – *Wolves From the Sea: Readings in the Anthropology of the Native Caribbean*. Leiden: KITLV Press.

Whitehead, Neil L., 1999 – Native society and the European occupation of the Caribbean islands and coastal *Tierra Firme*, 1492–1650. In: Pieter C. Emmer and German Carrera Damas, eds., *General History of the Caribbean*, vol. 2: *New Societies: The Caribbean in the Long Sixteenth Century*: 180–200. London/ Basingstoke: UNESCO/MacMillan.

Whitehead, Neil L., 1999 – The crises and transformations of invaded societies: The Caribbean (1492–1580). In: Frank Salomon and Stuart B. Schwartz, eds., *The Cambridge History of the Native Peoples of the Americas*, vol. 3: *South America*, part 1: 864–903. Cambridge: Cambridge University Press.

Wilbert, Johannes, 1993 – *Mystic Endowment: Religious Ethnography of the Warao Indians*. Cambridge, MA: Harvard University.

Wilbert, Johannes, 1993 – *Mindful of Famine: Religious Climatology of the Warao Indians*. Cambridge, MA: Harvard University.

Williamson, James A., 1923 – *English Colonies in Guiana and on the Amazon 1604–1668*. Oxford: Clarendon Press.

Williamson, James A., 1926 – *The Caribbee Islands Under the Proprietary Patents*. Oxford: Oxford University Press.

Wise, Kendryk S., 1934/1938 – *Historical Sketches of Trinidad and Tobago*, 4 vols. London/Port-of-Spain: Historical Society of Trinidad and Tobago.

Amerindian cultural heritage

Baksh-Soodeen, Rawwida, 1986 – *Amerindian Toponyms of Trinidad; Linguistic Legacy of Past Amerindian Occupation*. Paper presented at the Sixth Biennial Conference of the Society for Caribbean Linguistics and The American Dialect Society, August 1986. St. Augustine, Trinidad: The University of the West Indies.

Besson, Gérard A., 2001 – *Folklore and Legends of Trinidad and Tobago*. Port-of-Spain: Paria Publishing Co.

Boomert, Arie, 2001 – Names for Tobago. *Journal de la Société des Américanistes* 87: 339–349.

Boomert, Arie, 2010 – Kaíri, Trinidad: The one true island. *Archaeology and Anthropology: Journal of the Walter Roth Museum of Anthropology* 16 (2): 29–42.

Boomert, Arie, 2011 – The oldest place names of Tobago. *Archaeology and Anthropology: Journal of the Walter Roth Museum of Anthropology* 17 (1): 1–21.

Chauharjasingh, Archibald S., 2008 – *A Dictionary of Trinidad and Tobago Folklore*. La Romain, Trinidad: The author.

Friederici, Georg, 1960 – *Amerikanistisches Wörterbuch und Hilfswörterbuch für den Amerikanisten: Deutsch – Spanish – English*. Universität Hamburg, Abhandlungen aus dem Gebiet der Auslandskunde 53. Hamburg: Cram, De Gruyter & Co.

Lance, Cheryl, 2001 – *Creole Remedies: Case Studies of Ethnoveterinary Medicine in Trinidad and Tobago*. PhD dissertation, Wageningen University, The Netherlands.

Laurence, Kemlin M., 1975 – Continuity and change in Trinidadian toponyms. *Nieuwe West-Indische Gids* 50 (1): 123–142.

Laurence, Kemlin M., 1980 – The survival of the Spanish language in Trinidad. *Nieuwe West-Indische Gids* 54 (1): 213–228.

Newel Lewis, John, 1983 – *Ajoupa: Architecture of the Caribbean – Trinidad's Heritage*. Port-of-Spain: The author.

Seaforth, C.E., C. Dennis Adams and Y. Sylvester, 1983 – *A Guide to the Medicinal Plants of Trinidad & Tobago* (revised ed.). London: Commonwealth Secretariat.

Thompson, R.W. 1957 – A preliminary survey of the Spanish dialect of Trinidad. *Orbis* 6: 353–373.

Thompson, R.W. 1959 – Pre-British place-names in Trinidad. *De West-Indische Gids* 39 (1): 137–165.

Winer, Lise, 2009 – *Dictionary of the English/Creole of Trinidad & Tobago On Historical Principles*. Montréal/Kingston: McGill–Queen's University Press.

Appendix. Institutions and museums with significant archaeological holdings from Trinidad and Tobago

- British Museum, London, UK
- Cambridge University Museum, Cambridge, UK
- National Museum of the American Indian, Washington/New York, USA
- National Museum and Art Gallery, Port-of-Spain, Trinidad*
- Harris Collection, Pointe-a-Pierre Wildfowl Trust, Petrotrin Ltd., Trinidad*
- Tobago Historical Museum, Fort King George, Scarborough, Tobago*
- Harris Collection, John Donaldson Campus, University of Trinidad and Tobago, Port-of-Spain, Trinidad
- Harris Collection, Zoological Museum, Department of Life Sciences, University of the West Indies, St. Augustine, Trinidad
- Archaeological Research Laboratory, Department of History, University of the West Indies, St. Augustine, Trinidad
- Yale Peabody Museum, New Haven, Connecticut, USA

Collections with exhibitions of archaeological finds from Trinidad and Tobago, which are open to visitors, are marked with an asterisk.

Index

C

D

E

F

I

J

K

L

M

N

R

S

Curriculum Vitae

Dr. Arie Boomert (1946) worked as an archaeologist at the Surinaams Museum, Paramaribo, Suriname; Leiden University and the University of Amsterdam, The Netherlands; and the University of the West Indies, St. Augustine, Trinidad. In 2011 he retired as an Assistant Professor and Senior Researcher from the Faculty of Archaeology, Leiden University. At present he is a Honorary Research Fellow at Leiden University and a Curatorial Affiliate in the Division of Anthropology, Peabody Museum of Natural History, Yale University, New Haven, USA.